Chinese Law & Religion Monitor

中国法律与宗教观察

（July – December 2018）2018 年秋冬版

Chinese Law & Religion Monitor（July – December 2018）
Published by ChinaAid Association, Inc. (ChinaAid)
Website: www.chinaaid.org (English) | www.chinaaid.net (Chinese)
Address: 1300 Pennsylvania Ave. NW, Suite 700, Washington, DC 20004
Tel: 202-213-0506
ISBN-13: 978-1721828340 ISBN-10: 1721828346
Printed in the United States of America

《中国法律与宗教观察》2018 年秋冬版
对华援助协会出版
网站：www.chinaaid.net (中文) | www.chinaaid.org (英文)
本刊地址: 1300 Pennsylvania Ave. NW, Suite 700, Washington, DC 20004
本刊电话: 202-213-0506
ISBN-13: 978-1721828340 ISBN-10: 1721828346
美国境内出版印刷

《Chinese Law & Religion Monitor》
(July - December 2018 Vol. 11, No. 2)

Table of Contents

- Edward McMillan-Scott, former Vice-President, Human Rights and Democracy of the European Parliament; founder, Human Rights and Democracy Network
- Faith McDonnell, director of Religious Liberty Programs, Institute of Religion and Democracy
- Frank Wolf, Jerry and Susie Wilson Chair in Religious Freedom, Baylor University; founder and co-chair, Tom Lantos Human Rights Commission
- Katrina Lantos-Swett, president and chief executive officer, Lantos Foundation for Human Rights and Justice
- Scott Flipse, director of communications and policy, Congressional-Executive Commission on China; former Deputy Director for policy, U.S. Commission on International Religious Freedom
- William Inboden, Executive Director of the Clements Center for History, Strategy and Statecraft, University of Texas; former Senior Director, Strategic Planning on the National Security Council at the White House

Chinese Law & Religion Monitor

ISBN-13: 978-1721828340 ISBN-10: 1721828346

Address: 1300 Pennsylvania Ave. NW, Suite 700, Washington, DC 20004

Telephone: 1-888-889-7757

The *Chinese Law & Religion Monitor* is a biannual publication containing policy documents and academic works involving law, religion, and politics in China, with English translation.

Visit ChinaAid's website : www.ChinaAid.org

Editor's Note

By "Bob" Fu Xiqiu

As the world watched, in February of this year, China passed its new 'Religious Affairs Regulations' on its citizens. These new regulations impose further restrictions on its people, which now further encompasses unrelenting restrictions pertaining to China's education of its children. The right to education has been recognized in several international and regional legal instruments. These instruments include treaties (conventions, covenants, charters) and in soft law, which includes general comments, recommendations, declarations and frameworks for action. Additionally, on March 11, 2018, China's National People's Congress in Beijing adopted proposed amendments to the PRC Constitution, one of which valued the slogan "building a community of shared future for human beings" in the preamble. Relating to this proposal, the United States stated: "It is clear that China is attempting through this resolution to weaken the UN human rights system and the norms underpinning it. The 'feel good' language about 'mutually beneficial cooperation' is intended to benefit autocratic states at the expense of people whose human rights and fundamental freedoms we are all obligated, as States, to respect. For these reasons, the United States is calling a vote and will vote against this resolution. We encourage other countries not to support this resolution." By also seeing that China's resolution insists that governments be respected, the U.S. disputed the resolution by affirming: "A call for governments that abuse their own citizens' rights to be respected has no place in a forum dedicated to respecting and protecting the human rights and fundamental freedoms of the individual." The U.S. describes the resolution as an effort by China "to insulate itself from criticism of its human rights record by demanding 'respect.'" The U.S. further acknowledged: "The only way for any government to achieve respect is for that government to respect human rights and fundamental freedoms." https://chinachange.org/2018/04/09/with-

its-latest-human-rights-council-resolution-china-continues-its-
assault-on-the-un-human-rights-framework/.]

In view of this situation, this 2018 Fall-Winter issue of the Chinese Law and Religion Monitor will analyze the current situation of children's education in China. It needs to be recognized that education is a human right. This means: 1) the right to education is legally guaranteed for all without any discrimination; 2) states have the obligation to protect, respect, and fulfil the right to education; and 3) there are ways to hold states accountable for violations or deprivations of the right to education.

This issue contains the following articles and reports:

1. In *Children's Right to Religious Instruction and to Education about Religion*, Professor of International Law and Religion Jeroen Temperman's expertise in International Law is focused on laying the basis of understanding the International statements and builds a robust case for Children's Right to Religious Instruction and to Education about Religion. This understanding then can form a clarifying comparison to the situation as it exists in China today.

2. In *Religious Freedom in Education?*, Charles L. Glenn challenges the assumption that a faith-based education tends to make students unfit to be citizens of a liberal democracy.

3. Wang Yi's article, *Is it legal for the church to run a school?*, shows how in contemporary China running church schools and running house churches are both illegal. His argument is that the people in China are facing the clash of the Christian faith with the Constitution of China.

4. In *When the nest is overturned, can the eggs in it stay unbroken?" An overview of religious education for children in China*, writer Meng Yuanxin points out to readers that according to the U.N.'s covenants on human rights, the freedom of religious education is a component of the freedom of religion. This article also details the CPC's history of forcing the separation of education from religion and how the children's religious education in China is gradually disappearing from the public-school system.

5. Katherine A. Capps' article, *Liberty of Children's Religious Education in China at Risk*, analyzes how China is in clear violation of multiple international documents and how these violations ultimately affect the Chinese children's right to religious education. This article further contemplates what the Chinese

government should do to recognize the right of religious education and how the international community should react to the Chinese government if they fail to comply.

6. Japanese writer Sato Chitose's article, *ZuoTeng Qian Sui*, investigates the situation of the support and education of orphans and disabled children in the Christian "house church" and the Catholic "underground church" that are not registered with the government. This is written from the perspective of welfare education policy and religious policy, analyzes the difficult situation they face, the characteristics and social significance of Christians in the education of disabled children. The article points out that the religious management system of the Communist Party of China has become a cause of violation of children's basic human rights in the welfare education of children.

7. In "Summary of Police Actions - Yanyuan, Wangfu Ranch, Beiqijia township, Changping district, Beijing", the occupants of 2# Yanyuan were harassed by their tenant just for being a religious school.

8. "Notice - Maizhong Academy" – This document stated that the Maizhong Academy was investigated and told to rectify all their violations, which included them providing education illegally to children.

9. "Notice - Henan Provincial Catholic Patriotic Committee, Henan Provincial Catholic Committee on Educational Affairs" - This document says plainly that children are barred from entering a place of worship.

10. In *Xinjiang Authorities Jail Uyghur Imam Who Took Son to Unsanctioned Religious School*, the writer explains the CPC's determination to control the hearts of the Chinese people. Religious Liberty is a universal human right, even if it is not your religion.

11. In *Uyghur Schoolchildren, Parents Forced to Abstain From Fasting During Ramadan*, the writer details the intrusion of the CPC into the families right to Religious Liberty.

12. "Xinjiang Uygur Autonomous Region's Bureau of Education's Regulations about Banning On-campus Religious Activities" - This document displays the official stance concerning Religious Liberty in China, even before the new regulations came out in 2018. It further reiterates that schools maintain a certain number of hours of atheistic education.

13. "The Ministry of Education's Opinions about How to Properly Handle Religion's Disruption of School Education in Ethnic Minority Regions" – This is another CPC document that clearly shows the determined and continual restriction of the child's right to religious education.

14. In *Discrimination on the Basis of Religion or Belief in Education -Faith and a Future*, Christian Solidarity Worldwide conducted a thorough report how violations of freedom of religion or belief in educational settings are diverse and experienced in many countries around the world.

15. In part III of Special Rapporteur Heiner Bielefeldt's Report of the Special Rapporteur on freedom of religion or belief, it is recognized that the 'school constitutes by far the most important formal institution for the implementation of the right to education as it has been enshrined in international human rights documents'. Mr. Bielefeldt's report also clearly displays what role the teacher/student relationship should be and emphasizes that the role of families and parents are an essential factor in the education of children in the field of religion or belief.

To summarize, this particular issue of the Chinese Law and Religion Monitor contains carefully selected articles and reports that show the obvious disregard for the international human right pertaining to the religious education of children in China.

As always, ChinaAid will continue to dedicate itself to encouraging the improvement of religious freedom, human rights and the rule of law in China.

Editor-in-Chief:

Dr. Rev. Bob Fu, founder and president, ChinaAid Association

Midland, Texas, USA

Children's Right to Religious Instruction and to Education about Religion

By Jeroen Temperman
Professor of International Law and Religion, Erasmus School of
Law, Erasmus University Rotterdam

1 Introduction

Both at the universal and at the regional level the children's rights to education and religion are amply guaranteed. Focusing on the former, the universal realm, the United Nations' (UN) Convention on the Rights of the Child (CRC) is most explicit since it provides that 'States Parties shall respect the right of the child to freedom of thought, conscience and religion',[1] while on the right to education this convention moreover codifies that:

1. States Parties recognize the right of the child to education, and with a view to achieving this right progressively and on the basis of equal opportunity, they shall, in particular:

> (a) Make primary education compulsory and available free to all;
> (b) Encourage the development of different forms of secondary education, including general and vocational education, make them available and accessible to every child, and take appropriate measures such as the introduction of free education and offering financial assistance in case of need;
> (c) Make higher education accessible to all on the basis of capacity by every appropriate means;

---

[1] CRC, Article 14, para. (1). Convention on the Rights of the Child, G.A. Res. 44/25, annex, 44 U.N. GAOR Supp. (No. 49) at 167, U.N. Doc. A/44/49 (1989), entered into force 2 September 1990.

(d) Make educational and vocational information and guidance available and accessible to all children;

(e) Take measures to encourage regular attendance at schools and the reduction of drop-out rates.

2. States Parties shall take all appropriate measures to ensure that school discipline is administered in a manner consistent with the child's human dignity and in conformity with the present Convention.

3. States Parties shall promote and encourage international cooperation in matters relating to education, in particular with a view to contributing to the elimination of ignorance and illiteracy throughout the world and facilitating access to scientific and technical knowledge and modern teaching methods. In this regard, particular account shall be taken of the needs of developing countries.[2]

Taken in conjunction, then, it is tempting to argue that children's right to freedom of religion plus children's right to education automatically produce a "children's right to religious instruction". This contribution will engage with that notion and argue that such a right is a qualified right and secondly, that an alternative / complementary notion is emerging under international law, namely "education about religion", a notion which may or may not become a legal entitlement. The latter depends on which course both international legal benchmarking takes as well as the course of domestic state practice.

2   Right to Religious Instruction: Children's or Parents' Right?

There definitely exists under international law a "right to religious instruction", but this right is qualified and peculiar in a number of ways. First, international law reserves an important role, as

---

[2] CRC, Article 28.

intermediary if not as temporary rights-holder, here for parents or legal guardians. That is, relevant international clauses on religious freedom and on the right to education suggest that parents have an important say on the combined matters of religion and education as far as their children are concerned.

Accordingly, the UN International Covenant on Civil and Political Rights (ICCPR), in its freedom of religion clause, posits that 'States Parties to the present Covenant undertake to have respect for the liberty of parents and, when applicable, legal guardians to ensure the religious and moral education of their children in conformity with their own convictions'. [3] The European Convention on Human Rights (ECHR), similarly, albeit in the right to education clause in this case, stipulates that '[i]n the exercise of any functions which it assumes in relation to education and to teaching, the State shall respect the right of parents to ensure such education and teaching in conformity with their own religious and philosophical convictions'.[4] Even CRC, whilst on the one hand codifying an autonomous children's right to religious freedom as quoted above, emphasizes these concomitant parental rights: 'States Parties shall respect the rights and duties of the parents and, when applicable, legal guardians, to provide direction to the child in the exercise of his or her right [to freedom of religion or belief] in a manner consistent with the evolving capacities of the child'.[5]

So, this all rather begs the question whose right the right to religious instruction actually is, children's or rather a parental right? International law's ambiguous answer is: both. At one and the same time there exist autonomous children's rights to religious freedom and to education and parental rights to oversee the enjoyment thereof. Strictly speaking, one could make a case for the former being dominant, since CRC is both *lex posterior* (of a later date than for instance the ICCPR) and *lex specialis* (seeing to children's rights in a more specialized fashion than does for

---

[3] ICCPR, Article 18, para. (4). International Covenant on Civil and Political Rights, G.A. Res. 2200A (XXI), 21 U.N. GAOR Supp. (No. 16) at 52, U.N. Doc. A/6316 (1966), 999 U.N.T.S. 171, entered into force 23 March 1976.

[4] Protocol to the ECHR, Article 2 (second sentence). Convention for the Protection of Human Rights and Fundamental Freedoms, 213 U.N.T.S. 222, entered into force 3 September 1953; and Protocol to the Convention for the Protection of Human Rights and Fundamental Freedoms, 213 U.N.T.S. 262, entered into force 18 May 1954.

[5] CRC, Article 14, para. (2).

instance the ICCPR). That said, CRC *itself* reserves an important role, when it comes to the enjoyment of children's religious rights, for parents.[6]

The key to solving this conundrum, then, lies in such mediating notions codified by international law as "the best interest of the child"[7] and the "evolving capacities of the child". The latter notion is emphasized by Article 5 of CRC: 'States Parties shall respect the responsibilities, rights and duties of parents or, where applicable, the members of the extended family or community as provided for by local custom, legal guardians or other persons legally responsible for the child, to provide, in a manner consistent with the evolving capacities of the child, appropriate direction and guidance in the exercise by the child of the rights recognized in the present Convention.'[8] Importantly, it separately resurfaces in the religious freedom clause: 'States Parties shall respect the rights and duties of the parents and, when applicable, legal guardians, to provide direction to the child in the exercise of his or her right *in a manner consistent with the evolving capacities of the child*'.[9]

Accordingly, yes parents have an important say vis-à-vis their children's exercise of religious freedom, but this right of parents to direct their children recedes as the cognitive capacities of the child evolve. In other words, as the child matures and becomes in a position to articulate choices and opinions in this area, parental rights diminish.

While there is no way of pinpointing this moment to any absolute number of age (every child is different after all), the Committee on the Rights of the Child which oversees state compliance with CRC requires State parties to report on this matter as part of the state reporting procedure.[10] Some states have enacted legislation to ensure that the age for fully autonomously exercising one's religious and educational rights commences some years prior to

---

[6] Ibid.

[7] CRC, Article 3 (for the main principle) and recurring throughout CRC.

[8] CRC, Article 5.

[9] CRC, Article 14, para. (2), emphasis added.

[10] *General Guidelines Regarding the Form and Contents of Periodic Reports to be Submitted by States Parties*, adopted 11 Oct. 1996, U.N. GAOR, Commission on Right of the Child, 13th Session, U.N. Doc. CRC/C/58 (1996), para. 24.

reaching legal majority,[11] thus legally boosting and solidifying the significance of the legal notion of "evolving capacities of the child".

Having said all that, it goes without saying that the right to religious instruction under international law importantly hinges on parents, their choices, but also their pro-activeness and sense of initiative. Notably, states are under no obligation to organize (nor fund, see next section) religious instruction. The burden to organize and operate alternative education, beyond the scope of the state educational framework, lies on private individuals and not on the state. This is so, first and foremost, as the scope of the positive duty to organize education for the state simply is confined to *state-organized* education. Secondly, one could distil a rationale also from religious autonomy: Heavy state interference with or control over private education naturally rather defeats the purpose of organizing something outside the realm of the state-organized educational framework.

Consequently, when it comes to actually establishing private institutions catering to the needs of those who desire religious instruction international law expressly looks at parents to organize this.[12] For instance, the UN International Covenant on Economic, Social and Cultural Rights (ICESCR) provides that 'States Parties to the present Covenant undertake to have respect for the liberty of parents and, when applicable, legal guardians to choose for their children schools, other than those established by the public authorities, which conform to such minimum educational standards as may be laid down or approved by the State and to ensure the religious and moral education of their children in conformity with

---

[11] See e.g. German Federal Law of 1985 on the Religious Education of Children, BGBl 1985/155, setting this moment at age 14.

[12] This holds, *mutatis mutandis*, true for the regional European Convention on Human Rights too. It was established early on in the jurisprudence of the European Court of Human Rights, in the landmark *Belgian Linguistics Case*, that an individual cannot 'draw from [Article 2 of the Protocol to the ECHR] the right to obtain from the public authorities the creation of a particular kind of educational establishment'. *Case Relating to Certain Aspects of the Laws on the Use of Languages in Education in Belgium*, Application Nos. 1474/62; 1677/62; 1691/62; 1769/63; 1994/63; 2126/64, judgement of 23 July 1968, at section B, para. 9.

their own convictions'.[13] CRC, similarly, stipulates that '[n]o part of the present article or article 28 shall be construed so as to interfere with the liberty of individuals and bodies to establish and direct educational institutions, subject always to the observance of the principle set forth in paragraph 1 of the present article and to the requirements that the education given in such institutions shall conform to such minimum standards as may be laid down by the State'.[14]

From these formulations it is clear that, indeed, parents have a right to organize religious instruction for their children through establishing schools to that effect. While such a parental liberty also presupposes a fair degree of institutional autonomy, all relevant clauses do stipulate the possibility for states to enforce minimum standards. Such minimum standards pertain to the content and quality of the curriculum and teaching.

International human rights law does not stipulate a specific right for parents to organize religious instruction for their children within the realm of public schools. Should the state decide not to permit religious instruction in public schools, this would not necessarily amount to a breach of parental rights, seeing as the parental right to organize alternative schools precisely serves as a *residual right* to guarantee the religious needs of parents.

3   Funding

（1）   The right to religious instruction is qualified in other ways too. Notably, unlike public (primary) schooling,[15] the state is under no obligation to fund private schools, including privately-organized religious schools. For instance, the ICCPR, the UN Human Rights Committee has pointed out, 'does not oblige States parties to fund schools which are established on a religious basis.'[16]

---

[13] ICESCR, Article 13. International Covenant on Economic, Social and Cultural Rights, G.A. Res. 2200A (XXI), 21 U.N.GAOR Supp. (No. 16) at 49, U.N. Doc. A/6316 (1966), 993 U.N.T.S. 3, entered into force 3 January 1976

[14] CRC, Article 29(2). See also Article 5, para. 1(b), of the Convention Against Discrimination in Education, of 14 December 1960, UNESCO, 11th Sess., 429 U.N.T.S. 93

[15] Primary education must be made "compulsory and available free to all". CRC, Article 28(1)(a).

[16] *Waldman* v. *Canada*, Communication No. 694/1996, Views of the Human Rights Committee adopted on 5 November 1999, para. 10.6.

That said, if the state decides to fund religious instruction it must do so without discrimination based on religion or belief. For instance, in *Waldman* v. *Canada*, a case concerning the financially privileged status of Roman Catholic schools in Canada, the Human Rights Committee held that 'if a State party chooses to provide public funding to religious schools, it should make this funding available without discrimination. This means that providing funding for the schools of one religious group and not for another must be based on reasonable and objective criteria'. [17] In that particular case, the Committee found that the funding of Roman Catholic schools compared to other faith schools was in fact discriminatory under the ICCPR.

Elsewhere it has been shown that in practice it is often difficult for monitoring bodies to address equality in the area of funding, since states have found very intricate and covert ways of financially privileging the dominant or traditional religions of the country.[18]

4 Education about Religion: An Emerging Children's Right?

(2)   While positive international human rights law does not strictly provide for a right of the child to be *educated about religions*, a case to that effect might be indirectly based on some legal notions that are enshrined by international law. Notably, CRC demands the school framework be designed to prepare 'the child for responsible life in a free society, in the spirit of understanding, peace, tolerance, equality of sexes, and friendship among all peoples, ethnic, national and religious groups and persons of indigenous origin.' [19] Arguably, knowledge about the different religions present in a country is conducive to that aim.

"Teaching about religions", naturally, differs from traditional religious instruction into one particular religion. A number of best practices exist under international law, including the OSCE *Toledo Guiding Principles on Teaching about Religions and Beliefs in*

---

[17] *Ibid.*

[18] Jeroen Temperman, "Parental Rights in Relation to Denominational Schooling under the European Convention on Human Rights", 11:2-3 RELIGION & HUMAN RIGHTS: AN INTERNATIONAL JOURNAL (2017), pp. 142–152.

[19] Convention on the Rights of the Child, Art. 29(d).

Public Schools [20] and Council of Europe's *Signposts*, [21] other important examples include the European Union's REDCo project[22] as well as the work of the UN Special Rapporteur on freedom of religion or belief's in this area.[23]

Focusing on the Toledo Guiding Principles, this study that was prepared by the OSCE Office for Democratic Institutions and Human Rights (ODIHR), can be seen as a strong plea for the inclusion of courses about religions and beliefs into the curriculum of (public) schools in a way that respects children's rights. It is worth, in conclusion, to excerpt some of the key principles here for the benefit of the reader not yet familiar with this study:

1. Knowledge about religions and beliefs can reinforce appreciation of the importance of respect for everyone's right to freedom of religion or belief, foster democratic citizenship, promote understanding of societal diversity and, at the same time, enhance social cohesion.

2. Knowledge about religions and beliefs has the valuable potential of reducing conflicts that are based on lack of understanding for others' beliefs and of encouraging respect for their rights.

3. Knowledge about religions and beliefs is an essential part of a quality education. It is required to understand much of history, literature, and art, and can be helpful in broadening one's cultural horizons and in deepening one's insight into the complexities of past and present.

4. Teaching about religions and beliefs is most effective when combined with efforts to instil

---

[20] OSCE, *Toledo Guiding Principles on Teaching about Religions and Beliefs in Public Schools (2007)*.

[21] *Signposts - Policy and practice for teaching about religions and non-religious world views in intercultural education* (2014); and *Inclusive Study of Religions and World Views in Schools: Signposts from the Council of Europe* (2016).

[22] A Europe-wide study on religion in education involving some 10 universities.

[23] UN Special Rapporteur on freedom of religion or belief, *Freedom of Religion or Belief and School Education* (A/HRC/16/53, 2011).

respect for the rights of others, even when there is disagreement about religions or beliefs. The right to freedom of religion or belief is a universal right and carries with it an obligation to protect the rights of others, including respect for the dignity of all human beings.

5. An individual's personal religious (or non-religious) beliefs do not provide sufficient reason to exclude that person from teaching about religions and beliefs. The most important considerations in this regard relate to professional expertise, as well as to basic attitudes towards or commitment to human rights in general and freedom of religion or belief in particular.

6. Reasonable adaptations of policies in response to distinctive religious needs may be required to avoid violation of rights to freedom of religion or belief. Even when not strictly required as a matter of law, such adaptations and flexibility contribute to the building of a climate of tolerance and mutual respect.

7. Where compulsory courses involving teaching about religions and beliefs are sufficiently neutral and objective, requiring participation in such courses as such does not violate the freedom of religion and belief (although states are free to allow partial or total opt-outs in these settings).[24]

---

[24] *Toledo Guiding Principles*, pp. 13-14.

Religious Freedom in Education?

By Charles L. Glenn
December 2012

How far should and may the State go in prescribing how and to what ends children will be educated without violating the freedom of parents and of faith-based organizations?

Only over the past two hundred years or so, and much more recently in most of the world, has the State concerned itself with popular schooling. As I've shown in several historical studies (Glenn 1988, 1995, 2011), it has done so primarily as a means of social control and only secondarily to promote individual opportunity.

The first effective diffusion of popular schooling in France, for example, occurred in the wake of the revolution of 1830. As in other countries, the primary motivation for the extension of popular schooling was not economic but political; recent events had made it clear that an ever-larger share of the population would inevitably be drawn into political participation, if not through voting then through insurrection. It was urgent, for the protection of civil order and of property, that the common people be educated in the appropriate habits and attitudes. These reforms were overseen by François Guizot, who explained the role of public schools in these terms: "The state obviously needs a great lay body, a great association deeply united to society, knowing it well, living at its heart, united also to the state, owing its power and direction to the state, such a corporation exercising on youth that moral influence which shapes it to order, to rules." In each village, Guizot wrote, the State would govern bodies by the gendarme, and minds by the schoolteacher.

During the 1880s, Jules Ferry laid the definitive foundations for the *école de la République* which continues to be evoked by French politicians. Ferry and his allies were convinced, as a French historian has put it, "that a *spiritual power* was necessary to establish a republic" and that it was up to the school to inculcate what one education official called a *"Foi laïque,"* a secular religion. It is this continuing conviction that the public school, rather than being neutral as between conflicting systems of belief, should itself manifest and promote beliefs considered politically essential that led to recent bitter controversies over whether Muslim girls should be allowed to cover their hair in school, or Jewish boys to wear yarmulkes.

As recently as October 2012, a commission appointed by the government of François Hollande issued a report, *Refondons l'école de la République* (let us reestablish the school of the Republic), urging that citizenship should be developed on the basis of "a collection of common values, strong and providing structure, central reference-points of the national community – in the first rank of which is secularism." French *laïcité* is not simply the absence of religion, but an alternative belief-system; the present Minister of Education, Vincent Peillon, is author of a book about one of Ferry's allies, *Une religion pour la République: la foi laïque de Ferdinand Buisson* [A Religion for the Republic: The Secular Faith of Ferdinand Buisson].

Similarly, as I showed in *The Myth of the Common School* (1988), Horace Mann and his allies across the United States promoted with considerable resonance the conviction that public schools had a unique and indispensable role in forming citizens. With the waves of European immigration that began in the late 1840s, this conviction was directed particularly against what was perceived as the threat that Catholic schools would prevent the children of these immigrants from becoming loyal Americans. The myth of the common public school continues to have tremendous influence in political debates, despite the complete lack of evidence that graduates of private, including faith-based, schools are to the slightest degree less worthy citizens than those of public schools.

My contention is that giving primacy to the State in the formation of its future citizens represents a profound threat to freedom: not only religious freedom and that of parents, but also, over the long term, to that of liberal democracy itself. I will argue that the State has an unquestionable duty to ensure justice, including adequate preparation of every child in the academic competencies required for successful adult life, but that this does *not* mean that the State should itself seek to *educate* in the sense of forming the character and values of children. That task should be left to families and to the schools to which most of them entrust their children.

As context, it may be helpful to note how this issue has been posed in international law. The *Universal Declaration of Human Rights* (1948) states that "parents have a prior right to choose the kind of education that shall be given to their children" (article 26, 3). According to the *International Covenant on Economic, Social and Cultural Rights* (1966),

> the States Parties to the present Covenant undertake to have respect for the liberty of parents . . . to choose for their children schools, other than those established by public authorities, which conform to such minimum educational standards as may be laid down or approved by the State and to ensure the religious and moral education of their children in conformity with their own convictions (article 13,3).

Similarly, the *First Protocol to the European Convention for the Protection of Human Rights and Fundamental Freedoms* provides that "in the exercise of any functions which it assumes in relation to education and teaching, the State shall respect the right of parents to ensure such education and teaching in conformity with their own religious and philosophical convictions" (article 2).

This principle was incorporated into the constitutions of a number of the postcommunist nations of Eastern Europe. For example, the Bulgarian Constitution (1991) stipulates that "the raising and the education of children until they come of legal age is a right and an obligation of their parents; the state provides assistance" (article 47, 1). That of Estonia (1992) provides that "parents shall have the final decision in choosing education for their children" (article 37). Croatia (1990) provides that "parents shall have the duty to bring up, support and school their children, and shall have the right and freedom independently to decide on the upbringing of children" (article 63). Hungary states in its Constitution (1989) that "parents shall have the right to choose the type of education they wish to ensure for their children" (article 67, 2).

The context for such provisions in both international covenants and post-communist constitutions was a reaction against the abuses of education by totalitarian regimes that had been determined to eliminate any 'thought crimes' such as deviation from the party line through a thorough indoctrination of children and youth.

Let me give a little background to explain what brings me and what I bring to this topic. For more than twenty years I was the Massachusetts state official responsible for enforcing the laws on equal opportunity in education and managing the funding for the education of minority, immigrant, and urban youth in general; I thus became very familiar with the exercise of state authority, especially through enforcing desegregation in a dozen cities and drafting the regulations for bilingual education and sex equity. This practical experience made me always concerned to seek the right balance-point between conflicting rights and social goals, as reflected in the title of my latest publication (with co-editor Jan De Groof), *Balancing Freedom, Autonomy, and Accountability* in Education (Nijmegen: Wolf Legal Publishers 2012), a four-volume survey of policies governing k-12 schooling in 65 countries. Our contention is that public policies should seek to balance among the freedom of parents to choose an education for their children, the autonomy of educators to create distinctive schools, and the accountability of such schools (and homeschoolers) to government for the adequacy of the instruction provided, as measured by results.

Here it may be appropriate to emphasize a distinction that is clear in a number of languages but often overlooked in English, between *instruction* as the teaching of skills and information, and *education* as the development of character and life-orientation. Every young person needs both. The former, I argue, may be regulated by the State in order to ensure that every child will be able to function in further schooling and in adult life, while the latter should be entrusted to families and the educators they choose.

My first book, *The Myth of the Common School*, explored the historical background to the struggle between government and religious groups over schooling in France, The Netherlands, and the United States. I have continued to chew away at this issue in more than a dozen subsequent books, some historical and others comparative, exploring how, in Michael McConnell's characterization, "Advocates of the secular state, following in the tradition of Horace Mann and John Dewey, hold that the government's control over education should be used to inculcate a common set of democratic ideals in keeping with the principles of the regime" (106) and how that has been resisted by individuals and communities of faith. One of those books looked at the effects of government funding and regulation on faith-based schools and social agencies in the United States and several European countries; its title, *The Ambiguous Embrace*, gives an indication of my conclusions.

The issue has been given a new urgency for me by a number of meetings in Europe over the past several years, concerned with how education systems should respond to the challenge of Islam, as well as by emerging threats in several countries to the freedom of Protestant and Catholic schools to retain their distinctive character. I am serving on a new National Commission on Faith Based Schools; our first meeting was a few weeks ago at the headquarters of Agudath Israel in New York City, and included a representative of Islamic schools.

In contrast with the United States, every nation of Western Europe except Italy has some constitutional or statutory provision for funding non-public schools – mostly but not exclusively religious – chosen by parents. Although the popularity of such schools is evident from their continuing growth in 'market share', concerns are now being expressed that the ever-more-visible presence of Islam and the threat to social and civic concord which many believe that to represent is making parental choice a luxury that these countries can no longer afford. In the Netherlands, where 70 percent of pupils attend non-public schools, fifty of which are Islamic, the debate is especially acute.

The question comes down to this: is it necessary, for the sake of social peace and civic unity, for the State to use its authority and its resources to ensure that all children, from whatever religious or cultural background, receive an education that develops in them the same attitudes and a common civic identity, and that distances them from the beliefs and traditions of their parents? This view is currently most often associated with the political Left, though it has also been articulated by the Right; through much of the nineteenth century the Left was opposed to efforts by conservative regimes to use schooling to promote their interests, just as now the roles tend to be reversed. It would not be unfair to say that both sides promote the educational goals of regimes with which they approve and become opponents of state intervention when the other side is in power. My own position, as will become apparent, is aligned with neither Left nor Right, but with what I like to call the 'radical Middle,' the freedom claims of individuals and minority groups to be allowed to raise their children according to their own convictions while resisting the 'tyranny of the majority' of which Tocqueville warned.

Inevitably, any effort by the State to use its power and resources to impose upon children a government-defined model of personal character and values would derail the hopes and intentions that many deeply-religious parents have for their children. As Rob Reich points out, "[t]he demands and effects of liberal citizenship are decidedly nonneutral, favoring some cultural groups over others. Liberalism consciously and purposefully urges upon citizens a certain kind of character that outlines at least minimally the kind of person we are to be, which in turn affects the way cultural groups are able to form the character of their adherents" (38). The religious liberty of these parents to nurture their children in accordance with their deepest convictions would thus be frustrated by the State, which would in effect usurp the parental role.

Of course, there is nothing new about this program, or about the conviction that the child belongs to the State rather than to his or her parents, and it has been promoted as a key element of utopian projects of social and political reform since Plato had Socrates propose that infants be taken from their parents and raised in public nurseries. The project of creating a worthier public through education has appeared in many guises and under various political banners. What is perhaps curious is that many Liberals, with their strong commitment to individual freedom and forgetting the warnings of John Stuart Mill, should currently embrace a dominant state role in education.

I am not opposed to state authority or to vigorous state action, when it is appropriate. As a Calvinist, I believe that government is appointed by God to restrain evil and to ensure justice. I agree that the reach of government appropriately extends to faith-based schools and even to families when there is good evidence that children are being abused or neglected.

On the other hand, I agree with Abner Greene in challenging absolute state sovereignty in a Hobbesian or Hegelian sense, holding with him that

> Sovereignty . . . is permeable, not plenary. We the citizens are, first, human beings with an assortment of normative commitments, only some of which are to the state. There is no good reason to privilege the state as a source of norms … the state should sometimes let us live by lights other

than its laws, by crafting legislative accommodation or judicial exemptions (282).

In particular, I challenge the idea dear to Plato and Rousseau and to many contemporary Liberals, that society should be based on shared beliefs and that it is the State's business to use its authority and resources to promote such beliefs. Such, of course, is the essential totalitarian project. As Jules Steinberg put it in his study of Locke and Rousseau,

> the members of contemporary democratic societies do not comprise the kind of "community of belief," nor do they possess a shared set of common moral commitments, which are necessary conditions of the applicability of the idea of consent as a source of moral obligation and moral legitimacy. Instead, we confront societies whose members are divided into divergent "communities of belief" who, "far from being . . . homogeneous with one another, frequently hold values in conflict with one another's – even values antithetical to one another's" (124).

That being the case, it is important that the State act on the basis of strict neutrality toward alternative conceptions of the 'Good Life.' The term 'neutrality' is often abused, in fact, to justify a position on education which excludes religious perspectives while giving free rein to environmentalist, feminist, libertarian, or other 'comprehensive' perspectives. To quote McConnell again, "what passes for 'neutrality,' according to pluralist thinkers, is actually a deeply embedded ideological preference for some modes of reasoning and ways of life over others – rationalism and choice over tradition and conscience" (104).

We should heed Abner Greene's warning that "a mere desire for uniformity will almost never suffice as a compelling state interest, and we should also be cautious before accepting paternalistic justifications for the application of law to religious and other deeply-held, normative views" (118). Surely the experience of our profoundly pluralistic yet generally successful society shows that Nicholas Rescher is correct: [t]he stability and tranquility needed for the constructive management of a society's business need not root in agreement – and not even in a second-order agreement in the processes for solving first-order conflicts – as long as the mechanisms in place are ones that people are prepared (for however variant and discordant reasons) to allow to operate in the resolution of communal problems (168).

I am what Linda McClain refers to as a 'civil society-revivalist', in sympathy with Mary Ann Glendon, Bill Galston, and others committed to societal pluralism. Obeying the law, I contend, is a rational decision, not a moral obligation. Harold Laski wrote, nearly a hundred years ago, that

> [e]very government claims that it is wrong to break the law. To the pluralist that judgement can only be made when it is known what law is broken and under what circumstances. There are realms of conduct, both individual and collective, into which, under circumstances, he would deny that the state has a right to enter (215).

Just half that long ago, I spent some time in jail in North Carolina, and courted arrest in Selma, Alabama, by disobeying laws that I believed to be unjust, as measured against a higher authority than the State. People do that all the time, and Liberals often commend them, recognizing that the State is not always right. How is it, then, that the same Liberals tend to accept without question the superior wisdom of the State, acting through its officials, to that of parents in determining what is in the best interest of children? So long as it is not their own children.

Let me reiterate: the State does have a role, and an important one, in ensuring that every child can receive an adequate education, but the State should not itself be an educator, lest it overstep the limits of its appropriate role. A *pédagogie d'État* that concerns itself with what children and youth believe and to what they give their loyalty is a profound threat to freedom. We are the inheritors of a long and toxic tradition, in political thought, of the State as the benevolent shaper of a unified society in which, as Socrates puts it in *The Republic*, division of opinion is the greatest evil. Laski pointed out how pervasive this idea has been:

> The state is today the one compulsory form of association, and for more than two thousand years we have been taught that its purpose is the perfect life. It thus seems to acquire a

flavor of generality which is absent from other institutions. It becomes instinct with a universal interest to which, it appears, no other association may without inaccuracy lay claim. Its sovereignty thus seems to represent the protection of the universal aspect of men – what Rousseau called the common good – against the intrusion of more private aspects. There seems, at least today, no certain method of escape from its demands. Its conscience is supreme over any private conception of good the individual may hold. .... The area of its enterprise has consistently grown until today there is no field of human activity over which, in some degree, its pervading influence may not be detected (185).

Contrary to this tradition of political thought, an idea out of Catholic social teaching, subsidiarity, was adopted by the European Union in its founding Treaty of Maastricht; from the Latin *subsidium* (help or assistance), subsidiarity is taken to mean that authority should rest as close to those affected as possible, with the State in a helping role. I prefer a related concept out of the Dutch neo-Calvinist tradition, 'sphere sovereignty'. Abraham Kuyper taught that there are distinct 'orders of creation,' each with its own authority and responsibility direct from God: "the family, the business, science, art and so forth are all social spheres, which do not owe their existence to the state, and which do not derive the law of their life from the superiority of the state, but obey a high authority within their own bosom; an authority which rules by the grace of God, just as the sovereignty of the State does" (90).

One of these spheres, of course, is the State itself, which "possesses the threefold right and duty: 1. Whenever different spheres clash, to compel mutual regard for the boundary-lines of each; 2. To defend individuals and the weak ones, in those spheres, against the abuse of power of the rest; and 3. To coerce all together to bear personal and financial burdens for the maintenance of the natural unity of the State" (97).

The State must not seek, however, to occupy or usurp the function of any of the other spheres. As Herman Dooyeweerd insisted, sphere sovereignty does not merely prescribe a practical "hands off" policy; rather, the boundaries that separate the spheres are a part of the very nature of things. Neither the state nor the church has any business viewing the other spheres as somehow subordinate to them.

Education at all levels is such a sphere, and while schools and educators should cooperate with the family and may work closely with the church, as well as respond to legitimate requirements set by the State, it should not be thought of as branch offices of the State . . . or indeed of a church. This is why Dutch Protestant schools, which enroll one-third of the nation's pupils, do not 'belong' to churches but to independent boards, a pattern increasingly followed by Catholic and even municipal schools, each of which enroll about another third of the pupils.

What, then, is the role of government with respect to education? It is *not* to define for us the nature of the 'perfect life'; for that, we must be free to turn to religious or philosophical traditions, to the little platoons of trust and sharing within which we live, or to solitary wrestling in the midnight hour. Whether we speak of conscience, or of God, or of primary loyalties, we acknowledge claims upon us that 'go all the way down' and which enable us to judge whether what the State is asking of us in a particular instance is just or unjust, to be obeyed or to be disobeyed whatever the cost. No, the role of government is not to define what sort of person we should become, but to specify the required outcomes of instruction in measurable terms and hold schools (and homeschooling families) accountable for achieving those outcomes. These outcomes should include the skills needed for employment and for daily life, as well as an understanding of the framework of laws, procedures, rights, and obligations that undergird civic life. They should not include the beliefs, values, and loyalties that also make up an essential part of a good education but are the responsibility of civil society: families and the educators to whom they entrust their children, but also youth groups, sport programs, centers for recreation and the arts, and religious associations. These all perform essential functions that government should value and support – for example, by tax exemptions and by use of public facilities – but which it should not seek to direct. Do we need to be reminded of efforts by totalitarian governments to 'mobilize' youth through Hitlerjugend, Young Pioneers, and the like?

It may have been noticed that I used the term 'instruction' rather than 'education' in the preceding paragraph. This is a distinction that, as noted above, is quite clear in many languages, but not as clear as it should be in ordinary English usage. 'Instruction' is teaching someone how to do something or communicating facts and the relationships among them; 'education' is shaping the human beings, a life-long process that occurs in many different settings and relationships, what the Germans call *Bildung*.

Government in a liberal democracy should not seek to be an *educator*, nor should it prescribe the values that schools (public as well as private) seek to teach. Unfortunately, calling on government to do so seems to be an irresistible temptation for many contemporary Liberals who, in other domains, would strongly resist the idea of State prescription of beliefs and attitudes. A typical – and by no means extreme – example of this view is a book by Rob Reich, *Bridging Liberalism and Multiculturalism in Education* (2002). Reich's central concern, one he shares with Amy Gutmann and many other Liberals, is that every child should become 'autonomous,' making his or her own choices about the life to live and the norms by which to live it, since otherwise, they contend, a liberal democracy cannot thrive. Autonomy, Reich admits, "is culturally non-neutral, a trait that has transformative potential for the various allegiances and affiliations of individuals and that, moreover, is not desired or fostered in all cultures" (42). In effect, too bad for them! Reich is unapologetic about the fact that this project of civic education will have repercussions that extend into areas over which the State has no jurisdiction:

> In fostering the capacity for this free and equal citizenship, the liberal state asks its citizens to draw upon the political virtues and exercise skills and habits in the public sphere that have consequences for the plurality of ways of life led by the very same citizens in their private lives. ....
> Developing autonomous citizens is partial to those cultural groups that themselves emphasize or cultivate autonomy and potentially corrosive of those that do not (46-7).

Bottom line for Reich: "an education for autonomy and the political virtues runs counter to the very possibility of the Amish or Fundamentalist parents pursuing their own conceptions of the good" (48). But doesn't our constitutional and moral commitment to religious freedom and to multiculturalism and societal pluralism protect the right of these groups to live by their own sense of religious obligation? Not at all, he says, since "nurturing the capacity for and exercise of autonomy must come *before* we respect it. The state should violate respect for autonomy in efforts to foster its exercise" (108). After all, a "state that promotes minimalist autonomy will circumscribe and narrow the kinds of lives likely to flourish" (117), and this is as it should be.

Not that Reich has any illusions about how effectively public schools carry out what he considers their mission of promoting the civic virtue of autonomy and independent thinking. He generously concedes that, "some evidence suggests that in some circumstances, parents who homeschool their children may be better at achieving the state's and the child's educational interests than public or private schools," and he goes on to point out that "some and perhaps many schools do a poor job of countering the peer pressure to which children are so likely to succumb" (159). In fact, studies have shown that one of the primary reasons that parents and their adolescent children choose homeschooling is to avoid the pressures for conformity so characteristic of the peer culture dominant in public schools.

Reich is in fact prepared to allow homeschooling, but under state control not only of its *instructional* outcomes but of its *educational* goals and methods:

> the state should require parents to use multicultural curricula that provide such exposure and engagement. They must, in other words, convince relevant officials that the educational environment of the home fits somewhere within the ambit of the liberal multicultural education (169).

And this means, inevitably, that those parents and those educators in faith-based schools who do not conform to this liberal program but continue to insist upon the authority of religious tradition would be subject to an unspecified enforcement action to prevent them from continuing to frustrate the benevolent purposes of the State. "Certain kinds of homeschools and fundamentalist religious schools that consciously insulate children from the value diversity of a culturally plural state would be disallowed" (200).

A distinction made by Linda McClain in her book on families is helpful here. She writes,

> I accept political liberalism's tenet that government may persuade to promote the virtues (or values) characterizing the ideal of the good citizen, such as tolerance, civility, reciprocity, and cooperation. I also accept its caveat that government should not promote personal virtues characterizing ways of life belonging to particular comprehensive moral doctrines (or ideals of the good person) (47).

That seems to me an appropriate distinction, and it also seems evident that 'autonomy' as defined by Reich and others constitutes a 'personal virtue' that is a key doctrine of the 'comprehensive moral doctrine' of Liberalism; Reich makes very clear that it is intrinsic to being what he considers a good person.

The implication is that, just as government may not persuade with respect to religion (McClain 43), so it should not persuade with respect to a secular life-ideal that – as Reich admits – tends to undermine many of the ways of life of cultural and religious groups in a pluralistic society. These groups constitute what McClain characterizes as "'enclaves of protected discourse and action,' where 'counterpublics' can work out and nurture alternative conceptions of self, community, and justice" (82).

But what about 'autonomy'? Hanan Alexander has suggested, recently, that in fact the

> autonomous moral self-required for liberal democratic citizenship … is to be found not in Kant's universal rationality or in Rawlsian public reason, but in thick, dynamic ethical and religious traditions that offer concrete visions of what it means to be a good person and to live in a just society, acquired through subject-subject relations both among people – parents and children, teachers and students, children and their peers – and between students and the traditions into which they would be initiated. …. [Thus,] religious education, as well as other forms of moral and ethical education, should not merely be allowed or tolerated in a liberal democracy. It lies at the very heart of that which

is required to educate morally autonomous democratic citizens (160).

Similarly, Nancy Rosenblum, warning that "the Leviathan state should not aggregate to itself, destroy, or absorb functions that [faith-based] groups naturally perform with greater moral authority, vitality, and legitimacy" (17), has suggested how this might actually function:

> publicly supported religiously integrated education is actually a more reliable and effective form of democratic education than secular education offered in public schools. Because public education generally shies away from controversial comprehensive values of any kind, its civic education is "thin." By contrast, religious groups bring their own stories and sacred histories to bear in support of democracy, endorsing civic virtues and democratic institutions from their own points of view, and thickening the grounds of commitment to democracy (19).

She goes on to urge that the State not interfere with *how* these groups promote citizenship (162).

There is a curious paradox in the argument, by Reich and others, that autonomy in the young is to be developed through state-mandated instructional methods and goals, preferably in state-run schools. Thus, he warns that "rights to separate schooling or exemptions from education … have the potential to undermine the development of civic virtues, such as autonomy and mutual respect, that are fundamental to the legitimacy and stability of the liberal state" (7). So, autonomy of families and schools should be restricted to promote autonomy of children? One is reminded of Rousseau's insistence that citizens would have to be forced to be free! Is it not more likely that children and youth develop the skills and the confidence to act in appropriately autonomous ways by observing adults – their parents and their teachers – making authentic decisions with respect to their education? What sort of model of autonomous adulthood is a teacher in a bureaucratically-managed public school, with curriculum and teaching methods prescribed and every detail of teacher responsibility spelled out in a detailed contract?

As the communist regimes in Eastern Europe were crumbling, I was commissioned by the US Department of Education to write a report on the new developments which this permitted in schooling, subsequently published as *Educational Freedom in Eastern Europe* (1995). What was most striking about my findings was the energies that were released as groups of teachers and parents were able to create new schools to serve particular groups of children, and how in the process habits of trust and cooperation developed that had long been suppressed under regimes that had allowed little scope for civil society initiatives. We are seeing the same phenomenon today in the flourishing of charter schools in Boston and around the country, schools created around a shared, focused, and profoundly *local* vision of education.

An illuminating description of this process, and its power, is found in a new book by my Boston University colleague Scott Seider, *Character Compass: How Powerful School Culture Can Point Students Toward Success*. Seider provides a detailed description of how three charter public schools in Boston set about developing character in their students through instruction, rituals, and norms for relationships within the school. In each case, he argues (and the school leaders agree) character development is a crucial aspect of the success of these schools in producing remarkable results as measured by standardized tests, bringing their Black and Latino students to levels equal or above those of students in the most affluent suburbs. What is most noteworthy, for our purposes, is that each of the schools clearly articulates a set of character goals quite distinct from those of the other schools studied. These are public schools, and they conform to government requirements with respect to the *instructional* aspect of their mission, the common standards set for all public schools, but they make effective use of their freedom to determine their own *educational* goals.

By contrast, as sociologist Alan Peshkin has pointed out, often the "public schools' material advantages are overshadowed by their comparatively poor discipline, social problems, undedicated teachers, and indifferent parents, and also by their inability to develop character and to teach the truth" (84). As research by Peshkin, James Coleman, Anthony Bryk, and other distinguished social scientists has demonstrated, this focus on strong school culture has been a key characteristic of thousands of faith-based schools, enabling them to produce strong academic results on per-pupil budgets far below those of public schools. As Coleman observed, "[a] principal of a [public] school today in which attendance is based on residency has no set of dominant community values to uphold. Instead, there are a number of contending values, each claiming legitimacy, and at least some of them capable of being backed up by legal suits in court" (11-12).

Even Amy Gutmann, while insisting that "public, not private, schooling is an essential welfare good for children as well as the primary means by which citizens can morally educate future citizens" (70), concedes that, while the "evidence is scanty, . . . it suggests that private schools may on average do better than public schools in bringing all their students up to a relatively high level of learning, in teaching American history and civics in an intellectually challenging manner, and even in racially integrating classrooms" (65). Peshkin found, in studying a fundamentalist Christian school in Illinois, that its students were "significantly less alienated" than those at the local public high school (189).

Among the latter,

> 75 percent . . . responded that school should emphasize character development, but only 39 percent reported that in fact it did so (325). ... 59 percent of them said that "earning a lot of money" was very important to them, compared with 10 percent of the Bethany students (329). ... 93 percent of the Bethany students compared with 80 percent of the public high school students responded that they would approve of a black family moving next door (332). ... 93 percent of the Bethany and 95 percent of the public-school students agreed that "people who don't believe in God should have the same right to freedom of speech as anyone else" (333). ... 83 and 84 percent respectively disagreed with the statement that "only people who believe in God can be good Americans" (334). ... 72 percent of the public-school students but only 33 percent of the Bethany students agreed that "it's hard to get ahead without cutting corners here and there" (335).

It is not my intention here to make an argument for faith-based schools, but to challenge the common assumption that they tend to make their students narrow and bigoted, perhaps unfit to be citizens of a liberal democracy. The contrary seems to be the case, as has been demonstrated recently by a remarkable survey of many thousands of graduates of different types of schools in the United States (2011) and Canada (2012), available at https://www.cardus.ca/store/publications/. Indeed, can anyone confidently assert that the attitude in the typical evangelical school is more derogatory and intolerant toward gay marriage, for example, than the attitude in the typical public school in an affluent Boston suburb is toward fundamentalist Christianity?

What studies of faith-based schools and the more recent studies of charter schools make evident is that students flourish best, and develop the qualities that make for good citizens, in schools that offer a clear and shared value-orientation. Steven Vryhof suggests that

> I[i] an increasingly fragmented and community-poor world, children need both cultural memory – their story, their identity, their anchor points – and a cultural vision – their imagined future, their worldview and life view, providing purpose and meaning for a lifetime. Schools have a role in preserving and passing on the memory of the community and its vision for the future. But memory and vision are faith issues, deeply embedded into communities" (48).

Such communities provide rich soil for a good education, and a context within which young people can put down the roots that will enable them to resist the pressures of an often-toxic media and youth culture. Vryhof goes on to point out that a key assumption of the government school ethos is that an institution with no single dominating worldview is the best environment for young minds seeking and questioning and choosing. But is a smorgasbord of options best? Shouldn't an institution stand for something, whether that be a traditional religious faith or a secular but still distinctive ethos? Inquiry is most productive when it is in service to some pressing and deeply serious question. Teaching is more passionate and personal, and cuts more deeply, when it grows out of deep convictions, out of a strong identity (51).

Berkeley law professors John Coons and Stephen Sugarman made the same point in their now-classic 1978 argument for educational vouchers:

> The most important experience within schools of choice may be the child's observation of trusted adults gripped by a moral concern which is shared and endorsed by his own family. The content of that concern may be less important than its central position in the life of the institution. Even where particular values seem narrow and one-sided, a child's engagement with them at a crucial stage of his development might secure his allegiance to that ideal of human reciprocity which is indispensable to our view of autonomy (83).

Should we be concerned about faith-based groups that set themselves in deliberate opposition to the prevailing culture? Dutch policymakers have sought to ensure that only those immigrants be allowed into The Netherlands who are willing to accept topless beaches and other manifestations of cultural permissiveness. But, after all, there are many aspects of American society and American popular culture that I find objectionable, and I suspect that most of us could produce such a list; this surely does not disqualify us as citizens. Melissa Williams has suggested that some – the deeply religious, perhaps – will decline to praise the principle of individual liberty or autonomy because they see it used to justify self-indulgence and licentiousness rather than a strong sense of moral responsibility. Others will reject the idea of citizenship itself because they have been told – as Macedo and Feinberg tell them – that citizenship requires a primary loyalty to the political community, and they are not willing to give primacy to that community over their cultural communities.

Why consider such resistance to the prevailing culture a threat to the orderly and successful functioning of society (so long, of course, as the group in question is not planning or enabling threats to public safety)? After all, "these individuals are not necessarily enemies of democracy, indeed, they might be quite eager to participate in democratic dialogue if the price of admission were not conformity to a particular vision of citizen identity" (234).

Surely a liberal pluralistic democracy has no business making such a demand!

Nor does it have any business seeking to use the authority and resources of the State to require all those charged with the education of youth – whether parents or teachers – to seek to cultivate in them a single, government-approved, model of character ....

References

Coleman, James S. and Thomas Hoffer. 1987. *Public and Private High Schools: The Impact of Communities*. New York: Basic Books.

Coons, John E. and Stephen D. Sugarman. 1978. *Education by Choice: The Case for Family Control*, Berkeley: University of California Press.

Glenn, Charles L. 1988. *The Myth of the Common School*. Amherst: University of Massachusetts Press.

--------. 1995. *Educational Freedom in Eastern Europe*. Washington, DC: Cato Institute Press.

--------. 2000. *The Ambiguous Embrace: Government and Faith-based Schools and Social Agencies*. Princeton University Press.

--------. 2011. *Contrasting Models of State and School*. New York: Continuum.

Greene, Abner S. 2012. *Against Obligation: The Multiple Sources of Authority in a Liberal Democracy*. Harvard University Press.

Gutmann, Amy. 1987. *Democratic Education*, Princeton University Press.

Kuyper, Abraham. 1931. *Lectures on Calvinism*, Grand Rapids: Eerdmans.

Laski, H. J. 1989. "From *The Foundations of Sovereignty and Other Essays* (1921)." In *The Pluralist Theory of the State*. Paul Q Hirst, editor. London: Routledge.

McClain, Linda C. 2006. *The Place of Families: Fostering Capacity, Equality, and Responsibility*. Cambridge: Harvard University Press.

McConnell, Michael W. 2000. "Believers as Equal Citizens." In *Obligations of Citizenship and Demands of Faith: Religious*

Accommodation in Pluralist Democracies. Edited by Nancy L. Rosenblum. Princeton University Press. Pp. 90-110.

Peshkin, Alan. 1986. *God's Choice: The Total World of a Fundamentalist Christian School*. Chicago: University of Chicago Press.

Reich, Rob. 2002. *Bridging Liberalism and Multiculturalism in American Education*. University of Chicago Press.

Rescher, Nicholas. 1993. *Pluralism: Against the Demand for Consensus*. Oxford: Clarendon Press.

Rosenblum, Nancy L. 2000. "Introduction." In *Obligations of Citizenship and Demands of Faith: Religious Accommodation in Pluralist Democracies*. Edited by Nancy L. Rosenblum. Princeton University Press. Pp. 3-31.

--------. "*Amos*: Religious Autonomy and the Moral Uses of Pluralism." In *Obligations of Citizenship and Demands of Faith: Religious Accommodation in Pluralist Democracies*. Edited by Nancy L. Rosenblum. Princeton University Press. Pp. 16595.

Seider, Scott. 2012. *Character Compass*. Cambridge: Harvard Education Press.

Steinberg, Jules. 1978. *Locke, Rousseau, and the Idea of Consent: An Inquiry into the Liberal-Democratic Theory of Political Obligation*. Westport, CT: Greenwood Press.

Vryhof, Steven C. 2012. "Between Memory and Vision: Schools as Communities of Meaning." In *Commitment, Character, and Citizenship: Religious Education in Liberal Democracy*. Edited by Hanan A. Alexander and Ayman K. Agbaria. New York: Routledge.

Williams, Melissa S. 2007. "Nonterritorial boundaries of citizenship." In *Identities, Affiliations, and Allegiances*. Edited by Seyla Benhabib, Ian Shapiro, and Danilo Petranoviæ. Cambridge University Press. Pp. 226-56.

This article was reprinted from http://www.champion.org/pacape-drupal/ReligiousFreedominEducation.pdf.

Is it legal for the church to run a school?

By Wang Yi

You "who pursue righteousness and who seek the Lord" (Isaiah 51:1), peace be with you.

On and off some coworkers and parents inquired or had discussions about the legal status of our Reformed School. Can it ever be registered? Is it a violation of the Compulsory Education Law for the church to run a school? What risks do the school principal and teachers have to face? And what risks will parents face?

In Xinjiang, many mosques run Muslim schools. Recently, the local anti-riot police busted a Muslim school and caused the outbreak of violent resistance. According to a government document, some imams proclaimed during worship service that "you won't be able to go to heaven if you only study at school, but do not read the scriptures", "which caused many children to drop out of public schools and start attending underground Muslim schools."

In Tibet, there are also many temples providing religious education. This year, a group of young Tibetan monks set themselves on fire one after another to protest the government's control over religion, and the death count has gone up to over ten. Most recently, the 17th Karmapa Lama in India cordially called on the monks in Tibet to stop self-immolation.

In Hong Kong, about 25% of elementary schools and middle schools are church-affiliated. From June to September this year, social protests the Hong Kong government's championing of "citizen education class" also broke out to defend the independence of education from the government. Among them, several major Christian denominations, such as Catholicism, Anglicanism and Lutheranism were among the first resisting the entry of "ideological class" into schools. When 130,000 Hong Kong people took to the street and students all over Hong Kong staged a strike, the government had to cancel the "citizen education class" which was to start in September in elementary and middle schools.

Truly I pray to the Lord that every Christian family in this church will set their minds on sending their children in elementary school or middle school to the Reformed School to receive "Christian education." Truly also will I tell you, however, the first step will always be difficult. The legal risk we're facing matches our geographical location, which is between Xinjiang, Tibet and Hong Kong.

In places where the freedom of religion is present, the Hong Kong society employed "non-violence" to decline the government's "illegal" demands about education, whereas in places where the freedom of religion is absent, imams and lamas risked all they had to resist the government's demands. If we worship the true God and proclaim the Truth, yet the price we're willing to pay for the souls of our children is no more than the price those zealous pagans have paid, how is it possible for use to share the Gospel with those devout Tibetans and Muslim who believe in God but reject Jesus Christ?

If you are a Muslim who is willing to lay down your life to provide your children with religious education, and someone from Chengdu who sends their children to atheists to receive education shares the Gospel with you and claims that what he's sharing with you in the true "Gospel", will you believe it?

Or if you're a Hong Kong-based mother who took to the street to protest against "political ideology class", and a Christian from Chengdu whose children grew up receiving the education of dialectical materialism shares the Gospel with you and claims that what she's sharing with you in the true "Gospel", will you believe it?

No, mostly like they wouldn't believe it. They would say to you, "If what you believe is the Good News, why do you let your own children stay in the Bad News? Although we're not good, we don't give our children a stone when they ask for bread or give them a snake when they ask for fish. If what you share is the true Gospel, die you do your best to deliver your children from the evil of the world? At least we fought for them and risked our futures, jobs and even lives, but how do you who claim to be the followers of Jesus show your true faith in Him? You may feed your children with poisonous milk powder and God will protect your children, but how can you give your children poisonous education?"

To this, I have two responses for you to consider.

First, in contemporary China, running church schools and running house churches are both illegal. In terms of the topic of Christin education, our dilemma is similar to the dilemma of Daniel's three friends. In other words, what we're facing is not the challenges regarding administrative review and approval or registration. What we're facing is the clash of the Christian faith with the Constitution of China.

Article 36 of the Constitution added an important restriction about education to the statement "Citizens of the People's Republic of China enjoy freedom of religious belief", i.e. "No one may make use of religion to interfere with the educational system of the state." How can religion interfere with the "educational system of the state"? Unless the "educational system of the state" assumes a particular religious and ideological stance. And this stance is articulated in Article 24 of the Constitution, i.e. "The state advocates the civic virtues of love for the motherland, for the people, for labor, for science and for socialism; it educates the people in patriotism, collectivism, internationalism and communism and in dialectical and historical materialism; it combats the decadent ideas of capitalism and feudalism and other decadent ideas."

In other words, the two articles of the Constitution clearly show that China by far is still a theocracy upholding atheism as its state religion. Therefore, I must tell you, our church's (Blessings of Autumn Rain Reformed Church) running of "Covenant Reformed School" is not only illegal, but also a direct violation of the Constitution. The bottom line is, in contemporary China, the Christian faith is an unconstitutional faith. From the day you get baptized, you have embarked on the "unconstitutional" road of no return. Apostle Paul talked about "forgetting what is behind and straining toward what is ahead". It shows that the "reformed" road is a road of no return. Either the Constitution will be changed someday, or you will be changed someday.

Consequently, the regulations in Article 8 of the Education Law is based on Article 36 of the Constitution, which goes, "The state shall separate education from religion. Any organization or individual may not employ religion to obstruct activities of the state education system." Regulations in Article 3 and Article 6 derived from Article 24 of the Constitution, which goes, "In developing the socialist educational undertakings, the state shall uphold Marxism-Leninism, Mao Zedong Thought and the theories of constructing socialism with Chinese characteristics as directives and comply with the basic principles of the Constitution... The state shall conduct education among education receivers in patriotism, collectivism and socialism as well as in ideals, ethics, discipline, legality, national defense and ethnic unity."

In light of this church's confession of faith and the call I have received from the Lord, I have to tell you that the elders of this church and I, as well as the brothers in Christ who will someday take the positions of pastor and elders after us, all strongly oppose "separating education from religion" until the Second Coming of our Lord Jesus. If the Lord sees it as good, may He help us pay a greater price than those paid by the people in Hong Kong, Tibet and Xinjiang. I'm also saying this to you and your descendants: do not elect anyone who doesn't have this resolve or show this gift of faith to be the elder of this church.

Finally, Article 62 of the Compulsory Education Law allows "private schools operated by any social organization or individual to implement compulsory education." Therefore, "compulsory" means the state should provide free education, not that citizens must receive public education. Nevertheless, based on the stipulations of the Constitution and Education Law, Non-state Education Promotion Law again reiterates in Article 4, "Non-state schools shall abide by the principle of separating education from religion; No organization or individual may make use of religion to conduct activities that interfere with the educational system of the State." This Article is the equivalent of Deuteronomy for the atheist education, which runs through the Constitution and the Non-state Education Law, and hence our violation of the law has been consistent.

Now do you see the crookedness of this policy? If the proposition that "citizens have the freedom of religious belief" and the proposition of "separating education from religion" are both valid, it implies that our children are not citizens of this country. In other words, "citizens under 18 years old do not have the freedom of religious belief," which is also why the "Three-Self" churches refuse to baptize believers under 18 years of age. Jesus said,

"Therefore go and make disciples of all nations, baptizing them in the name of the Father and of the Son and of the Holy Spirit," (Matthew 28:19) but according to this policy, "those under 18 years of age" are not considered men, let alone citizens, because all men shall be baptized, "and teaching them to obey everything I have commanded you". (Matthew 28:20)

If Christians are "second-class citizens" according to the Constitution, their under-age children are actually "third-class citizens".

Why? Because the principle of "separating education from religion" not only robs the church and Christian parents, but also directly robs our children. God's church is left with no choice but to reject the public education system "separating education from religion" and to rebuild church schools outside "the state education system" to restore Christian education. I once said in my microblogging that "Even imprisonment can't stop us from running schools", because "We must obey God rather than human beings!" (Acts 5:29) The forerunners of house churches all paid prices for their faith, and now it's our turn to pay the price for our children. Members of house churches have all paid prices for the present of the church, and now it's our turn to pay the price for the future of the church.

Jesus said, "Yet a time is coming and has now come when the true worshipers will worship the Father in the Spirit and in truth, for they are the kind of worshipers the Father seeks." (John 4:23) Dear brothers and sisters, let us not forget that Christians' children are not only humans, but this "kind of worshipers".

Second, in contemporary world, running church schools is as illegal as running house churches.

First and foremost, the "Constitution" of Christians and the church is the Bible. When we consider whether an issue is "legal" or not, we primarily think about whether it agrees with the Bible. Outside the state education dominated by atheism, running church schools is legal while not running church schools is actually illegal. In other words, for parents and the church, "start children off on the way they should go, and even when they are old they will not turn from it", (Proverbs 22:6) is not a right that can be renounced, but rather a responsibility that shall not be given up. The meaning of "starting children off on the way they should go" is not a process dictated by parents' choice. The original meaning of the phrase is "dedicating". When King Solomon and his people finished building the temple, they "dedicated the temple of God" (2 Chronicle 7:5). "Starting children off on the way" means dedicating children to God as the temple of God. "Education" is a process of dedication, or worship. Education free from worship and dedication is not education, but rather "anti-education" or "illegal education." In circumstances beyond our control, we could only rely on God's mercy granting us grace in the midst of "illegal education"; but in circumstances where we do have choices, if we continue to let our next generation receive "illegal education", we are openly testing God with our children's futures.

Secondly, between the Constitution and China's current effective Constitution and laws, there occurs a secular and "legal" space for the existence of church schools, i.e. a series of international covenants the Chinese government joined or signed. If the Bible cannot hold the Chinese government accountable in the sense of secular laws and neither can it convict the state in the sense of secular laws for the time being, those international covenants have greater legality than China's domestic laws. In the context of the government dishonoring its promises, the church's obligation to obey the king is manifested in its compliance and obedience to the United Nations' human rights convention.

1. Article 18 of Universal Declaration of Human Rights goes, "Everyone has the right to freedom of thought, conscience and religion; this right includes freedom to change his religion or belief, and freedom, either alone or in community with others and in public or private, to manifest his religion or belief in teaching, practice, worship and observance." Regarding education, Article 26 says, "Parents have a prior right to choose the kind of education that shall be given to their children." In other words, it is parents, not the state, who have the right to choose the kind of education that shall be given to their children.

2. Article 18 of International Covenant on Civil and Political Rights adopted the expression about freedom of religion in Universal Declaration of Human Rights, but Clause 4 of Article 18, in addressing parents' right to choose the kind of education for their children, makes a point to include religious education, "The States Parties to the present Covenant undertake to have respect for the liberty of parents and, when applicable, legal guardians to ensure the religious and moral education of their children in

conformity with their own convictions."

3. Article 14 of Convention on the Rights of the Child further specifies that children are humans who enjoy the freedom of religion, "States Parties shall respect the right of the child to freedom of thought, conscience and religion."

4. Article 13 of International Covenant on Economic, Social and Cultural Rights gives a more comprehensive illustration about religious education and children's education, "The States Parties to the present Covenant undertake to have respect for the liberty of parents and, when applicable, legal guardians to choose for their children schools, other than those established by the public authorities, which conform to such minimum educational standards as may be laid down or approved by the State and to ensure the religious and moral education of their children in conformity with their own convictions."

Lastly, although China's Education Law established the principle of "separating education from religion", Article 82 of Education Law

does mention "religious schools", i.e. "Regulations governing education of religious schools shall be formulated separately by the State Council."

This regulation shows: 1) Education Law recognizes that "religious school" is a legal concept; 2) Education Law recognizes that the existence of religious schools is not necessarily in conflict with the regulation that "no one may make use of religion to interfere with the educational system of the state"; 3) Education Law recognizes that it is not applicable to the management of religious schools; 4) Currently there is no existing law to govern the establishment of registration of religious schools because the State Council hasn't formulated any regulations governing religious schools.

Therefore, let's boldly proclaim that the legal status of the Reformed School is a "religious school" mentioned in Education Law. For this, we pray to the omnipotent and omniscient God who governs both human history and human hearts: like house churches anticipating and waiting to be registered with the state's civil affairs agency as independent entities someday, the Reformed School is also anticipating and waiting to be registered with the state's education affairs agency someday because its legality far exceeds the legality of any secular education, which comes from both the commandment of the Lord Almighty denied by the

Chinese government and the universal human rights covenants accepted by the Chinese government. Therefore, before the principle of "separating education from religion" is altered, the Reformed School and our church will uphold Christ as our sole Sovereign, stick to our identity, and will not seek a third road, because the principle we stick to is the principle of "separating church and the state", which is also in our confession of faith. As far as education is concerned, this principle implies "separating education from the state" instead of "separating education from religion." It means the content of education is determined by the conscience and faith of citizens, not the state. Some parents mistakenly believe that they choose education for their children, which is a lie deceiving themselves and others. As a matter of fact, before church schools became available, we didn't have a choice at all. Sending your children to the Reformed School is your choice whereas sending your children to public schools is not your choice, because it's a choice made by the state on your behalf.

Our Lord, we ask for truth, wisdom and faith. Our God help our children, our church, and our government. On his knees for the revival of religious schools.

God's servant

Wang Yi

10/18/2012

"When the nest is overturned, can the eggs in it stay unbroken?"
An overview of religious education for children in China

By Meng Yuanxin

According to the United Nations' covenants on human rights, the freedom of religious education is a component of the freedom of religion. What is religious education? According to the International Encyclopedia of Education complied by T. Hu-sen, etc., there are two kinds of religious education: religious instruction and instruction about religions. (Husen,T.& Postlethwaite T.N.,1994,4996) The Encyclopedia of Education published in Taiwan defines religious education by the content of education, "It is education about religious doctrines and religious rules." (Shi Hengqing, 2002). In this article, religious education for children is defined as instruction about religions provided to children regarding religious doctrines and rules. According to Law of the People's Republic of China on the Protection of Minors, minors refer to "citizens under the age of eighteen," which is identical to the definition of children in the United Nations' covenants on human rights. References cited in this article use "minors", "citizens under the age of eighteen" and "children" interchangeably due to their identical connotations. As a matter of fact, the Communist Party of China (CPC) and the Chinese government still do deny the concept of "religious education for children." This author has not yet found any academic publications in Chinese about religious education for children in mainland China except for a few published discussions and news articles, compared to a large number of anti-religion and pro-atheism articles published by the CPC government.

By providing a panoramic overview of the mainland China's policy regarding religious education for children since CPC took power in 1949, including policies and regulations about religion and education mostly during Deng Xiaoping's era and Xi Jinping's Administration, as well as some exposed cases, which are only the tip of the iceberg, this article attempts to give a detailed account of the policy evolution and actual development of religious education for children in China, and make a simple comparison of China's policies and the United Nations' covenants on humans rights and the polices and regulations adopted by the majority of countries in the world. This author believes that in the so-called Xi's New Era, religious education for children in China is experiencing a dark age and will be dealt with more harshly in the future like in Mao's era.

I. Mao's era: With the skin gone, to what can the hair attach itself? Politics wiped out religion and dominated education, not to mention religious education for children.

During the three decades between 1949 and 1978, the Constitution of the People's Republic of China promulgated in 1954 has nothing concerning religious education; neither was any law or regulation concerning education passed during this period of time. As a result, religious education was subject to the control of CPC's policies due to the absence of laws or the rule of law concerning it. In his "Speech at the Meeting with Representative of CPC and Workers in Moscow" delivered on November 18, 1957, Mao said, "Materialism must replace Idealism and Atheism must replace Theism." On September 19, 1958, CPC Central Committee and the State Council pointed out in "Instructions about the Work Concerning Education", "CPC's guiding principle for the work concerning education is to make education serve the political agenda of proletariats…" CPC had full control over education and children in China were forced to receive CPC's anti-religion, atheistic education centered round materialism and communism. During the Cultural Revolution, all Buddhist temples, Daoist temples, mosques and churches across China were forcibly shut down and religious clergy were forced to leave their profession. Religious activity disappeared from public life. With politics dominating religion and aiming to eradicate religion, religion was on the verge of extinction, and thus there was no room for religious education, not to mention religious education for children.

A. Catholicism and Christianity: church-sponsored schools "taken over, handed over and reformed"

Church-sponsored schools appeared in China as early as in the Qing Dynasty long before 1949. After 1949 when CPC took over China, the government took over these schools, which marked the end of church-run schools and Christian education. Although "CPC's Instructions about Catholicism and Christianity" released on August 19, 1950, required that "church-run schools be perceived as privately-owned enterprises and be treated by the government equally in the same way as public schools. (But) church-run schools are mandated to offer political class and church-run higher education institutions must offer religious class as an elective... And church-run schools shall not stage pro-religion or anti-religion exhibitions or gatherings on campus." On November 30, 1950, however, Wang Liangzao, a priest from the Catholic Church's Chengdu parish in Guangyuan county, Sichuan province, jointly released "The Declaration of Independence and Reform" with a few other people, and soon after, the Chinese government took schools sponsored by the Catholic School under state control. On December 29, 1950, the Political Affairs Council passed "Decisions Regarding How to Handle Cultural and Educational Relief Agencies and Religious Groups Subsidized by the United States of America" at its 65th Meeting, and thereafter took over schools receiving financial assistance from America. On January 14, 1951, the Political Affairs Council's Culture and Education Committee issued "Regulations about the Registration of Cultural and Educational Relief Agencies and Religious Groups Receiving Subsidies and Funding from Foreign Countries", starting to register schools receiving subsidies from foreign countries or operating on funds from foreign countries before a given date. On June 15, 1951, Shanghai-based Liberation Daily proclaimed that "the term 'church-run schools'" had been sent to the History Museum. According to the "Instructions about Taking Over Private Elementary Schools and Middle Schools" issued by the Ministry of Education on August 10, 1952, and incomplete statistics, over 200 church-run middles schools and 1,700 church-run elementary schools had been taken over by the government and turned into public schools, and thereafter, all church-run schools had been taken over, confiscated or reformed by the CPC government.

B. Religious education for minority ethnic groups

Prior to 1949, religion and education were blended in the Buddhist temples among the Tibetan and Tai people. Among Uyghur and Hui people, there were both religious schools and non-religious schools. After 1949, religious schools were gradually dismissed and religious class in non-religious schools was also canceled.

The "democratic" reform of religious system between 1958 and 1960 mainly targeted Islam among Hui people and Buddhism among the Tibetans. Hui people mainly lived in Ningxia Hui Autonomous Region and the Muslim region in Gansu, Qinghai and Shaanxi. Tibetan Buddhism was prominent mainly in Yunnan, Sichuan, Gansu and Tibet where the Tibetans congregated. On August 10, 1958, the CPC Central Committee's Ministry of the United Front issued "Opinions about Reforming the Religious System among Hui People", and on December 7, 1958, Ministry of the United Front approved and forwarded "The Report of CPC in the Ethnic Affairs Committee on Problems regarding How to Handle Islam and Lamaism". According to this report, "Temples shall not force...children to learn scriptures or become Manlas(students of Islam)... and Imams and other religious professionals shall not interfere with the state education", and hence the practice of sending Muslim children to mosques to study scriptures and become Manlas was abolished in regions inhabited by minority ethnic people believing Islam.

1) Xinjiang: religious schools banned

When CPC first took power in the 20th century, there were still two types of education in Xinjiang: regular education and religious education. Both public schools and schools run by the Ethnic Culture Promotion Committee offered religious classes. In 1950, Xinjiang's education departments took over and reformed elementary schools and explicitly outlawed religious schools, which was not effectively implemented though. In 1952, in response to the requests by religious communities, the CPC government in Xinjiang restored two religious classes per week in elementary schools, which was taught by school teachers and attended by students on the voluntary basis. In 1953, the development of religious schools exceeded their scale in 1949, so the government mandated at the end of the year that religion should not interfere with school education. With the completion of the socialist reform in 1956, some elementary-level religious schools were shut down in Xinjiang. In 1958, Xinjiang government again explicitly outlawed religious schools and classes. During the Cultural Revolution, all the Islamic religious schools in Xinjiang were banned.

2) Regions inhabited by Tibetans: Tibetan Buddhist temples almost all wiped out and religious education no longer in existence

Temple-run education as the major form of traditional education in regions inhabited by Tibetan Buddhism believers had lasted 1,200 years and the relationship between temple-run education and religious education was closely interconnected. Since the religious reform in 1958, this tradition was systematically destroyed, and many Tibetan Buddhist temples were appropriated by government-run schools. Among the 618 Tibetan Buddhist temples in Qinghai, up to 597 of them disappeared. After the onset of the Cultural Revolution, only 8 out of 2,713 temples survived in Tibet, and only a dozen out of 6,000 temples survived in the entire Tibetan Buddhist region, including Qinghai, Sichuan, Gansu and Yunnan. Consequently, only a few Tibetan Buddhist temples remained before the "Reform and Open-up", and the traditional temple-run education which included religious education for children had been canceled entirely.

II. Deng's Era: the confusing mix of "policy vs. law and illegal vs. legal"

The beginning of Deng's Era is not clearly defined. As far as the management of religion goes, Deng's Era started in 1978 when Deng Xiaoping officially became the supreme leader of CPC's and lasted through the Hu Yaobang-Zhao Ziyang Administration, the Jiang Zemin Administration, and the Hu Jintao-Wen Jiabao Administration, during which the government maintained the policy of keeping religious education out of public education as was done previously. There was one difference though, i.e. this policy was incorporated into the legislature about education and presented in the cloak of law and legality, and even more confusingly, the cloak of "the rule of law." In regard to the various forms of religious education for children that existed outside the state's education system and in the gray area whose legal status was interpreted in opposite ways by the authorities and common people, the government toned down the harshness in its rhetoric, but the practice of suppression of religious education was selective and only carried out in a few regions. The intensity and extent with which such policies were carried out also varied from region to region.

A. National education: regulations followed by policies; sustained rejection of religious education

Regarding this, the Ministry of Foreign Affairs of the People's Republic of China also admitted in May 2010, in "The People's Republic of China's Third and Fourth Report about the Implementation of Convention on the Rights of the Child" that "China's national education doesn't include religious education."

1) Connotations of the two major principles regarding education and religion: subtle differences between policy and regulation

a) "The principle of separating education from religion"

This principle can be traced back to the origin of CPC because as early as in June 1923, CPC asserted in Article 12 of the "Constitution of the Communist Party of China's" (Draft) passed on CPC's 3rd National Conference, "Practice compulsory education and the separation of education from religion." The Education Law of People's Republic of China passed on March 18, 1995, at the 3rd Plenary Session of the 8th National People's Congress mentioned religion in four articles, including Article 8, Part 2, which says, "The State separates education from religion. No organization or individual may make use of religion to conduct activities that interfere with the education system of the State."

What is the "principle of separating education from religion" then? In the section "Interpretations of law and Q&A" on the National

People's Congress' website (www.npc.gov.cn, 12/17/2000), the answer to the question "why must education be separated from religion" is given in prohibitive statements:

"No religious organizations or individuals shall illegally interfere with the educational and teaching activities of schools and other educational institutions in the national education system. No organizations or individuals shall utilize religion to engage in illegal activities that interfere with the state's education system, interfere with the natural science education and political education offered in schools, spread religious ideas in schools and other educational institutions, conduct religious ceremonies, or use schools to inoculate students with religious ideas and convert students to religion…"

CPC Central Committee's Department of United Front, which is the actual and direct supervisory organ of religion in China, used both prohibitive and advocatory statements in its answer to this question, as shown in "Regulations on Adherence to the Principle of Separating Religion from National Education" posted on the Department of United Front's website (12/08/2008).

"No organizations or individuals shall use religion to interfere with national education or proclaim religion in any manner in schools; further reinforce education about atheism and materialism among faculty and students of all ethnicities; never cease to increase faculty's and students' ability to voluntarily resist superstitions and cults; non-state schools shall implement the principle of separating education from religion. No organizations or individuals shall use religion to engage in activities to interfere with the state's education system."

b) "Religion shall not interfere with education"

The wording of CPC Central Committee's decrees is slightly different from the wording of the Constitution and the series of laws and regulations about education and the difference lies in this: the extension of the concept "education" in CPC Central Committee's documents is broader than that of the concept "education" in the Constitution and the series of laws and regulations about education.

III. The stipulations in CPC Central Committee's degrees

On June 27, 1981, the Resolution on Certain Questions in the History of Our Party since the Founding of the People's Republic of China adopted at the 6th Plenary Session of the 11th Central Committee of the Communist Party required that "…religion shall not intervene in… education."

Documents following this expanded the meaning of education to include both "school education" and "social and public education." According to The Basic Viewpoint and Policy on the Religious Question during Our Country's Socialist Period issued by the Secretariat of the Central Committee issued by CPC Central Committee on March 31, 1982, widely known as Document No. 19, "The political power in a socialist state…will never permit religion… to intervene in the schools or public education. It will be absolutely forbidden to force anyone, particularly people under eighteen years of age, to become a member of a church, to become a Buddhist monk or nun, or to go to temples or monasteries to study Buddhist scripture." This decree was repeated word by word in the "Instructions by CPC Central Committee on Properly Handling Religion in the Campaign of Purging Spiritual Pollution" issued on December 31, 1983.

On July 14, 1990, CPC Central Committee's Notification about Reinforcing the Work of the United Front reiterated, "…religion shall not intervene in… school education as well as social and public education."

The Notification about Several Questions regarding Further Improving Religious Work issued by CPC Central Committee's State Council in 1994 also emphasized, "No one shall use religion to interfere with… school education as well as social and public education or use religion to impede the activities of compulsory education."

IV. Stipulations in the Constitution and the series of laws and regulations regarding education

The gist of those stipulations can be summarized as "No organization or individual shall use religion to engage in activities that interfere with the educational system of the state or the activities of compulsory education", which is expressed in Clause

2, Article 36 of Constitution of the People's Republic of China, Article 11 of the Law of the People's Republic of China on Regional Autonomy by Ethnic Minorities which took effect on October 1, 1984, Article 16 of Compulsory Education Law of the People's Republic of China which took effect on July 1, 1986, Article 8 of Education Law of the People's Republic of China which took effect on September 1, 1995, Article 3 of Regulations on Religious Affairs (2004), and Article 4 of Regulations on Religious Affairs (2017).

A. Non-state schools - Regular non-state schools: the principle of separating education from religion reiterated

Clause 2, Article 4 of the Non-state Education Promotion Law of the People's Republic of China which took effect on September 1, 2003, says, "Non-state schools shall abide by the principle of separating education from religion. No organization or individual may make use of religion to conduct activities that interfere with the educational system of the State."

B. Schools involving foreign organizations: involvement of religion strictly forbidden and religious education singled out

Article 7 of the Regulation of the People's Republic of China on Chinese-foreign Cooperative Education which took effect on September 1, 2003, says, "Foreign religious organizations, religious institutions, religious universities and colleges, and religious instructors may not engage in cooperative education activities within China"; and "Sino-foreign cooperative education institutions may not engage in any religious education or carry out any religious activities".

C. Christianity and Catholicism targeted
1) legal schools and illegal religious education: non-state schools run by Christians experience "7-year's itch."

Since the Regulations on Schools Run by Social Forces took effect in October 1997, schools run by various social forces, including Christians, started to emerge.

Among the first batch of schools run by Christians, Beijing-based "Morning Star" founded by Xu Yanyi in 2004 is well-known and influential. It is a non-residential school starting from 1ˢᵗ grade to 12ᵗʰ grade. On May 10, 2005, Xu obtained an official permit to run the school, but in June 2010, the school was shut down, which, according to Xu, was caused by the government's excessive caution and suspicion. "The Ministry of Education showed up unannounced and accused us of making students read and memorize bible verses. That is nothing but a rumor, only because we posted some character-building materials on classroom walls and some happen to be bible verses in Chinese and English."

On July 30, 2009, Christian-run Hualin Foreign Languages Experimental Kindergarten obtained the administrative permit from Guangxi Zhuang Autonomous Region's Yufeng District's Bureau of Education. According to the news from Zhongxin Net on July 17, 2015, the kindergarten was outlawed by the Bureau of Education which announced that investigation showed that the kindergarten had long used books of religious content as textbooks.

2) "Gray" schools and illegal religion: facing investigation and shutdown anytime

There are two other types of Christian education in China: parents-run homeschools, and unregistered schools facilitated or run by urban churches which mainly admit the children of church members. Homeschools, such as ACE (Accelerated Christian Education), are often available only to a small number of elite middle-class Christian families in cities. Christian schools run by churches, on the other hand, have no avenue to get registered according to the law or get approved by the government, and therefore can only register themselves as "art schools", "tutoring centers", or "early-stage education centers". Some even run without any form of registration. Existing in a gray area, they are often tolerated by the grassroots government, but are often under pressure from the government and at risk of being investigated or shut down. The investigation and shut-down by the government are often based on accusations that these schools operate outside their allowed scope of business operations. Child educated in these two types of Christian schools cannot transfer to public schools in China, so some parents who send their children to such schools to receive Christian education will still have their children registered with public schools and even have to pay tuition to public schools.

3) Religious education by church Sunday schools: overall tolerance and sporadic suppression

The church's administration of religious education to children has a long history in China. In 1940, the Chinese Sunday Schools Association was founded and made a great contribution to providing early-stage religious education to children in China.

In early 1980s, to prevent children from disrupting the adults' worship service, some churches in mainland China started to separate adults and children during Sunday service, which marked the reemergence of Sunday school for children in mainland China. However, the reality is not always as described in "The Combined 3rd and 4th Report by the People's Republic of China on the Implementation of Conventions on the Rights of the Child", "The law of China doesn't forbid parents and legal guardians from giving their children religious education; neither does the Chinese government interfere with this kind of behavior. The government has never interfered with believing parents taking their children to venues of religious activities to participate in religious activities. In regard to Catholic churches' Catechism and Christian churches' Sunday schools and other religions offering special religious education according to their religious traditions to a small number of children, the government neither encourages it, nor forbids it."
The external challenge to children's Sunday school mainly lies in the grassroots government in a few regions often interfering with children's attendance of Sunday schools and depriving children of their right to be exposed to the Christian faith.

D. School education and religion in minority ethnic regions

In February 1983, to address the widespread issue of school education and religion in ethnic minority regions, the General Office of the Central Committee of the Communist Party of China and the General Office of the State Council forwarded the Ministry of Education's Opinions about How to Properly Handle Religion's Disruption of School Education in Ethnic Minority Regions (Document No. 16), which made six requests: 1) No spread of religion or religious ideas among students in schools; 2) Schools shall not cancel classes for the sake of religious activities; 3) No one shall force students to believe in religion or become monks, lamas or manlas; 4) No religious classes of any form shall be offered in schools; 5) No one shall use religion to disrupt or interrupt school's normal teaching activities; 6) No one shall in any way interfere with or resist school's teachings about Marxism-Leninism, Maoist ideology, science and culture.

On November 2, 1992, the Ministry of Education issued "Opinions about Strengthening the Education of Ethnic Minority Groups in Ethnically Mixed and Scattered Regions", which says, "Adhere to the principle of keeping religion away from education and persist in educating students about atheism and materialism to make students foster scientific worldviews and views about religion."

1) Featured area: Xinjiang
a) "Underground" (non-official) Islamic schools: ever changing policy content and policy effects causing escalation of conflicts

Muslims' traditional form of education is "scriptural hall education", also known as Mosque education and mainly provided by scriptural schools. There are three levels of scriptural schools: the advanced-level scriptural schools specialize in cultivating elite religious figures, the medium-level scriptural schools educate adult Muslims, and the primary-level schools provide education to children and teenagers. These schools teach religious ceremonies, Arabic language, Koran, the Sacred Teachings of Islam, as well as Islamic philosophy, law and literature. The "underground" scriptural schools in this article refer to primary scriptural schools not authorized or approved by the Chinese government, also known as privately set-up scriptural classes (locations) or "non-official" scriptural schools. Since the Chinese government bans evangelizing minors, all "underground" scriptural schools are deemed as "illegal". Xinjiang's policy about "underground" scriptural schools changed from "channeling and dissembling" to "banning and outlawing" and intensified from "focusing on religion's interference with education and impact on children's development" to the level of "preventing the spread and mobilization of extremist religious forces."

Since the "Reform and Open-up" in late 1970s, CPC's policy aiming to wipe out religion started to loosen up and Islamic scriptural schools started to come back to life in Xinjiang. In 1980s, a large number of "underground" scriptural schools quickly emerged in Xinjiang.

In February 1983, the General Office of the Central Committee of the Communist Party of China and the General Office of the State Council forwarded the Ministry of Education's Opinions about How to Properly Handle Religion's Disruption of School Education in Ethnic Minority Regions (No. 16 Document), which specifically mentioned "underground" scriptural schools, saying "privately set-up scriptural schools without governmental approval must be handled step by step; no approval shall be given to the request for Arabic language class by some ethnic elementary and middle schools in certain regions; no restoring of religious class in the name of learning the Arabic language shall be allowed."

In 1984, Xinjiang Uygur Autonomous Region's CPC Party Committee public decreed that it is absolutely forbidden to set up scriptural schools without government's permission", and such schools (classes) as well as the practice of privately teaching children scriptures at home must be "aggressively channeled and dissolved."

With the emergence of "underground" scriptural school in areas with a concentrated Muslim population in Xinjiang and the rapidly growing social influence of "underground" scriptural schools, the government's policy shifted from "channeling and dissolving" to "banning and outlawing" and started to portray the issue of "underground" spiritual schools as reflective of the external conflicts between the enemy and us people instead of an issue of internal conflicts within the people themselves.

In 1988, Xinjiang Uygur Autonomous Region issued a decree to strictly prohibit underground scriptural schools and launched a series of actions to ban and outlaw them. Since 1990, about 1,000 "underground" scriptural schools have been outlawed every year, mostly attended by students of public schools. According to the

Regulations of Xinjiang Uygur Autonomous Region on Religious Affairs promulgated in 1990, "No organization or individual is allowed to set up religious schools and scriptural schools (sites) without government's approval."

Around 1997, Xinjiang Uygur Autonomous Region struck certain regions with harsh measures, but "underground" scriptural schools did not cease to exist. From Jan to Oct 1999, Xinjiang shut down 118 "underground" scriptural schools. From January to October 2004, Xinjiang outlawed 420 "underground" scriptural schools. From January to May 2006, a total of 112 "underground" scriptural schools were shut down across Xinjiang. Lizha, a graduate student of People's Public Security University of China, disclosed in "A Preliminary Study of the Illegal Religious Activities in Xinjiang", "In 2008 alone, 1,320 people were caught for involvement in underground scriptural studies in three areas of southern Xinjiang."

b) Legal schools: public decrees issued to ban religious activities

It was in Xinjiang in 1996 that the rule "Religious activities are prohibited in schools" first appeared in the government's documents. On February 2, 1996, Xinjiang Uygur Autonomous Region's Bureau of Education released Regulations about Banning On-campus Religious Activities (applicable to schools of all levels and all types except religious schools), which says, "(In)socialist schools... all forms of religious activities are prohibited and no religious groups or individuals shall build or set up mosques, Buddhist temples or Daoism temples on school campuses, including school-run factories, farms, internship sites, etc., and those preexisting ones must be demolished or relocated within a certain time. No students shall be recruited to study religious texts. There shall be no interfering with school-conducted education about dialectical materialism, historical materialism, atheism, and scientific or cultural knowledge." Regarding teachers, "Teachers shall not participate in religious activities, spread religious ideas among students, or coerce and organize students to join religious activities. Those who violate this regulation will be subject to school's criticism and education and those who refuse to mend their ways will lose their teaching qualifications. Those who commit severe violations shall be removed from the faculty team."

Students "shall not participate in religious activities, attend scriptural schools or choirs, cite scriptures, sing worship songs, fast, or wear religious symbols, and those who participate in religious activities "will be criticized and educated by schools and those who refuse to mend their ways are subject to discipline and penalty."

c) Minors prohibited from entering mosques

Mosques in Xinjiang's Urumqi and Altai have this government-issued sign posted on their doors all year long, "No government employees and minors allowed to enter".

2) Special attention: children's religious education in Tibetan-inhabited regions

In May 1980, Tibetan Autonomous Region's CPC Party Committee's Department of the United Front promulgated "Several Specific Regulations about Continuing to Implement the Party's Policy on the Freedom of Religion and Belief" and Tibetan Autonomous Region's CPC Party Committee issued "Opinions about Comprehensively Implementing the Party's Policy on the Freedom of Religion and Belief and Reinforcing the Management of Religious Activities". Per these two documents, temples should provide quality education on classical texts and culture to children whose parents willingly send their children to temples to become monks and nuns; when children reach 18 years of age, it is up to them to decide whether to leave the temple or stay." Based on this, the Tibetan branch of the Buddhist Associations of China gradually restored scripture chanting classes and scripture study classes and began to offer religious classes in some major Buddhist temples. On November 22, 1980, however, Tibetan Autonomous Region promulgated "Instructions on Further Implementing the Party's Policy on Religion Comprehensively", stating that "The rare cases of using religion to interfere with administration and education... must be corrected and forbidden."

In February 1983, the General Office of the Central Committee of the Communist Party of China and the General Office of the State Council forwarded the Ministry of Education's Opinions about How to Properly Handle Religion's Disruption of School Education in Ethnic Minority Regions (No. 16 Document). One of the six opinions in this document singled Tibet out, "No one shall force students to believe in religion or to become monks, lamas or manlas."

Since 1996, the government has launched the so-called "patriotic education campaign" in Tibet and government-run media aggressively promoted atheistic education on children and defamed Dalai Lama.

Part 1 of Article 27 of "Methods for Managing Tibetan Buddhist Temples" promulgated by the State Religious Affairs Bureau on September 30, 2010, which became effective on November 1, 2010, says, "Students admitted by temple-run scripture study classes… should in general be above 18 years of age". This regulation almost rips all children of the opportunity to join the scripture study class in temples.

V. Since Xi Jinping's ascent to power: both religion and religious education for children suppressed on all fronts

As far as the management of religion is concerned, Xi's administration went through two stages. The first stage from CPC's 18th National Conference in November 2012 to CPC's 19th National Conference in October 2017 is marked by the State Council's Legal System Office openly collecting feedback online about the Regulations on Religious Affairs (Draft for Review) submitted by the State Bureau of Religious Affairs in September 2016 and the release of the new Regulations on Religious Affairs in August 2017. The second stage began on October 24, 2017, when Amendment to CPC Constitution was adopted on CPC's 19th National Conference and Xi Jinping's Thought on Socialism with Chinese Characteristics for a New Era was written into CPC Constitution, which officially ushered in Xin Jinping's Era as far as CPC's intergenerational power transmission is concerned. In the second stage, CPC launched a series of policies and measures against the Constitution and laws made by themselves to suppress religious education for children and forbid children to convert to religion, causing a massive outbreak of persecution cases across China, which is a great regression nearly to the extent of entirely eradicating children's religious education

A. Impending storm: prelude of the so-called "new era"
1) Regression instead of progression of reforms and revision of laws concerning religious education

a) Pilot free trade zone vs. intensified control on religious education

The Special Management Measures (Negative List) for Foreign Investment Access in Pilot Free Trade Zones (2017), i.e. Document No. 51, which took effect since July 10, 2017, not only reiterated Article 7 of the Regulation of the People's Republic of China on Chinese-foreign Cooperative Education, which says, "Foreign religious organizations, religious institutions, religious universities and colleges, and religious instructors may not engage in cooperative education activities within China; Sino-foreign cooperative education institutions may not engage in any religious education or carry out any religious activities,", but also added a new stipulation, "They are prohibited from investing in religious education institutions in China." The control over religious education has regressed instead of improving in the so-called pilot free trade zones.

b) The new Regulations on Religious Affairs announced the separation of civil and public education from religion.

Article 44 of the new Regulations on Religious Affairs released in August, 2017, "forbids evangelizing in schools and other educational institutions other than religious schools and institutions, conducting religious activities, establishing religious organizations, and setting up venues for religious activities", and the new Regulations devotes a separate chapter to "religious schools" which used to be in the chapter about "religious groups" in the old Regulations, thus emphasizing the separation of religious education and training from national education for citizens. As pointed out by Freedom House, a non-governmental organization, in its report "Freedom in the World 2018", the new Regulations further narrowed the scope of religious freedom, especially "religious education" for children.

2) Xinjiang: escalation from "banning religion from campus" to "resisting and preventing religion's infiltration into campus"

The policy of "banning religion from campus" mainly targets open and direct religious activities while the policy of "resisting and preventing religion's infiltration into campus" targets both that and the expression of covert and indirect religious messages.

This author found three documents issued between 2011 and 2013 but failed to find the original publications despite painstaking efforts. The three documents are: Document No. 18 issued by CPC's Central Committee's Office (2011), Xinjiang Autonomous Region's Party Committee's Opinions about Resisting and Preventing Religion's Infiltration into Campus, i.e. Document No. 27 by Xinjiang's Party Committee (2012), and Several Instructions and Opinions about Further Managing Illegal Religious Activities and Containing the Infiltration of Religious Extremist Ideology" (Trial), i.e. Document No. 11 by Xinjiang's Party Committee (2013). This author believes that it is the above three documents, especially the second and third one, that shaped up the policy of "resisting and preventing religion's infiltration into campus" in Xinjiang, which is reinforced by two "shall nots", i.e. No one shall use religion to interfere with the activities of the state's education system, and no organizations or individuals shall conduct religious activities in schools. As far as the "six strict prohibitions" goes, this author only found five of them, i.e. spreading religious ideas and converting someone to religion are strictly prohibited on campus; setting up venues for religious activities and conducting religious activities are strictly prohibited on campus; founding religious groups and organizations by faculty or students is strictly prohibited; faculty and students are strictly prohibited from attending or organizing religious activities off campus; wearing religious attires and religious symbols is strictly prohibited. In another online article titled "The Six Strict Prohibitions Implemented by Aketao County's Nekeqi Elementary School", this author found the "six prohibitions" as follows:

1)Prohibit religious activities from entering schools; 2)prohibiting religious behaviors from entering schools – faculty and students are prohibited to practice religious behaviors at school or at home and violations with adverse effects will cause the expulsion of the violators; 3)prohibiting religious speech from entering schools; 4)prohibiting religious attires and decorations from entering schools – faculty and students shall not wear hijab or strange clothes; 5) prohibiting religious ideas from entering schools – faculty and students shall not accept religious ideas or become religious believers; 6) prohibiting religious beliefs from entering schools – faculty and students shall not join any religious activities.

According to Corps Daily dated October 31, 2014, the education system of Kashgar launched "the Oath-taking and Signing Ceremony by A Thousand School Principals to Resist Religion's Infiltration into School Campus."
On May 6, 2016, Yaxin Net published an article under the title "Xijiang Kashgar No. 1 Middle School: Relentlessly Keeping Religion Out of Schools", according to which, "Every day, the head teacher of every class will warn students against converting to religion or participating in religious activities; the four intersections in front of the school are guarded every day by school teachers half an hour before and after school hours to identify students wearing religious clothing or demonstrating other improper behaviors."
The Notice of Issuing "Instructions about Focusing on the Overarching Goals and Safeguarding Schools' Safety and Stability", i.e. Document No. 1 (2017) was promulgated by Xinjiang Uygur Autonomous Region's Education Bureau on April 11, 2017, which demands "relentlessly resisting and preventing religion's infiltration into schools and implementing the 'six strict prohibitions' in schools' rules, regulations and daily management work."

3) Gansu province strictly prohibits religious activities

In early May 2016, a video titled "Cute Gansu girl citing scriptures" went viral on the internet showing kids of a kindergarten in Gansu's Linxia citing Koran. Soon after, Gansu province's Bureau of Education required the education department of all level to strictly forbid the entrance of religious activities into schools and made six commands to schools of all levels and all types except for government-approved religious schools and institutions: 1) no religious activities are allowed; 2) no religious classes or spreading of religious ideas to students are allowed, no organizing students to visit religious sites for teaching activities and field trips, and no interfering with or blocking the schools' conducting of ideological, moral, scientific and cultural education; 3) no forcing or enticing students to convert to religion, or engaging in any activities to evangelize students, form religious groups and organizations; 4) no religious ideas in textbooks used in medium-level and lower-level schools; 5) students are not allowed to attend illegal religious organizations and religious gatherings; 6) teachers are not allowed to use their positions to teach about religion in class or take students to religious activities; foreign teachers are strictly forbidden from engaging in the spread of religion on campus.

4) Multiple provinces bar children from attending religious activities in and outside religious venues

In many provinces, children are barred from attending any religious activities and church has become the third type of public place following singing/dance clubs and internet cafes that prohibit the minor from entering. Christian website "World Observatory" reported in August 2017 that in Inner Mongolia, Henan, Jiangsu, Zhejiang and Fujian, children were disallowed to join summer camps promoting Christian faith.

On June 15, 2016, the Sunday school of Huqiu House Church in Tongzi county, Huizhou province, was harassed by the local public security agents and the township PCP officials who demanded children to stop attending church service. On June 23, all the parents in Huaqiu township received a "notice" from the elementary schools and middles schools in town, which prohibits parents from taking minors to church according to a ruling from the above. Huaqiu township's Comprehensive Management Office and Public Security Department also threatened the church repeatedly warning that minors will be barred from going to college or joining the military if they don't stop attending church.

On August 4, 2016, Zhou Yanhua, leader of a church in Xinjiang Uygur Autonomous Region's Xinyuan county, and Gao Min, a member of the church, were detained for 15 days and 10 days respectively for organizing church members' children to take a tour to join a summer camp. They were detained on the charge of teaching minors religious and superstitious ideas.

On July 13, 2017, the government-run Three-Self Patriotic Movement (TSPM) and China Christian Commission (CCC) in Henan province issued a notice to their subsidiary TSPM and CCC, forbidding the two organizations and churches affiliated with them to host summer camps for students and minors, which was done every year in previous years and never caused any concerns from the government.

In early August 2017, government employees and public security agents of all the counties and townships in Zhejiang province's Wenzhou city sent a notice to churches in their jurisdiction to prohibit parents from taking their children to church for Sunday schools or sending them to summer camps. Government officials also presented to every church to monitor and inspect, even installing someone at churches to monitor them.

5) Church-run classes for children prohibited

In July 2017, a private family-style academy founded by a house church in Henan province's Zhuzhuang village to build children's character was shut down by the local public security and religious affairs agents.

B. Déjà vu: Xi Jinping's new era or Mao Zedong's old era ?
1) CPC controls religion: congruence of form and substance

In Deng Xiaoping's era, although it was known to all that the management of religion was in CPC's hands, the nominal government agency in charge of religious affairs, i.e. the State Bureau of Religious Affairs, was subordinate to the State Council. The Plan to Deepen the Reform of CPC and Government Agencies released by CPC's Central Committee after the Two Sessions in 2018 annexed the State Bureau of Religious Affairs to the Central Committee's Ministry of the United Front. Separating the agency in charge of religious affairs from the government's State Council and putting it under the CPC Central Committee's Ministry of the

United Front implies that the Atheism-endorsing CPC has got onto the stage from behind the scene to take over the control of religion from the so-called government, blatantly and undisguisedly.

2) Non-state schools: facing "CPC's control"

On April 20, 2018, the Ministry of Education issued a public notice to collect feedback on The Regulations on the Implementation of the Non-state Education Promotion Law of the People's Republic of China (Draft for Revision and Feedback Collection). The main change about the new edition is the addition of Article 4, which says, "Non-state schools shall adhere to the leadership of CPC and the direction of guiding education with socialism, adhere to the non-profit nature of education, and implement the fundamental task of building character and people. The grassroots CPC organizations in non-state schools must carry out the Party's guiding principles and policies, functioning as the political core, and participate in and monitor schools' important decision-making process according to the law, regulations in this law, and other relevant government regulations." This is also reflected in other major revisions to this document. The upcoming new edition of The Regulations on the Implementation of the Non-state Education Promotion Law (Order of the State Council No. 399) clearly is going backwards, subjecting non-state schools to the same control imposed on state-run schools. The so-called non-state schools will actually become CPC-controlled non-state schools.

3) Children are prohibited from attending religious activities in and outside religious venues – a campaign spreading from remote ethnic minority regions to provinces inhabited by Han Chinese and potentially to the whole nation

On January 19, 2018, AFP quoted China's state-run Global Times, "Guanghe county in Gansu's Linxia Hui Autonomous Prefecture issued a notice to kindergartens, elementary schools and middles schools to forbid students to enter religious sites to participate in religious activities or go to scriptural schools to study or chant scriptures, and to, and demand schools to reinforce ideological and political education for students and conduct effective propaganda."

On April 8, 2018, Henan Provincial Patriotic Catholic Association and Henan Provincial Administrative Commission of the Chinese Catholic Church issued The Notice to Limit/Bar Minors from Entering Church, stating that "According to the 'principle of adhering to the separation of religion from education' issued by the Provincial Bureau of Religious Affairs on April 3, and in implementing the stipulation in Regulations on Religious Affairs, i.e. 'Sites for religious activities are prohibited from hosting any form of training sessions to provide religious education to minors', Chinese Patriotic Catholic Association and Chinese Administrative Commission of the Chinese Catholic Church in all areas shall implement the following regulations: 1) All sites for religious activities across the province shall not provide religious education and training to minors, or classes in the name of summer camps or winter camps; 2)Persuade believers who go to churches to attend worship services or Mass to find their own childcare instead of taking their children to church; 3)Take these regulations seriously. They used to be communicated through propaganda and education, but now are implemented as legal mandates; 4) People in charge of the sites for religious activities will be held responsible for the violations of the regulations above, which may lead to the clergy's loss of registration with the government and the shutdown of the sites for religious activities." As a matter of fact, however, one of the grounds this notice is based on, i.e. "sites for religious activities are prohibited from hosting any form of training sessions to provide religious education to minors", does not even exist in the New Regulations on Religious Affairs. It was fabricated to justify the regulations listed in the notice.

On the walls and door of Qi County's Catholic Church hang posters and banners saying, "No Sharing Religious Ideas with Minors at the Sites of Religious Activities".

On Easter, April 1, 2018, during a Mass held at a Catholic church in Henan's Zhengzhou parish, government employees broke into the church openly to drive out children attending the mass. On subsequent Sundays, there was always a police vehicle parked at the entrance of the church and police officers guarding the church gate to bar children from entering with their parents, including little children held in their parents' arms.

In early April 2018, the government forcibly put up a sign saying "minors not allowed in church" at the entrance of the main church in Anyang parish, Henan province. On Sundays, law enforcement agents guarded the entrance of the church. Teachers of schools in Anyang district asked students for information about their parents' religious belief and asked parents to come to schools to register their religious belief status. On April 11 and April 12, 2018, Linzhou No. 9 Elementary School in Henan's Anyang city and Chengguan No. 1 Elementary School in Zhengzhou's Xingyang sent an open letter respectively titled "An open letter to all the parents of elementary schools and middle school students in this city: why should minors be barred from sites for religious activities?" According to the letter, it is illegal for any organization or individual to guide, support, allow and condone the conversion of minors to religion or involvement in religious activities, and both believing and non-believing parents ought to tell their children not to enter sites for religious activities and not to engage in religious activities and trainings. Parents were also required to sign this letter and put down their children's names and class.

In early April 2018, the government of Shangqiu, Henan, delivered the message to each resident's door, "Religious belief is forbidden now. If you don't quit, your children can't go to school and your seniors will lose public assistance. If you still refuse to quit, you'll be fired if you work for the government and your retired family members will lose their pension."

On April 17, 2018, children's bibles and books were confiscated by government agents from Beixishang Church in Jiaozuo, Henan.

A red-headed document (high importance) titled "Plan for Implementing Sites for Religious Activities in Zhongning County" (No.2 Document by Dazhancheng township's CPC Party Committee, 2018) raised eight points regarding scrutinizing the scope of religion. The 4th point prescribes "minors under 18 years of age are not allowed to study in temples" and the 5th point says, "elementary school children are barred from temples during both summer and winter break."

On April 30, 2018, an internet posting titled "Chinese churches' circumstances and appeal: raise your hands in prayer for current and upcoming environment" listed in 18 points the various degrees of persecution that occurred in different parts of China. Two of the 18 points involve religious education for children: 1) church youth groups are all canceled, and students are told to remove pictures and posters of the cross from their homes; 16) people under 18 years of age are barred from church, all Sunday school classes are canceled, and teachers must find out what make Christian students believe in Jesus."

4) Widespread campaign to resist and prevent religion in elementary and middle schools across China

The Notice about Effectively Handling Safety and Education in Elementary and Middle Schools in 2018 issued by the Basic Education Bureau of the Ministry of Education emphasizes "preventing the infiltration of religion into schools" and specifically requires "increasing the intensity of propaganda about our country's religious policies and related laws and regulations, strengthening the management of school education, effectively handling students' moral education and the ideological and political education for faculty and staff, increasing the awareness and ability to prevent religion's infiltration into schools, deepening the education about atheism, science and culture, and organizing a great variety of themed educational activities to guide students in establishing scientific and right worldviews, outlooks on life, and values.

On January 11, 2018, Guangxi-based Hezhou Daily reported that Zhaoping county's Commission of Politics and Law joined hands with the county's Propaganda Department, Department of the United Front, Public Security Bureau, Education Bureau and Religious Affairs Bureau in conducting a campaign called "keep religion out of campus", which covered eight schools and 900 teachers, including Zhaoping Middle School and Zhaoping No. 1 Elementary School.

In March 2018, there was a Notification about Religious Policies Concerning Schools circulating on the internet, allegedly released by Henan's education departments. Content of this Notification includes: school is a place for education and a battlefield to foster constructors of Socialism for CPC and China; no organizations are allowed to spread religious ideas in schools; the act of praying individually or as a group as well as discussing religion are all considered illegal activities; students are forbidden to take their classmates or friends to religious activities off campus; head teachers must explain every regulation in this Notification to their students and make them comply; students must write down the name of the person delivering the Notification, the name of the person it is delivered to, and the time and location this happens.

In late April, 2018, the elementary schools teachers in Shandong province's Jining city and Zoucheng city all received a notice from their schools demanding them to fill out "Survey on Students' Religious Belief", "Survey on Faculty' Religious Belief", "Information Sheet about Students' and Teachers' Religious Belief", and "Information Sheet about Resisting and Preventing Evangelization on Campus" in accordance with A Notice about Implementing the Request of the Superiors Regarding Conducting Research on the Management of Religion and Submitting Basis Data about Religion issued by the Ethnic and Religious Affairs Bureau of Jining city and Zoucheng city. Teachers were required to fill out the four forms in paper and electronically and submit them by 11A.M., April 18. This notice also required teachers to "conduct thorough investigation, fill out the forms and submit them in good faith. It also warned teachers against missing the deadline and threatened consequences on those who fail to submit truthful information.

5) Unprecedentedly harsh restrictions on schools run by church

On Feb 14 and March 14, 2018, Tian'ai Kindergarten operated by Zhifang Church in Anyang, Henan, was sealed off twice by public security agents citing "incomplete permits" and eventually outlawed, while a few other kindergartens with worse facilities and without a church background have not been investigated.

A few months ago, the government of Beijing's Changping district constantly pressured the landlord who leased property to Bafu (Beautitude) School run by Beijing-based Aijiabei Church to revoke the lease. Due to intolerable pressure, Bafu Elementary School had to relocate in Jan 2018. At 5 A.M. on March 29, a dozen of security guards escorted by the police surrounded Bafu School and blocked the entrance of the school's kindergarten. They cut off the metal locks on the door to break into the kindergarten, drove out staff on duty, took away children's desks, books and other teaching equipment, used shields, mental forms and other anti-riot equipment to intimidate teachers and parents, drive away teachers, beat up and injured some parents and church members.

On April 16, 2018, about 20 staff of the religious affairs bureau and education bureau came to the church-operated kindergarten in Xiamen to investigate the classes, textbooks and students enrolled, and register religious publications. The person heading the group claimed that this school is not registered with the government and guilty of "illegal operations", and that the investigation was incurred by "reports from some people."

VI. Temporal and spatial comparisons
A. Temporal comparison: essential sameness and difference between Mao, Deng and Xi

1) **Essentially the same: "The magistrates are free to burn down houses" – education is dominated by the anti-religion government's ideology of "atheism", "materialism" and "socialism"**

Since CPC took power in 1949, its official ideology has remained materialism which has an innate anti-religion tendency. The concept of "school-provided religious education" does not exist in China, so the compulsory education (elementary and middle school education) provided to children from either atheistic or theistic family backgrounds, regardless of what kind of religion, is the same, i.e. atheistic education. The atheistic propaganda in CPC's education system is full of opposition and criticism of religion, defaming it as "spiritual opiate", "feudal superstition", "foolishness" and teaching children to hate, despise and avoid religion.

Chapter One (General Provisions) of Education Law of the People's Republic of China mentions "ism" 12 times, "socialism" nine times, "Marxism and Leninism" once, "Patriotism" once, "Collectivism" once, and "Mao Zedong Thought" once. It highlights taking Marxism, Leninism, Mao Zedong Thought and the theory of building socialism with Chinese characteristics as the guidelines for education for the purpose of developing the cause of socialist education. It has "patriotism, collectivism, and socialism" as the main content of education. According to Article 6 of

"Regulations on the Management of Elementary Schools" (No. 26 Document promulgated by the State Education Commission on March 9, 1996), the primary goal of elementary schools if to cultivate students into people "with basic thoughts and sentiments around loving our country, loving our people, loving physical labor, loving science, and loving Socialism…"

2) So-called difference: "the common people are forbidden even to light lamps" – the magnitude of resistance to religion varies slightly

From Mao's era to Xi's era, CPC's policy of banning religion on school campus and interfering with children's involvement in religious activities outside schools has persisted without much change, and the only difference lies in the extent of policy implementation which varies due to the unique personality traits and demands of each supreme leader since after all, China is a nation ruled by man, not the law. It is this author's belief that Xi Jinping seems to deliberately emulate Mao Zedong in every aspect. For example, the great importance Xi attached to young people's conversion to religion might come from his familiarity with Mao's famous saying "Young people are like the rising sun at 8 or 9 o'clock in the morning and his knowledge about Mao's successful use of the young people (the red guards) to advance his own agenda. In addition, The Plan to Deepen the Reform of CPC and Government Agencies released by CPC's Central Committee after the Two Sessions in 2018 separated the State Bureau of Religious Affairs from the government's State Council and put it under CPC Central Committee's Ministry of the United Front. Since CPC has blatantly taken over the management of religion, it might have increased the intensity of policy implementation.

B. Spatial comparison with other countries

a) Outright departure from the stipulations of UN's covenants on human rights concerning children's religious education

Clause 3 of Article 26 of Universal Declaration of Human Rights goes, "Parents have a prior right to choose the kind of education that shall be given to their children." Article 5 of Declaration on the Elimination of All Forms of Intolerance and of Discrimination Based on Religion or Belief goes: 1)The parents or, as the case may be, the legal guardians of the child have the right to organize the life within the family in accordance with their religion or belief and bearing in mind the moral education in which they believe the child should be brought up; 2) Every child shall enjoy the right to have access to education in the matter of religion or belief in accordance with the wishes of his parents or, as the case may be, legal guardians, and shall not be compelled to receive teaching on religion or belief against the wishes of his parents or legal guardians, the best interests of the child being the guiding principle. Part 4 of Article 18 of International Covenant on Civil and Political Rights which the Chinese government endorsed recognizes parents' right to choose education for their children. It says, "The States Parties to the present Covenant undertake to have respect for the liberty of parents and, when applicable, legal guardians to ensure the religious and moral education of their children in conformity with their own convictions." Article 13 of International Covenant on Economic, Social and Cultural Rights which the Chinese government also endorsed goes, "The States Parties to the present Covenant undertake to have respect for the liberty of parents and, when applicable, legal guardians to choose for their children schools, other than those established by the public authorities, which conform to such minimum educational standards as may be laid down or approved by the State and to ensure the religious and moral education of their children in conformity with their own convictions." Article 14 of Convention on the Rights of the Child which the Chinese government also endorsed specifies that children enjoy the right of religious education from children's perspective, "States Parties shall respect the right of the child to freedom of thought, conscience and religion. States Parties shall respect the rights and duties of the parents and, when applicable, legal guardians, to provide direction to the child in the exercise of his or her right in a manner consistent with the evolving capacities of the child."

The stipulations above show clearly that the Chinse government has failed to observe any one of the provisions endorsed by the international community concerning children's right and freedom to receive religious education. For a long time, the Chinese government has ignored and trampled on hundreds of millions of Chinese children's rights to religious education, and is continuing to do so with more blatant, unscrupulous, and alarming policies.

b) Deviate further away from the international trend of religious education for children

If public schools and private schools are two separate systems, sine the formation and development of modern nation states, they have emerged two types of religious education for children in the world. The first type is nations of religious plurality in which religious education is forbidden in public schools but allowed in private schools, such as the United States of America, Japan, South Korea, etc. The second type is countries with an official religion in which the government promotes education of the official religion and religious education is compulsory in public schools and optional schools, such as many Islamic countries and some Buddhist countries including Thailand.

Countries in the first category, i.e. countries that bar religious content from public schools, are showing the tendency to consider restoring religious education in public schools. For example, France used to strictly adhere to the separation of religion from public schools and see the denominational education as purely private and ecclesiastic affairs but is not considering bringing religious education back into public schools. Article 137 of The Basic Law of the Hong Kong Special Administrative Region of the People's Republic of China and Article 128 of The Basic Law of the Macau Special Administrative Region of the People's Republic of China both stipulate, "Schools run by religious organizations may continue to provide religious education, including courses in religion."

Therefore, the mainland China's policy of curbing religious education for children is diametrically opposed to the trend of the global religious education for children and the gap between the two keeps widening.

VII. Foresight: "When the nest is overturned, can the eggs in it stay unbroken?"

Nothing comes from nowhere! As early as 2006 when Xi Jinping was CCP's Party Secretary in Zhejiang province, he orchestrated the "Xiaoshan Religious Case", known as the largest-scale religious case since the end of the Cultural Revolution, which stunned the world. The government of Xiaoshan district in Zhejiang province's Hangzhou city forcibly demolished the church building constructed by Xiaoshan Church, beating up a dozen of Christians and illegally taking a dozen of Christians into custody, among whom eight were given heavy sentences. Unsurprisingly, after Xi Jinping became the leader of CPC in 2012, the campaign of forcible cross demolition started in Zhejiang province in 2014, which is the province governed by Xi for five years and thus, people can't help but wonder whether Xi was behind this campaign. Xiao Baolong, the Party Secretary of Zhejiang during the campaign, was promoted to become the Deputy Chairman and Secretary-in-general of the Chinese People's Political Consultative Conference in 2018 at the Two Sessions, thus ranking as a top leader of CPC and second in the line of power just behind Wang Yang, who's a member of CPC's Standing Committee of Political Bureau and in charge of religious affairs. Anyone with an impartial view of the religious persecution in China will admit that the brutality of religious persecution by CPC peaks in Tibet. Due to his "governance success" in Tibet from 2011 to August 2016, Chen Quanguo was transferred to Xinjiang in September 2016 and promoted to become a member of the Political Bureau at CPC's 19th National Conference. He then carried all his "governance experiences in Tibet" persecuting Tibetan Buddhism over to Xinjiang to persecute Islam. At CPC's 19th National Conference, Xi's name was put in CPC's Constitution and at the Two Sessions in 2018, presidential term limits, which was the only indicator of political progress since the Reform and Open-up, were removed.

This is far from the end of insanity! In late March 2018, the major online stores all over China received a notice that starting from March 30, 2018, Taobao, Jingdong and WeChat will stop selling Bibles. On April 23, 2018, CPC Central Committee's Political Bureau headed by Xin Jinping gathered for the 5th time to study Manifesto of the Communist Party and its significance in current times. This is the first and only time out of 125 occasions since December 26, 2002, when the 16th CPC Central Committee's Political Bureau first gathered to study together, that they studied the Manifesto of the Communist Party, which centered around the "phantom" of Communism. This author searched "CPC leaders study the Manifesto of the Communist Party" on the internet and got nothing exactly the same back, except for one entry titled "CPC leaders and the Manifesto of the Communist Party" dated 12/01/2017, which was published on Anhui Daily (rural edition, Hepei) and mentioned that "the Manifesto of the Communist Party was read by CPC leaders Mao Zedong, Liu Shaoqi, Zhou Enlai, and Deng Xiaoping."

Nowadays, all religions in China under the rule of Xi Jinping are facing the greatest challenges since the end of the Cultural Revolution, as if the nightmare of the darkest days in the Cultural Revolution when religion disappeared from the public realm is coming back. Not only is children's religious education gradually disappearing from the public-school system, the non-state schools that emerged since the "Reform and Open-up", especially schools run by Christians and foreigners, and existed spottily in a grey area to provide religious education, have nearly lost space for existence. Even more so, children and their parents have been stripped off the freedom to experience religion together at religious sites or attend recreational activities organized by religious groups outside schools and religious sites.

This author thinks of the environment of religion and religious education for children as a bird's nest and a baby bird who needs a shelter from the rain and wind to survive. When the nest is overturned, eggs in it are surely broken. Religious education for children in China is again in a desperate situation and believing parents once again face the crisis of not being able to pass their faith to the next generation. All the religions in China are facing the crisis of not being able to pass their faith to the next generation! Although we have faith that religion that transcends reason cannot be attained by the thinking capacity of CPC and its leader Xi Jinping, and the supreme One will not let religious education for children vanish from China, we are will deeply concerned because "when the nest is overturned, how can eggs in it stay unbroken?" Perhaps the question that demands a more urgent response from us is: faced with hundreds of millions of children being deprived of the freedom and right to receive religious education, what actions can religions in China, international religious groups and the international community that does enjoy the freedom of religious education for children take to make a change?!

References:

1. "Options for religious education in our country from the viewpoint of contemporary religious education theory of the West" by Fang Yongquan (Taiwan)
2. "A study of how school education and temple education complement each other in Tibetan-inhabited regions under the principle of 'separating education from religion'" by Jing Dongge
3. "The disappearance of church-run schools in mainland China" by He Yiping, (http://www.open.com.hk/content.php?id=953#.Wu57HaSFPIU)
4. "The co-existence of ethnic religious education and public education in Xinjiang during Republic of China" by Zhou Hong, "*Northwestern Ethnic Studies*", 2nd edition, 2001
5. "An explorative analysis of the religious policy model in the public schools of western countries" by Teng Zhiyan, "*Foreign Education Studies*", 9th edition, 2008
6. "The past and present of underground scripture teaching in Xinjiang" by Li Xiaoxia, (http://blog.caijing.com.cn/expert_article-151687-68866.shtml)

Liberty of Children's Religious Education in China at Risk

By Katherine A. Capps

Note: The purpose of this article is to recognize China's violation of human rights concerning Chinese children and their right to religious education. This study is part of a growing body of research on the abuses that have occurred since the release of the new regulations this year. The findings may be useful in drawing attention to how religious education for children is a guaranteed liberty and that the international community should understand the ramifications for what China is imposing on its citizens and the affect it will have on the following generations.

I. Introduction

For many decades Chinese citizens have suffered under religious rules and regulations. At present, under Xi Jinping, many of these practices have expanded exponentially. Since February 1, 2018, crackdowns on unregistered and state-sanctioned places of worship and their religious leaders have increased. Furthermore, these new regulations have amplified the restrictions to the Chinese children and their ability to participate in any 'religious' activities inside and outside their homes.

These new regulations have extended to include the children's educational system. Any type of 'religious education' is currently under attack at an extreme level. These regulations have mandated that students must not read scriptures in class or in religious buildings and that all students and teachers should work to strengthen political ideology and propaganda. In addition, these new regulations have banned children from attending any and all religious events over spring or winter break.

It is an indisputable fact that education is one of the most important foundations of all human societies. In other words, the way a society regards raising the next generation is reflected first and foremost in its educational system.

II. The worldwide understanding of the term 'child'

Historically, the term 'child' comes from the Latin word 'infans' which means "the one who does not speak". During the Roman times, this term designated the child from birth up to the age of seven years. This notion evolved through the centuries. The negative effect was that the term 'child' was viewed widely and the accepted age of adulthood varied from one culture to another. Currently the term 'child' is defined as anyone below the age of eighteen years.[25]

III. International law concerning the rights of children, religious liberty and education

The protection of religious education has been in effect for centuries. However, children's rights in the international arena were not officially recognized until after World War I with the adoption of the "Declaration of Geneva" in 1924. It then continued to gain international approval with the "Declaration of Children's Rights" in 1959 and these rights have become even more explicit through the years.[26]

1. UN The Declaration of Human Rights of 1948

This Declaration was adopted by the UN General Assembly as a result from the international involvement of World War II. It sets out, for the first time, fundamental human rights to be universally protected. In accordance with the original intent regarding religious liberty, Article 18 in the Declaration states: "[e]veryone has the right to freedom of thought, conscience and religion; this right includes freedom to change his religion or belief, and freedom, either alone or in community with others and in public or private, to manifest his religion or belief in teaching, practice, worship and observance."[27] This document continues to be an inspiration whether in addressing injustices in times of conflicts, or

---

[25] *Rights of the Child*, Humanium, https://www.humanium.org/en/declaration-rights-child-2/.

[26] *Id* at

[27] *Universal Declaration of Human Rights*, United Nations, http://www.un.org/en/universal-declaration-human-rights/.

in societies suffering repression and also in efforts towards achieving universal enjoyment of human rights.

2. The Convention against Discrimination in Education (1960)

Articles 1, 2 and 5 state that the establishment and maintenance of separate educational institutions for religious reasons cannot be discriminatory if it keeps with the wishes of parents or legal guardians and that these institutions conform to educational standards developed by competent authorities. These institutions are also to be engaged to the full development of the human personality and to strengthening respect for human rights and fundamental freedoms.[28]

3. The UN Declaration on the Elimination of Intolerance and Discrimination based on Religion or Belief (1981)

This document reinforces the concept of religious liberty and was adopted by the UN General Assembly. Article 5 of the United Nations' declarations on religious intolerance concerning a child includes that:

- "The parents or, as the case may be, the legal guardians of the child have the right to organize the life within the family in accordance with their religion or belief and bearing in mind the moral education in which they believe the child should be brought up.
- Every child shall enjoy the right to have access to education in the matter of religion or belief in accordance with the wishes of his parents or, as the case may be, legal guardians, and shall not be compelled to receive teaching on religion or belief against the wishes of his parents or legal guardians, the best interests of the child being the guiding principle.
- The child shall be protected from any form of discrimination on the ground of religion or belief. He shall be brought up in a spirit of understanding, tolerance,

---

[28] *Religious Freedom and the International Community*, Seventh-Day Adventist Church: Public Affairs and Religious Liberty, http://www.adventistliberty.org/current-issues.

friendship among peoples, peace and universal brotherhood, respect for freedom of religion or belief of others, and in full consciousness that his energy and talents should be devoted to the service of his fellow men. ...."[29]

Additionally, Article 8 of this Declaration goes even further by stating "[n]othing in the present Declaration shall be construed as restricting or derogating from any right defined in the Universal Declaration of Human Rights and the International Covenants on Human Rights."[30] The idea of religious liberty in education comes from the idea that parents must be the decision makers regarding their children's education.

4. Convention on the Rights of the Child (1989)

This treaty confirmed the idea that the child is a human being with rights and dignity. In this perspective, multiple texts from the international community proclaim the protection of the child. Article 14 identifies the rights of the child to freedom of religion or belief and places an emphasis on providing direction in a manner consistent with the "evolving" capacity of the child.[31] This is the first internationally binding text recognizing all the fundamental rights of the child.

As shown above, there are multiple documents that have been agreed upon by the international community concerning religious liberty in education for children. This area has grown in importance, however, there are vast variations of how these principles are ultimately practiced.

IV. Analysis of the topic and its relevance to China

China is currently governed by the Chinese Communist Party and has for many years had a restrictive attitude towards religion. Their attitude concerning religion stems from the basic

---

[29] *United Nations' Declarations on Religious Intolerance*, Religious Tolerance (Sept. 7, 2006), http://www.religioustolerance.org/un_dec.htm.

[30] *Declaration on the Elimination of All Forms of Intolerance and of Discrimination Based on Religion or Belief*, United Nations Human Rights, http://www.ohchr.org/EN/ProfessionalInterest/Pages/ReligionOrBelief.aspx.

[31] *Religious Freedom and the International Community*, Seventh-Day Adventist Church: Public Affairs and Religious Liberty, http://www.adventistliberty.org/current-issues.

philosophical (Marxist) dogma against religious conviction, historical patterns of societal organization and control and concerns that religion may disrupt ethnic stability and territorial integrity.[32] Chinese leaders, perceiving a threat to their power, now openly reject the universality of human rights and characterize these ideas as a foreign intrusion and penalizing all who promote them.

It has been argued that religious identity is determined at birth but then it is fostered through education. This is because education influences the way individual choices are made. The regulation of choice of religious education by China is subsequently another way in which their law will shape the lack of control that parents have over the foundation of a child's religious identity.

According to the 'Religious Affairs Regulations', which was released in China this year, there are eight Articles that any religious affiliated educational organization for children have to abide by. Particularly, Articles 11, 12 and 18 of the new regulations mandate:

- "Religious schools are established by national religious groups or by the religious groups of provinces, autonomous regions, and directly-governed municipalities. Other organizations or individuals must not establish religious schools.

- The establishment of religious schools shall be by upon application of the national religious groups to the religious affairs department under the State Council, of application of the religious groups of provinces, autonomous regions, directly-governed municipalities to the departments religious affairs for the people's government of that province, autonomous region, or directly-governed municipalities. The religious affairs departments of provincial, autonomous region, or directly governed municipality people's governments shall make a recommendation within 30 days of receiving the

---

[32] *People's Republic of China: Law and Religion Framework Overview*, Religlaw (2017), https://www.religlaw.org/common/document.view.php?docId=7279.

application; and report to the department of religious affairs under the State Council.

- Religious groups and temples, Taoist temples, mosques, and churches (hereinafter temples and churches), carrying out religious education and training to cultivate religious professionals where the training period is 3 months or more, shall report for review and approval to the religious affairs departments of local people's governments at the districted city level or higher."[33]

The question is this, how do these violations ultimately affect the Chinese children's right to religious education, what should the Chinese government do to recognize the right of the children's religious education and how should the international community react to the Chinese government if they fail to comply?
This is a complex question that requires our effort to address.

1. How do these violations ultimately affect the Chinese children's right to religious education?

These violations remove one of the most positive influences promoting virtue, morality and primary building blocks for a good society. The freedom for a child to learn religious principles must be made available, must be unhindered and actively promoted for the good of the Chinese culture. If these regulations are enforced China would suffer consequences of a citizenry that was deficient of the concepts of positive ethical influences.

2. What should the Chinese government do to recognize the right of the children's religious education?

The government, ideally, should comply with the "UN The Declaration of Human Rights", "The Convention against Discrimination in Education", "The UN Declaration on the

---

[33] Note from Website: All translations on this site are unofficial and are provided for reference purposes only. *Religious Affairs Regulations 2017*, ChinaLawTranslate (Sept. 9, 2017),
http://www.chinalawtranslate.com/%E5%AE%97%E6%95%99%E4%BA%8B%E5%8A%A1%E6%9D%A1%E4%BE%8B-2017/?lang=en.

Elimination of Intolerance and Discrimination based on Religion or Belief" and the "Convention on the Rights of the Child".

3. How should the international community react to the Chinese government for these violations?

Being that the People's Republic of China was in fact re-elected to the United Nations Human Rights Council in 2016, they should be eager to bring nation-states together to protect and promote human rights instead of their wish to divide, conquer, and silence opposition.[34] To be fair, the Council should reject China's efforts to challenge UN human rights forums and should also address the many human rights violations occurring inside and outside of China. If China does not comply, consequences from other nation-states should be implemented and China should not be one of the nation's serving on the Council for human rights.

V. Conclusion

In summary, China's current policy regarding religion is regularly approved to further state economic and social goals rather than to encourage religious liberty. Their government requires all religions to conduct their activities within the range prescribed by law and to adapt to what they consider social and cultural progress. This view has negatively influenced the current situation in China concerning religious liberty in education.

People often find themselves in a ridiculous 'politically correct' world where today's children are taught anti-religion but not allowed to learn or practice religion. Historically, one would see that religious education was important to civilization many centuries ago. According to the Talmud, the first school for children was established about 100 B.C. Children were taught to read and to write even in families of moderate means as early as 600 B.C. Great stress for their education was laid on the study of the Torah (the law of Moses). Religious training of the boy began in his fourth year, as soon as he could speak distinctly. The

---

[34] *UN Rights Body Needs to Challenge Powerful—and Abusive—China*, HumanRightsWatch (March 14, 2018), https://www.hrw.org/news/2018/03/14/un-rights-body-needs-challenge-powerful-and-abusive-china.

religious life of the girl also began early. Later the children took part in the Sabbath and Passover festivals and boys attended synagogue and school regularly.[35]

Christians in China have been repressed ever since the People's Republic was created in 1949 with the government's imposition of the Communist Party's atheistic values. Yet, there is a significant population of Christians and other religious minorities that are sustained by the positive force of their faith.

"But the Lord God helps me; therefore I have not been disgraced; therefore I have set my face like a flint, and I know that I shall not be put to shame."[36] To truly have liberty in all areas of life, including education, is to be trusting on no other than the author of our destiny, Almighty God.

---

[35] *Child: International Standard Bible Encyclopedia*, BibleHub (2017), http://biblehub.com/topical/c/child.htm.
[36] *Isaiah 50:7* (ESV).

The Christian Faith and the Education of Children with Disabilities: Challenges and Possibilities for Grassroots Christian Organizations Regarding the Underprivileged

By Sato Chitose

Abandoned infants are the most underprivileged social group in human society[1], and among them, the abandoned infants with physical disabilities, such as respiratory function impairment, are the most underprivileged of the underprivileged. The faint flicker of their lives can easily be swallowed by the darkness if no external help is available.

In China today, the social welfare system designed to preserve the lives of such abandoned infants and support their growth is still under construction. In the meantime, the shortage of orphanages, the inefficiency of child welfare system, the great discrepancies between the education systems in different regions, the government's dereliction of duty and many other factors have jointly created the pervasive problem of abandoned children not getting any support from the government. It is some Christian civil groups that have stepped in the place where parents and the government are absent and have taken on the responsibility of raising these children who fall through the cracks of the public policy.

From the Christian civil groups involved in the rearing and parenting of orphans and children with disabilities for a long time, this author selected and listed out Christian groups and Catholic groups separately to examine the Christian characteristics of this cause and its social significance. Groups listed in this article all have a close connection with churches that are unregistered with and unrecognized by the government, i.e. Christian "house churches" and Catholic "house churches, and therefore are significantly impacted by the Xi Jinping Administration's tightened control over house churches.This article will investigate the dire circumstances of these two groups from the viewpoint of policy on welfare, education and religion, and to illustrate the point that the Communist Party of China's system for managing religion has violated children's basic rights in the cause of child welfare and education.

I. Abandoned infants: the most underprivileged group in Chinese society

A. The current situation of orphans in China and religious groups

According to statistics from China's Ministry of Civil Affairs, there were 502,000 orphans in China by the end of 2015, including 92,000 orphans living in facilities and 410,000 orphans scattered around in society.

An orphan here refers to a minor under 14 years old with both parents deceased or declared dead by the people's court. Orphans "scattered around in society", i.e. orphans living in the homes of their grandparents, relatives, or foster parents, accounted for 80% of the total number of 500,000 orphans. The rest of the 20% are targets of "centralized adoption" and they live in welfare facilities run by the local government and civil charity groups.

The majority of the institutions involved in centralized adoption are "orphanages" run by the local government. In the meanwhile, about 10,000 orphans and abandoned infants live in charity organizations operated by civil charity groups or individuals across China. It is worth noting that of all the civil organizations that adopt orphans and abandoned infants, 74% of them have a connection with churches or temples. While child welfare organizations are mainly orphanages run by the government, many civil charity organizations are groups and individuals with a religious background.

Per the regulations of China's Ministry of Civil Affairs, citizens who find an abandoned baby must notify the neighborhood committee or villagers' committee, and after the public security agency issues the "certificate of abandoned baby", the state-run orphanages will take over the abandoned baby. Because the grassroots government employees in charge of the process are not familiar with the process of taking over abandoned infants or having their hands tied by China's family planning policy, the public security agency encounters great difficulties in issuing the "certificate of abandoned baby", which in turn, causes the problem that some abandoned infants have difficulties being admitted to orphanages.

It is the charity organizations and individuals with religious background that have taken in the "orphans" not recognized as such by the law who are abandoned and without a legal status. Besides Catholic and Christian groups, Buddhist and Islamic communities and individuals also adopt abandoned infants and orphans. According to people working in the adoption business, Buddhist and Islamic groups and individuals tend to take in healthy children while children with severe disabilities are mainly adopted by Christian groups and individuals. In terms of adopting children with disabilities, Christian groups have made a great contribution whether it has been recognized or not.

B. The "gray area" in China's child welfare policy

UNICEF defines an orphan as a child under 18 years of age who has lost one or both parents to any cause of death.

The Chinese government, however, adopted a narrower definition of orphan which has led to the remarkable social problem that "de facto orphans" are not receiving any assistance and protection they desperately need. "De facto orphans" refer to minors without guardians who have difficulties surviving but are deprived of assistance and the opportunity to receive education because they do not qualify as "orphans" according to the law.

These de facto orphans include: 1) orphans not possessing their parents' death certificate or the certificate of orphans for various reasons; 2) orphans with one living parent who is not able or willing to raise the child due to military service or illness causing mental or physical disabilities; and 3) orphans with both living parents who are not able or willing to raise the child due to military service or illness causing mental or physical disabilities.

According to Procuratorate Daily, China has at least 610,000 such "de facto orphans" and most likely, the actual number of such orphans are much greater. The number of "government-recognized" orphans who fit with China's legal definition is 500,000, a gap of 110,000 children with the number of 610,000 "de facto orphans". It has been disclosed that even some orphans recognized as such by the law end up not receiving any public assistance due to "the local government's dereliction of duty and the absence of supervisory organs. Xiong Bingqi (2013) exposed such cases as the local government in Henan province which did not set up orphanages due to poverty.

The "de facto orphans" mentioned above are actual "orphans" but deprived of government assistance. In other words, they are children falling through the cracks of the safety net due to the imperfection of child welfare system and their existence revealed the "gray area" in China's child welfare system.

C. Comparison with Japan

In the first half of the 20th century, because of the rapid increase of children orphaned by Japan's defeat in WWII in 1945, the Japanese government passed Child Welfare Law in 1947 which led to a quick establishment of child care system which covered the welfare of children orphaned by the war. In today's Japan, children under 18 years of age who need parenting are all recipients of the child care system which provides protection, assistance and financial security. Besides abandoned children with no living parents or parents whose life or death is unknown, the system also covers children with living parents who are not able or willing to raise them due to military service or illness, as well as children abused by their parents. A local government agency called "Consultation Office Regarding Children" is responsible for investigating the concerned child's case to decide whether the child shall receive child care and how to take care of the child. As you can see, Japan's system is more inclusive than China's system which requires the orphan to provide the "certificate of abandoned baby" or "death certificate of parents", and such an inclusive system is the product of accumulated experiences since the inclusive system is the product of accumulated experiences since the foundation of the system 70 years ago. Compared with the western countries, however, the Japanese government's budget for child's welfare is still low.

Most Japan's orphanages are operated by civil groups (social charity legal persons) sanctioned by the local government while the local government only operates or takes over charity organizations for children with severe disabilities or takes over charity organizations involved in unethical practices or violence against children. The expense on personnel and service by civil/social charity legal persons are entirely funded by the government, and these legal persons are answerable to the government for their organizational operations.

As for religious groups, Christian groups or Buddhist groups have been well recognized as social charity legal persons in history. Whether an organization has religious background or not is not linked with whether it will be approved by the government or not. In Japan, traditional Christian and Buddhist groups' operation of charity work preceded WWII and hence they tend to have a stable source of funding, which makes them more likely to be approved by the government as social charity legal persons.

II. Civil organizations formed by house church believers

Through persistent research in the field, this author examined the cases of Christians providing care and education children with disabilities. The following case is about a civil child charity organization (referred to as agency B[11]) located in the suburbs of a metropolis in northern China. My research so far has revealed two characteristics of Christian-run charity organizations: 1) such organizations have developed their own independent guidelines for education and care based on the Christian faith; 2) such organizations have a complicated "state vs. religion" relationship with the local government.

A. Located in the suburbs of big cities and parenting children with severe disabilities

Since the 19th century, many Christian denominations founded churches in metropolis A in China and some missions' committees in Europe and America supported the local relief and education work for children through church-affiliated schools and orphanages. From the socialist revolution to the Cultural Revolution, the number of Christians dropped temporarily but rose again in 1980s like many others place in China. After 1990s with the rapid advance of urbanization, "emerging urban house churches" independent of the government-sanctioned "Three-Self system" have been established one after another.

These emerging urban house churches attracted white-collar professionals, students and intellectuals who have a burning passion for social causes and volunteer activities. Charity agency B is one of the grassroots non-profit organizations founded by this kind of believers from emerging urban house churches.

In China, a high percentage of abandoned infants have disabilities, a serious social problem acknowledged by the Chinese government as well. Children with disabilities need advanced medical care and nursing techniques as well as special education tailored to their needs. Cultivating a healthy personality in abandoned children, including children with disabilities, starts from helping these children cultivate a one-on-one, trusting relationship with their caregivers at the orphanage. At present, however, orphanages in China suffer the shortage of both funds and personnel, which renders one-on-one care focused on relationship-building impossible. Many children with disabilities are children with cerebral palsy and other conditions which require regular medical evaluation, but the shortage of funds and personnel makes it impossible and sometimes even causes the loss of lives.

In response to this situation, the relief practice of taking children with disabilities out of orphanages, placing them in a regular family for a period of time and sending them to medical institutions for assessment by specialists was developed and promoted in 1990s. Ms. Zhang, founder of agency B, got involved in this after she took in a boy with whole-body paralysis from an orphanage in a different part of China and became his foster mother. She found that the child, though without facial expressions previously, became able to express joy, anger, sorrow and happiness in a short time due to her consistent companionship. Humorously, Ms. Zhang described this experience as her "first love." She saw the paramount importance of building a personal relationship with children with disabilities when providing them with care. Therefore, she contacted her friends in some house churches and jointly founded agency B to focus on the care of children with disabilities.

Agency B currently is home to 20 children with disabilities under 20 years of age, all released officially by orphanages from different parts of China due to the challenge of care-giving. These children all have physical or mental disabilities such as cerebral palsy, seizure disorder, or Down Syndrome, and need intensive care around the clock. Ms. Sun, co-founder of the agency and Ms. Zhang's friend, is in charge of the agency's operations and fund-raising. The 15 employees hired by the agency provide intensive care to these children on day and night shifts, feeding them and attending to their incontinence. In the meanwhile, other Christians in city A and their friends volunteer their time on the weekends to help take care of these children.

The activities of agency B is funded by money and resources donated by people inside and outside China, and half of the donors are Christians. Many non-Christians in China also donate money and resources to this agency.

The salary of agency B's employees, including Ms. Zhang's, is "slightly lower than the salary of people doing the same type of work in city A." Although not affiliated with any particular church, the founder and employees of this agency are all Christians.

B. Faith-based "simulated family"

The trademark characteristic of agency B is its family-style care-giving model that children and care-givers maintain a "long-term relationship." As described above, Ms. Zhang founded agency B after she realized that "big orphanages with too many children can't afford to give children the care they need", thus agency B's focus on the model of "simulated family." Ms. Zhang is called "mom" by both the children and care-givers and she plays the role of a mother, while the role of father is assumed by Ms. Sun who has more male personality traits. Certainly, it is impossible for any mother to maintain a close relationship with 20 children though they are all her "children", so the main care-giving work falls on the shoulders of the employees who are "aunts" and "uncles" to these children.

In agency B, children are placed in different rooms according to their age, gender and severity of disability, usually 3-5 children sharing one room. Each room has a responsible person who maintains a lasting and stable relationship with the children in this room. Many children cannot speak, but care-givers can read what they attempt to express by observing the subtle changes in their expression and voice, such as "hold me", "I'm hungry", or "I want to listen to music." Care-givers tend to develop stronger attachment to children they started caring for during their infancy, so each care-giver has their own "favorite" child. Likewise, every child has their own favorite care-giver. The development of such one-on-one emotional intimacy is conducive to promoting these children's mental growth.

A detail observed in the room of children with cerebral palsy melted this author's heart. While helping change a child's diaper, this author accidently glanced over the ceiling of the room and saw the whole ceiling covered by pictures of giraffe, lion, chimpanzee and other animals liked by children. We "healthy" people never stare at the ceiling in our daily life, but bed-ridden children with cerebral palsy do that every day and even in their entire life. This ceiling decorated with pictures of animals shows the care-givers' incredible thoughtfulness and consideration of the children's needs.

The lack of education opportunities for abandoned infants and orphans is a nationwide problem, which also plagues agency B. Special education schools are not accessible because agency B is in the suburbs. Besides, the household registrations of most kids with agency B are still with the orphanages they came from and not in city A, so it is very challenging to get them into schools in city A. As a result, agency B send their children with disabilities to a special school founded by Christians, which focuses on teaching a trade to children with physical disabilities.

As for children with both physical and intellectual disabilities, the employees and volunteers of agency B provide them with some elementary education. For example, painting class is taught once a week by a volunteer who is also a professional painter. Physical disability makes it difficult for some children to maintain one posture, so caregivers secure their bodies on home-made chairs. Some children have the painting brush fastened to their foreheads, and others need help to grasp the painting brush with misshapen hands for three hours straight so that they could finish a painting.

Ms. Zhang feels strongly that children with moderate disabilities should be able to achieve independent living through training at vocational schools. Although these children need assistance with eating meals, using bathroom and taking a shower, they are capable of doing simple tasks in the service industry or manufacturing industry. Since she cannot find the right school to provide such training, she has to find creative ways to provide vocational training to children under her care.

Agency B obtains funds and resources to cover the agency's operation and volunteer teachers and doctors through a Christian website. Donors of funds include Christians in China and Christians overseas who learned about agency B through their friends or the internet. Medical service needed by children with disabilities is provided by a top private hospital as a charity cause. There are also non-Christians who learned about this agency through their Christian friends and thus got involved in volunteering or the donation of money and resources.

As a matter of fact, it is through some Christian websites that agency B identifies and receives abandoned children with disabilities who need special care. Christians volunteering at orphanages across China, especially government-run orphanages, will contact agency B when they encounter children labeled by orphanages as "severely disabled and beyond our ability to care for." After obtaining permission from the orphanage and the local government, these children will be transferred to agency B.

Although not affiliated with any particular church, all the employees of agency B are Christians and the agency regularly and spontaneously hold internal prayer meetings, and Christian music is often played on the site. Employees and children singing worship songs and dancing together has become a part of their daily routine.

This author also had a first-hand experience caring for these children as a volunteer and learned that each child's disability is different in severity and each child has a different way to express moods and emotions. This author was too tired to even speak after helping these children eat a meal. It is by their Christian faith that agency B's employees have been able to do such labor-intensive work 24/7 all year long. At their prayer meetings and in their prayers, what they repeatedly say are "equal value" and "interaction."

At the prayer meeting one day, Ms. Zhang prayed, "Lord, we can see these children have a spirit and they're sacred. Living in this world, they are no different from us... The employees here are the same as the children with disabilities and they are all equal in your eyes." She went on to pray, "Every person here, care-giver or care-receiver, we all need God's care and God's protection, protection for our hearts and our bodies." The Christian doctrine of "everyone is equal before God" makes them emphasize the equal value of all lives before God, and both children with disabilities and "healthy people" are God's creation. This concept of "equal value" is a shared belief in agency B and children with disabilities are often referred to as "valuable and precious life" in the agency.

Since children with disabilities and healthy people have the "same value", the relationship between them is not a one-sided "healthy-people-caring-for-children-with-disabilities" relationship, but rather an "interactive" relationship. More than just a slogan, "interaction" is a reality in the employees' daily experience with children. Ms. Sun, co-founder of agency B, said, "I learned about love and faith through these children." Due to her personality style and occupational requirement as a teacher, she "often repressed emotions and ended up becoming a bystander of life." Through her involvement with agency B, she said, "I'm able to engage in relationships with people now because of these orphans and children with disabilities." To this day, she will still often give up sleep at night to take care of the children.

C. Expansion of support network and deterioration of church- and- the- state relations

Located in the suburbs of city A, agency B is a child welfare organization focused on children with disabilities which was founded by Christians from house churches. Behind this agency is a massive support network involving Christians and non-Christians, state-run organizations and non-government groups, and Christians in China as well as Christians overseas. The agency is scarce in personnel, funding, educational and medical resources, but various people from inside and outside China have stepped in out of various motivations to support this agency, and therefore, agency B has become the focal point of this massive support network that connects people in various places. This network formed through agency B is different from the pyramid-shaped structure of a nation's government. Although horizontal, it is a massive global network across spanning regions and nations, which can be seen as a characteristic of the Christian church composed of people from all over the world, including the Chinese people.

The Christian concept that "all creations are equal before God" endorsed by agency B is also a magnet to various people involved in this agency. Through the Christian lens of seeing Children with severe disabilities and communication difficulties as "precious lives blessed by God", agency B championed the concept of engaging in relationships with these children out of "joy" instead of obligations or profits.

As we turn our eyes to the circumstances of the Chinese society agency B is situated in, however, we will see that the church-and-the-state relationship around agency B is tensing up.

For 20 years, agency B has taken in children with severe disabilities that state-run orphanages are not capable of taking care of and provided these children with as much as education as possible, which is a supplement to the functionality of state-run orphanages. In the meanwhile, agency B deems it as a mission entrusted by God and an inalienable duty to care for and educate children with disabilities. Therefore, state-run orphanages that transfer children with disabilities to agency B have formed an interdependent relationship with agency B. As the patron of orphanages, the local government acquiesces to this kind of interdependence.

From the legal perspective, agency B as a charity organization is without a legal status. According to the regulations of the Ministry of Civil Affairs and State Bureau of Religious Affairs, only "organizations run by religious communities" operated by "registered religious groups, sites for religious activities, and certified religious clergy according to the law" are recognized and allowed to run child welfare organizations.[13] Therefore, agency B founded by believers from unauthorized "house churches" is not recognized as an "organization run by religious communities." If approved by the county-level government, civil groups can also function as "social welfare groups" to operate child charity organizations,[14] but the criteria for approval are extremely complicated and the process of getting approved is a "black box operation". Despite the many attempts agency B made to obtain the approval, the county government always denied it. It is very likely that the government's decision was informed by the fact that agency B was founded by believers from house churches.

In addition, the outbreak of fire in a private orphanage in Henan province's Lankao county in January 2013, which killed seven children, is a tragedy that alarmed the whole nation. Grabbing this opportunity, the Chinese government asked the local government to reinforce control over civil organizations which adopt abandoned infants and orphans. Agency B in city A was also affected by this new order. Some of the children adopted by agency B were sent back to the orphanages they came from and the number of children in agency B dropped.

Agency B used to be interdependent with state-run orphanages in other cities and relatively distanced from the government of city A. In the wake of the tragedy that happened in Lankao in 2013 and the Xi Jinping Administration's tightened control over religion, agency B has been distanced by state-run orphanages in other cities and treated with hostility by the grassroots government of city A. The church-and-the-state relations have deteriorated.

III. Child welfare organizations outside the state-sanctioned Catholic Church system

A. Founded by priests of "underground" churches in the rural area

To study civil groups with Catholic background, this author examined unauthorized church D, i.e. one of the so-called "underground churches", in county C in northern China. Also founded on the Christian faith and its values like agency B, church D's charity organization also specializes in the care and education of children with severe physical and intellectual disabilities. As far as the church-and-the-state relationship goes, since it is directly operated by an underground church, church D's charity organization is facing a more strained relationship with the grassroots government than agency B.

Like Hebei province and Fujian province, county C became a recipient of Catholic missionary activities as early as in the 17th century. In this rural area, the Catholic faith has been passed down from generation to generation among peasants who make up the majority of the members of the Catholic Church. Archbishops, priests and nuns all come from families of these believers and the Catholic faith has blended into the rural society. Currently, 10% of county C's population is Catholics.

Church D was up and running at its current location even before the "liberation" in 1949. After the founding of New China in 1949 and under the leadership of the Communist Party of China, some Catholic groups in China began to appoint their own bishops, i.e. the so-called "self-election and self-ordination" of bishops. The priests and sisters of church D saw this practice as "blasphemous to the Pope", so they refused to comply and refused to recognize the self-elected and self-ordained bishops. During the Cultural Revolution when all religious activities were cracked down on, the priest of church D died in prison. After 1980s when Reform and Open-up policy was implemented, religious activities resumed, but the priests and sisters of church D remained loyal to bishops appointed by the Pope and refused to accept the bishops appointed by the Chinese government or participate in state-sanctioned Catholic Church activities.

As a result, church D as a house church has been subject to various forms of persecution from the county government. The county's public security bureau places the church under 24-hour surveillance and the priest of the church is still under house arrest at the church. When the National People's Congress, G20 and other significant political activities were held before and after the Chinese government's diplomatic negotiations with the Vatican, the local government will always take the priest of church D into custody. All these are done out of fear that as a "sensitive figure", the priest of church D will expose the Chinese government's violation of human rights and citizens' religious activities to overseas political or religious figures or western media.

D church's operation of the child welfare facility started when babies with hearing and vision impairment were left at the doorstep of the church in 1980s. Because of that, the church built a simple house in its courtyard to take in and take care of abandoned infants dropped off at the church's door. When the word "a local church will adopt abandoned infants with disabilities" went out in C county, more babies were left at the church's door. The children with severe disabilities taken in by agency B discussed in chapter 2 are adopted from orphanages from all over China while the children with disabilities adopted by church D were all found at the church's door. At its highest number, more than 100 children with cerebral palsy, seizure disorder and deformed body parts lived on church D's facility. The number dropped to 50 or so after some children were adopted by Christian families and some died.

The operation of the facility and care-giving are on the shoulders of 30 sisters from church D. Taking care of children with severe disabilities around the clock is labor-intensive, and these sisters live in the church's dorms, receive no extra pay besides a pension to cover their living cost, and they have to work on the weekends. Funding of the facility comes from offerings from domestic believers, financial assistance from overseas Catholic churches and non-believing Chinese citizens.

B. Research findings

The activities of church D's charity organization abide by the Catholic Church's teaching about "acting with the power of prayer", and blends into the Catholic Church's religious activities. Abandoned children are named after Catholic saints, such as St. Francis. Sisters and priests confirm the children's faith every day through Mass. Children who can get into a wheelchair must attend Mass every Sunday and receive blessings from the priest. For sisters of the church, devoting their lives fully to children with disabilities is a manifestation of their faith in Jesus.
Let's look at the facility of this charity organization. Compared with agency B introduced in chapter 2, church D's charity organization has even less human and financial resource. Its facility is right next to the church. When this author first visited the facility a few years ago, the most striking impression was the stench of saliva and feces mixed and flies flying around in a poorly-lit room. Then this author saw some sisters feeding a little boy without pants. Clearly, the facility's cleanup crew was understaffed.
As far as education is concerned, it is very difficult for the children in the organization to get schooling because many of them have severe disabilities, such as cerebral palsy, which makes going to school a great challenge, and there are no special education schools for children with disabilities in county C which is in the rural area. As for children with less severe intellectual disabilities, the nuns provide on-site education, since church D does not have a support network agency B obtains its educational resources from, church D's charity organization has very little education resources available for children under its care.
The root cause of church D's plight is the denial of its legal status as religious group because it is an underground Catholic church.

The grassroots government of county C installed public security agents in the church to monitor the church's visitors and capital flow. On top of that, citing "underground churches are illegal", the government of county C also sees church D's welfare organization as illegal and orders church D to shut down the facility every year since 10 years ago, claiming that "The children church D takes in are not orphans because church D adopts them without government's approval, so these children are products of violating the government's 'one-child policy'". In the meanwhile, county C's public security department refuses to grant these children household registration and hence they are "undocumented people." As a result, these children with disabilities have no ID, have little access to medical treatment, and have no access to school education.

Despite these challenges and very limited human and financial resources, church's D's efforts made a deep impression on this author who saw some sisters spoon-feeding the abandoned children with disabilities. On church D's welfare facility, children are put in different rooms based on their gender and severity of disabilities. In a room for girls, this author saw the sisters chop up mushy noodles and patiently fed it to girls with a spoon. One girl made painstaking effort to feed her noodles to another girl who seemed younger and had disabilities, although the older girl herself had trouble eating her own food due to paralyzed hands caused by cerebral palsy. She emulated the sisters' care-giving behavior and took care of the younger children around her. Through their interactions with the sisters, these children with physical and intellectual disabilities acquired the emotion of "love" and the action of "caring for others" and are practicing them.

C. Catholic traditions and deterioration of church and the state relations

Church D's charity organization inherited the Catholic tradition of engaging in child welfare activities across China since the 19th century. The Catholic Church's tradition of manifesting faith through engagement in social causes is carried out all over the world. Through various channels, church D has receiving donations from some overseas Catholic groups as well as some consistent support from inside China, including some Buddhists. As a result, church D and its child welfare organization have been expanding their support network which goes beyond the region, the national border and religious border.

Nevertheless, church D's support network is often disrupted by persecutions from the grassroots government. In the meanwhile, due to the Xi Jinping Administration's harsh measures against Catholic house churches, church D and its child welfare organization are also affected by the tension in the church-and-the-state relations. Unlike agency B which has established an interdependent relationship with a few local governments, church D doesn't have any government agency's support. Since the local government simply wishes for unauthorized church D and its child welfare organization to disappear completely, the tension between the two keeps increasing.

IV. Summary: increasing tension in church and the state relations and "illegal dominos"

The Chinese government always has a small budget for children's welfare and education and the care and education for abandoned infants with disabilities, the most underprivileged social group, has always been supplemented by the efforts of civil groups. Many civil groups are without legal status and existing in the gray area. Unlike government agencies subject to many rules and regulations, however, such civil groups are able to recruit talents and resources from various overseas groups and foundations.

Christian civil groups are part of a global Christian network and boasting a century-old tradition of providing relief to abandoned infants in China. In 2000s, a quiet consensus about the division of functions regarding orphans' welfare and education has been reached, i.e. "state-run organizations adopt orphans and abandoned infants who are easier to care for while civil groups, especially Christian-run organizations adopt children with severe disabilities and needing more intense care." Christian groups have utilized their abundant public and secret networks to collect financial and medical resources to be expended on the care and education of children with severe disabilities, including getting resources from overseas.

The church-and-the-state relationship around Christian-run child welfare organizations reflects the diversity of government policy in different regions. Some local governments with inadequate budget for child welfare and education tend to use Christian-run child welfare organizations that adopt children with severe disabilities as a "welfare safety valve", and therefore barely consider whether these Christian organizations are authorized by the government or not.

The Chinese government sits on the fence between "management" and "acquiescence" when it comes to unregistered welfare organizations run by civil religious groups. When the central government loosens up religious policy to allow unregistered religious groups to function to a certain degree, some local governments will use welfare organization with religious background to supplement their policy on welfare and education. Existing in the gray area where "no legal status is granted but activities are acquiesced by the government", civil welfare organizations, especially Christians groups and individuals, continued to play this role.

However, in the wake of the "Lankao Incident", which happened in a non-government child welfare organization in 2013, and the Xi Jinping Administration's tightening control over religion, more measures have been taken to reinforce and standardize the management of civil child welfare organizations.

After 2013, the central government became sterner in outlawing unregistered religious groups. In the wake of "Lankao Incident" and public outrage demanding "never having this kind of tragedy happy again", the Ministry of Civil Affairs promulgated new guidelines to "standardize the management of" and "clean up" non-government child welfare organizations. Regarding religious groups operated by Christians, the Ministry of Civil Affairs clearly articulated that only religious groups registered with the government are allowed to operate child welfare organizations. As for child welfare organization operated by unregistered religious groups, grassroots government required children under their care be removed and transferred to state-run orphanages. Presently, welfare organization run by unregistered religious groups and individual Christians all face the dilemma of either getting registered or getting shut down.

Civil groups without any religious background also need approval from county-level government and above. However, due to the vague criteria for approval, the probability of unauthorized religious groups associated with house churches and underground churches being approved by the government is minimal.

Since these child welfare organizations are not recognized by the law, violations of basis human rights frequently occur in these organizations. If the church patronizing a child welfare organization operated by Christian group or individuals is not registered with the government, the church itself is "illegal" according to the law of China. Under this circumstance, these child welfare organizations, be they "civil religious organizations" or regular "social welfare organizations", will have no legal status in China. As a result, the grassroots public security agency will not grant household registration to children under the care of these organizations, and as "undocumented people", these children have no right to access medical services and school education. Neither are they protected by the law or entitled to human rights. This is a concrete example of how under the Chinese Communist Party's management of religion, religious activities outside the government-approved "patriotic religious groups" are deemed as illegal by the law. In other words, since China's religious policy limits religious freedom, the basic human rights of the most underprivileged social group, i.e. orphans and abandoned children with disabilities, are left unprotected. This is the "illegal dominos' effect", which runs contradictory to the Chinese government's public stance of "implementing people-centered governmental concept and the principle of 'children first' and promoting the healthy growth of abandoned infants."

V. Significance of Christian-run civil child welfare organizations and their opportunities

In today's China, in keeping with its economic development and the advance of social pluralism, more and more religious groups outside the state-sanctioned system have participated in education and charity cause, and the social network supportive of these causes is also expanding in and outside China. The stories told here of believers from churches outside the state-sanctioned system engaging in the education and charity work for children, especially orphans and children with disabilities, are typical examples of these changes.

What impact has such social causes championed by Christians had on the overall Chinese society and what opportunities are available in this area?

The mainstream society's belief that prioritizes productivity and actual benefits will not be able to explain the act of providing thoughtful and thorough care to children who are not your own, especially when it is unknown whether these children will become contributing members of society. Children with disabilities that need intensive care around the clock are often abandoned first in a productivity-oriented society. The Bible, however, stands for an opposing value system. The weak and the strong are equal and sometimes, the former hold more value than the latter. The Christian belief that deems the weak in human society as sacred and invaluable is reflected in such bible verses as found in Matthew 25, "Whatever you did for one of the least of these brothers and sisters of mine, you did for me".

Why can Christians share life with children with disabilities? Not out of obligation or the expectation for rewards. Christians interviewed by me said they believe "all lives share the same value and all lives are blessed by God." It is such a belief in "the value of life" and "blessings from God" that drives that decision to share one's life with orphans and children with disabilities. Adult care-givers are not just providing "children" with care; they are also blessed by these children. Life shared with these children also produces changes in the hearts of the Christian care-givers, and such changes felt in heart in turn convert to words naturally through prayer or Mass.

The Christian faith has transformed the quality or care and education given to children with disabilities, and the experience of caring for and educating these children gives life to the care-givers' faith. The charity and education cause by Christian groups for children with disabilities has created and practiced a new value through the interaction of faith and works. The Christian groups that provide care and education to orphans and children with disabilities not only display to the mainstream society the significance of the mutual support between the sick and the "healthy", but also take on these responsibilities.

The two child welfare organizations introduced in this article attach great importance to the interpersonal relationship between care-givers and children with disabilities. Providing care and education according to each child's personality can be a shining example to other child welfare organizations in China. Some local governments have informally visited agency B to study their model of care.

In addition, the support network of Christians also helps these agencies raise educational, medical and human resources. Non-government child welfare organizations are often short in funds and talents compared with government-run organizations, but such shortage also attracts the flow of human and material resources across the religious and national borders to fill up the gaps. This shows how people in various fields can be drawn together and form connections, as opposed to bureaucratic organizations under a government with highly centralized power.

References

Notice about Further Improving the Work Regarding Abandoned infants (Document No. 83, 2013) issued by Ministry of Civil Affairs, National Development and Reform Commission, Ministry of Public Security, Ministry of Justice, Ministry of Finances, National Health and Family Planning Commission, State Bureau of Religious Affairs.
Feng Hua & Zhu Junyi, "Help Old Orphans Better Integrate into Society (viewpoints)". People's Daily, 17th edition, 6/9/2017.
UNICEP: Orphans
https://www.unicef.org/zh/media/%E5%AD%A4%E5%84%BF%E9%97%AE%E9%A2%98.
"A conundrum that demands a quick solution: 600 thousand de factor orphans across China in desperate need for relief", The Procuratorate Daily, 11/22/2017.
Zhang Hui (2014), "The current situation and problem of our country's orphan relief and assistance system", Journal of Central South University of Forestry and Technology, 2nd edition, 2014.
Xiong Bingqi (2013), "'Illegal adoption' and 'black kindergarten'" 2nd edition, 2013.
Ministry of Civil Affairs' "Temporary Measures on the Management of Social Welfare Organizations", No. 19 Decree by

the Ministry of Civil Affairs of the People's Republic of China, 12/30/1999.
Daniel H. Bays (2012), A New History of Christianity in China, Wiley-Blackwell。

Original material of BaFu school event

BaFu school

1. Summary of Police Actions March 15, 2018

Yanyuan, Wangfu Ranch, Beiqijia township,
Changping district, Beijing - March 15, 2018, 5:00pm

A vehicle with the logo of security guards and the license plate of EM8780 broke into the gathering at 2# Yanyuan, and about 8-9 people coming out of the vehicle claimed to be dispatched by Beiqijia township government. Refusing to show any government papers, they took pictures of children leaving school to go home without asking for their permission first.

After the police was called by some parents, a police officer surnamed Yao with the badge number of 055857 arrived at the scene. After making a call to Beiqijia township government, the police officer claimed that the security guards were indeed sent over by the government, stating that he wasn't at liberty to tell why he believed so.

After checking and documenting every security guard's ID number, the police officer verbally asked them to delete the pictures they had taken, stating that the police had everything on the record and lawsuits against these security guards can be filed to the People's Court. No one followed through to make sure that these security guards had indeed deleted pictures before they left the scene in the vehicle they arrived in.

2. Information Bulletin March 21, 2018

We signed a 10-year rental lease in July 2016, with the owner of 2# Yanyuan and after we moved in the property, we have spent a large amount of money remodeling it and have maintained a good relationship with the landlord. However, the landlord suddenly asked to terminate the lease in February 2018, without giving us a clear reason. Recognizing that the landlord might be facing some challenges and for the sake of focusing on our long-term goals and maintaining the peace in the community, we were willing to find a solution through negotiations, but the landlord just went ahead to sue us to Changping district's People's Court on March 1, 2018. The court has accepted the case and is going through the civil law procedures.

Nevertheless, ignoring the fact that our dispute is being processed by the court, the landlord broke the law wittingly and provoked a conflict in such a rush that shocked us because our lease is still legal and valid at that point. In the afternoon of March 12, 2018, the landlord parked vehicles at the entrance of the property to block us from getting in or out. Despite that we reported this to the police who made a written record of the incident, the landlord still refused to move the vehicle away, which undermined our respect for the landlord, and caused a negative impact on our existing conflict as well as the harmony and stability of the community.

We call on our neighbors and residents in this community to join hands in defending the community's harmonious environment and support problem-solving through negotiations and judicial justice. We also reiterate that we have always been willing to negotiate with the landlord friendly and we have refrained from reacting to his actions. Hereby, we strongly urge the landlord to remove the vehicles blocking our entrance or the landlord will be held responsible for any legal consequences and the condemnation from the public should he refuse to do so and hence bring harm to either the vehicles or people.

Tenants of 2# Yanyuan - March 21, 2018

We once got along, but why fight each other now?
You press me so hard, but for what purpose?
Breaking the law wittingly, you shall be held responsible!

3. Urgent prayer requests

"Start children off on the way they should go, and even when they are old they will not turn from it". (Proverbs 22:6)

Children are the inheritance from God and educating children according to the Bible is every Christian's desire. Please join us in united hearts and minds to pray for the persecutions Beatitude

School is facing and pray that we can stand firm in our faith. Since Jan. 3 this year, Beatitude School has endured pressure from multiple sources. Despite that pastors, teachers and parents prayed and stood together, and earnestly asked to dialogue with the relevant government agencies, the challenges faced by parents and children have been ignored. On Jan. 30, while the lease was still effective, the elementary school children were forced to leave the school they had attended for five years. Up to this day, the lease is still effective, but the landlord has kicked the teachers and students out, which seemed to be an action orchestrated by someone behind him. Besides refusing to pay a fine induced by breach of the lease agreement, forty security guards forced their way into the school and moved desks, books and other school facilities to the street curb of the community. Such radical actions constituted severe violations of the public order regulations and China's civil and criminal laws! Brothers and sisters in Christ, please pray for Beatitude School.

All the parents of students attending Beatitude School
March 30, 2018

4. The Declaration of Tenants

We signed a 10-year lease with the landlord of 2# Yanyuan in July 2016, and according to the lease agreement, the lease is still effective, and we still enjoy the legal rights of tenants spelled out in the lease.

After the lease was signed, we had maintained a good relationship with the landlord and we invested heavily into remodeling the place based on mutual agreements spelled out in the lease contract. In Jan. 2018, without any clear reasons or advance notice, the landlord suddenly asked to terminate the lease agreement. We learned that the landlord had to do so due to reasons he was not at liberty to tell us. He did tell us that his radical actions were dictated by certain people. To keep our priorities straight and to maintain the peace in the community, we the tenants still expressed understanding of the landlord's behaviors and agreed to cooperate in solving the problem according to the general principles in the General Principles of the Civil Law and the Contract Law regarding the compensation for contract violations.

According to the Contract Law, where a party failed to perform or rendered non-conforming performance, the amount of damages payable shall be equivalent to the other party's loss resulting from the breach; if the amount is less than the loss resulting from the breach, the other party can ask the People's Court or an arbitrator to increase or reduce the amount of damages.

But the landlord refused to pay for our loss and instead, filed a lawsuit involuntarily against us to Changping district's People's Court in Feb. 2018. As we the innocent, conforming party of the contract who had suffered a loss for no reason anticipated the court to make a just ruling, the landlord blocked the entrance of the rental property with vehicles on March 12, 2018. Although we notified the police the same day and the police made a written record of our complaint, the landlord had not moved the vehicles away. Such actions will likely escalate the conflict and disrupt the harmony of the community, and in the meantime, the landlord's illegal and irrational problem-solving methods and those behind him who supported such methods have caused significant adverse impact and the loss of interpersonal understanding and respect, which is detrimental to problem-solving.

Instead of engaging in negotiations initiated by us, the landlord continued to take radical actions and burglarized our property on March 23. On March 28, the landlord sent in 40 security guards who forced their way into 2# Yanyuan to prevent us tenants from entering, which frightened our students and their parents, and caused the normal teaching activities to have to stop. When such severe violations took place, the tenants called the police in three separate instances. To defend judicial justice, we will actively seek help and support from relevant government agencies, experts and scholars.

We want to reiterate our stance that we have always being willing and actively seeking solutions through friendly negotiations with the landlord. We ask the landlord and relevant government agencies to respect the law, recognize the importance of harmony in community, and avoid causing conflicts with illegal activities. Should any property damage or personal injuries be incurred, the landlord must be held morally and legally responsible. Earnestly we plead with our neighbors, the property management agency and people living in our community to monitor the situation fairly, openly and justly. We still believe in justice and people's conscience!

Tenants of 2# Yanyuan,

March 30, 2018

Persecution has never ceased.

In days of suffering, a feeble heart weakens your strength.

Notice from the Education Bureau of Siming District of Xiamen City on the "Maizhong Academy"

No. 01 (2018)

To Maizhong Academy,

Per investigation, you are found to provide education illegally, without license or permission, at Shangli Church located at 490, Luyue Apartment Complex, Longhu South Road, Siming District, Xiamen, and at another location, i.e. 57-804, Erli, North District, Qianpu.

According to Article 64 of The People's Republic of China's Law Regarding the Promotion of Education Sponsored by Individual Citizens, this bureau is sending you this notice to inform you about your violations and request you to rectify your violations by 4/28/2018.

Signature of the subject of investigation (inquiry):
Signature of the conductor of investigation (inquiry):
Phone number: 0592-5862712

The Education Bureau of Siming District, Xiamen city

4/13/2018

告知书

[2018]第 01 号

麦 zhong 学堂:

经查, 你单位存在下列问题: 无照无证, 未经许可, 在厦门市思明区上李龙虎南路 490 号鹭悦家园小区 "尚 11 教会" 和前埔北区二里 57-804 擅自办学。

我局根据《中华人民共和国民办教育促进法》第六十四条规定, 现告知你单位对上述问题, 于 2018 年 4 月 28 日前整改完毕。

被调查（询问）人签字:

调查（询问）人签字:

联系电话: 0592—5862712

厦门市思明区教育局

2016年 ll 月 l5 日

Henan Provincial Catholic Patriotic Committee
Henan Provincial Catholic Committee on Educational Affairs

Notice

According to the "principle of adhering to the separation of religion and education" issued by the Provincial Bureau of Religious Affairs on 4/3, and in implementing the stipulation in Regulations on Religious Affairs, i.e. "Sites for religious activities are prohibited from hosting any form of training sessions to provide religious education to minors", the Chinese Christian Council and the Three-Self Patriotic Movement Committee in all townships and cities are required to:

1.   All sites for religious activities across the province shall not provide religious education and training to minors, or classes in the name of summer camp or winter camp.

2.   Persuade believers who go to churches to attend worship services or Mass to find their own childcare instead of taking their children to church.

3.   Take these regulations seriously.   They used to be communicated through propaganda and education, but now are implemented as legal mandates.

4.   People in charge of the sites for religious activities will be held responsible for the violations of the regulations above, which may lead to the clergy's loss of registration with the government and the shutdown of the sites for religious activities.

5.   The Chinese Christian Council and the Three-Self Patriotic Movement Committee in all townships and cities shall communicate the content of this Notice to churches in their jurisdiction in a timely manner.

Henan Provincial Catholic Patriotic Committee
Henan Provincial Catholic Committee on Educational Affairs
4/8/2018

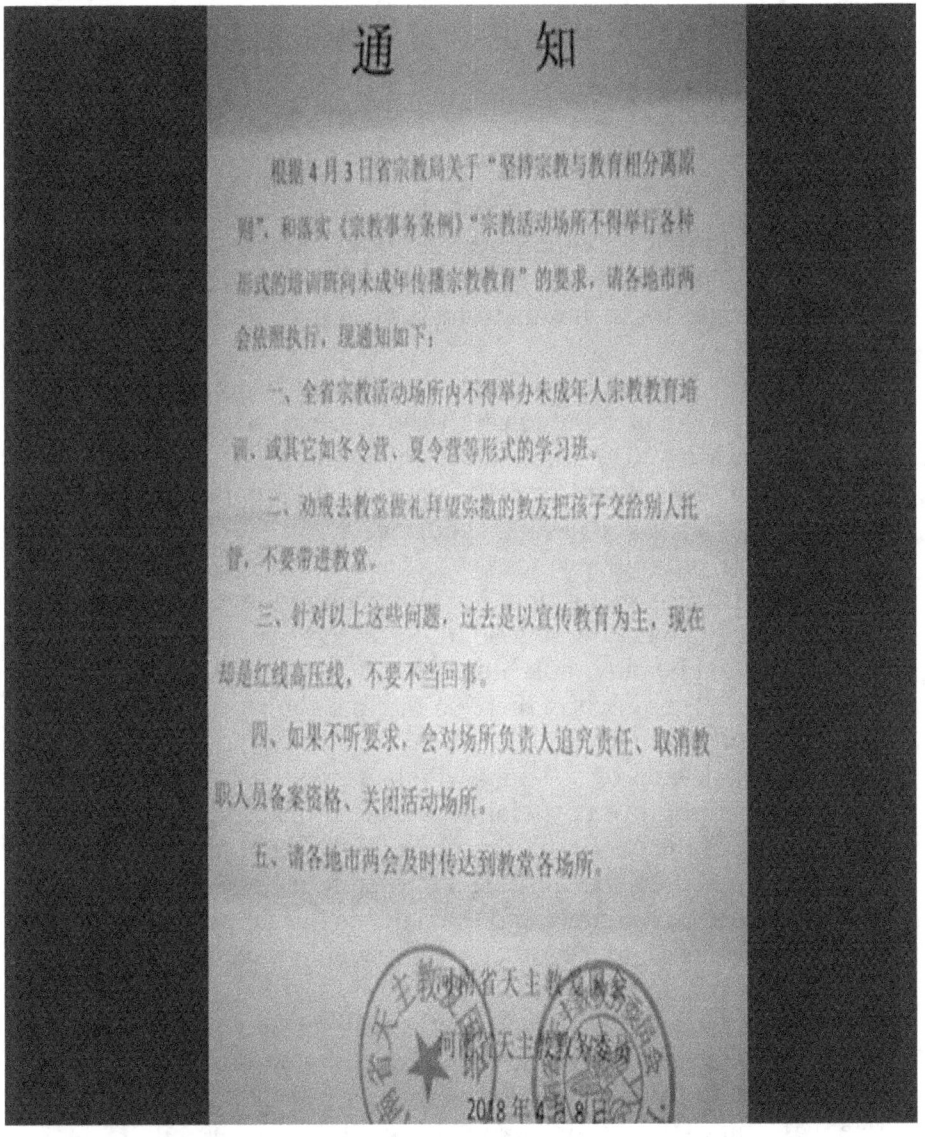

通　　知

根据 4 月 3 日省宗教局关于"坚持宗教与教育相分离原则"，和落实《宗教事务条例》"宗教活动场所不得举行各种形式的培训班向未成年传播宗教教育"的要求，请各地市两会依照执行，现通知如下：

一、全省宗教活动场所内不得举办未成年人宗教教育培训，或其它如冬令营、夏令营等形式的学习班。

二、劝戒去教堂做礼拜望弥撒的教友把孩子交给别人托管，不要带进教堂。

三、针对以上这些问题，过去是以宣传教育为主，现在却是红线高压线，不要不当回事。

四、如果不听要求，会对场所负责人追究责任、取消教职人员备案资格、关闭活动场所。

五、请各地市两会及时传达到教堂各场所。

2018 年 4 月 8 日

Henan Provincial Catholic Patriotic Committee
Henan Provincial Catholic Committee on Educational Affairs
4/8/2018

Xinjiang Authorities Jail Uyghur Imam Who Took Son to Unsanctioned Religious School

05-10-2018

Authorities in Hotan (in Chinese, Heitian) prefecture, in northwest China's Xinjiang Uyghur Autonomous Region (XUAR) have sentenced a prominent imam to more than five years in prison for taking his son to an unsanctioned religious school to meet other children.

Abduheber Ahmet, the imam of the Dongbagh Mosque in Urchi township, in Hotan's Qaraqash (Moyu) county, was initially detained in May 2017 and handed a five and a half-year jail term a month later, the ruling Chinese Communist Party secretary of Urchi township told RFA's Uyghur Service.

The 46-year-old father of four "took one of his sons to an underground religious school" in Dongbagh village, the party secretary said, speaking on condition of anonymity.

"It is said that he only took him once … I think it was four or five years ago … He took him there so that his son would meet and play with other children."

Ahmet, a state-approved imam who had previously received a "five star" rating from officials, "revealed [his crime] himself during one of the confession meetings," the secretary said, and received "leniency" because he admitted to it.

"Because the government and the party is fair, he was given a five and a half-year sentence, otherwise he would have received a seven-year prison term," he added.

According to the secretary, Ahmet is serving his sentence in Bayin'gholin (Bayinguoleng) Mongol Autonomous Prefecture at the Reform Through Labor Prison in Korla (Kuerle) city.

He was sent to the prison "about 11 months ago," he said.

'Two-faced' Uyghurs

Since April 2017, Uyghurs accused of harboring "strong religious views" and "politically incorrect" views have been jailed or detained in re-education camps throughout the XUAR, where members of the ethnic group have long complained of pervasive discrimination, religious repression, and cultural suppression under Chinese rule.

In the months since XUAR party chief Chen was appointed to his post in August 2016, he has initiated unprecedented repressive measures against the Uyghur people and ideological purges against so-called "two-faced" Uyghur officials—a term applied by the government to Uyghurs who do not willingly follow directives and exhibit signs of "disloyalty."

In October last year, RFA learned that authorities had jailed four grandchildren of Qurban Barat, the former imam of Hanliq Mosque in Qaraqash county, who was once recognized as a "Patriotic Religious Scholar" by the Communist Party for turning two alleged "separatists" in to the police.

The four received prison sentences of between five and a half and eight years because they "listened to religious teachings" and possessed "illegal religious materials," Barat's son told RFA at the time, adding that at least three other party members in his county have children or spouses who have been sentenced to prison or placed in re-education camps for religious violations.

China regularly conducts "strike hard" campaigns in Xinjiang, including police raids on Uyghur households, restrictions on Islamic practices, and curbs on the culture and language of the Uyghur people, including videos and other material.

While China blames some Uyghurs for "terrorist" attacks, experts outside China say Beijing has exaggerated the threat from the Uyghurs and that repressive domestic policies are responsible for an upsurge in violence there that has left hundreds dead since 2009.

Reported by Shohret Hoshur for RFA's Uyghur Service. Translated by RFA's Uyghur Service. Written in English by Joshua Lipes.

Uyghur Schoolchildren, Parents Forced to Abstain From Fasting During Ramadan

05-21-2018

Authorities in northwest China's Xinjiang Uyghur Autonomous Region (XUAR) are forcing Uyghur students and their parents to sign pledges that they will not fast during the holy Islamic month of Ramadan in a bid to further undermine the religious traditions of the mostly Muslim ethnic group.

Officials have typically forced restaurants to stay open and restricted access to mosques during Ramadan, and last year sources told RFA's Uyghur Service that Uyghur Communist Party cadres, civil servants and government retirees were made to sign documents that said they would neither fast nor pray during the holy month, ostensibly to set an example to other Uyghurs in the community.

But a student in Kashgar (in Chinese, Kashi) prefecture's Peyziwat (Jiashi) county recently told RFA that school officials made him and his classmates sign agreements with their parents that they would not fast during Ramadan—which falls between May 16 and June 14 this year—marking the first time authorities have been known to target school-age children with the measures.

The report suggest that authorities are making unprecedented incursions into the personal lives of Uyghurs to eliminate what they call signs of religious "extremism" in the region.

"As we are students, we don't fast," said the student, who spoke with RFA on condition of anonymity.

"We have signed a school agreement and also written a letter of promise."

When asked if his parents were fasting during Ramadan, the student said that they weren't because "they are not allowed to practice such things in front of … their children."

"To act as role models, of course they will not fast," he added.

A female cadre from Peyziwat county said that ahead of Ramadan "all cadres and party members were called to the county office for a meeting, in which we were told to 'be more vigilant' and to 'pay special attention' to anyone who complains about the government's policy regarding religious extremism."

"The cadres are working hard on … educating [residents] about the incorrectness of fasting," she added.

When asked whether fasting was considered an "illegal religious activity," the cadre acknowledged that it is not, but said "people shouldn't complain when living under such good conditions."

She also confirmed a report by New York-based Human Rights Watch (HRW) earlier this month that authorities are imposing regular "home stays" on Muslim Uyghur families of cadres who record information about their lives and political views, and subject them to political indoctrination, as part of an increasingly invasive "strike hard" campaign in the region.

"They are helping farmers get out of poverty," she said of the home stay policy, which the government says provides families with access to education about technical skills and teaches them Mandarin Chinese to help residents find better work.

Other sources, including an officer at a police station in Aksu (Akesu) prefecture, said increased security measures are in effect around the region during Ramadan.

"We have intensified patrols in order to retain stability, and at the moment there are no instability issues," said the officer, before hanging up the phone.

Existing measures

The new restrictions surrounding Ramadan are in line with existing measures targeting religious "extremism" that have been introduced in recent years.

Since April, thousands of Uyghurs accused of harboring "extremist" and "politically incorrect" views have been detained in political re-education camps and prisons throughout Xinjiang, where members of the ethnic group complain of pervasive discrimination, religious repression, and cultural suppression under Chinese rule.

Authorities have relied on a list circulated early last year of "75 Signs of Religious Extremism" to detain Uyghurs amid a string of harsh policies attacking their legitimate rights and freedoms enacted since Communist Party secretary Chen Quanguo was appointed to run the region in August 2016.

Among the signs of extremism on the list were "conducting business as usual" and "women who wear religious clothing to work" during Ramadan, "storing or purchasing large quantities of food for home" and "acting abnormal," and "praying in groups in public outside of mosques."

But party officials told RFA that they had been notified of several new "signs of extremism" in April last year, including people who stand with their legs wide apart while praying, dye their hair with henna, wear short trousers, wear a watch on their right wrist, and those suddenly abstaining from alcohol.

Another list informs officials to watch out for the so-called "28 Signs of Illegal Religious Activities."

Ahead of Ramadan this year, the Munich-based World Uyghur Congress (WUC) exile group issued a statement urging the Chinese government to ensure the right to religious freedom for Uyghurs, and to allow them to observe the holy month without restrictions.

"Each year, the month of Ramadan has been turned into one of fear and anxiety because of the increased restrictions, which has caused untold disturbance in the daily life of the Uyghur people," WUC president Dolkun Isa said at the time.

China regularly conducts "strike hard" campaigns in Xinjiang, including police raids on Uyghur households, restrictions on Islamic practices, and curbs on the culture and language of the Uyghur people, including videos and other material.

While China blames some Uyghurs for "terrorist" attacks, experts outside China say Beijing has exaggerated the threat from the Uyghurs and that repressive domestic policies are responsible for an upsurge in violence there that has left hundreds dead since 2009.

Reported by Gulchehra Hoja for RFA's Uyghur Service.
Translated by RFA's Uyghur Service. Written in English by Joshua Lipes.

Xinjiang Uygur Autonomous Region's Bureau of Education's Regulations about Banning On-campus Religious Activities

No. 5 regarding Protestantism (issued on 8/5/1996)

I. To preserve the socialist orientation of education and safeguard the normal order of school's educational and teaching activities, and in accordance with The Constitution of People's Republic of China, The Law of People's Republic of China on the Autonomy of Minority Ethnic Regions, The Law of People's Republic of China about Education, the Regulations of Xinjiang Uygur Autonomous Region on Religious Affairs, as well as the Party's and our country's regulations regarding ethnic, religious and educational affairs in conjunction with the reality of the schools in our region, the following regulations have been devised and passed.

II. Socialist schools are battlefields where we educate students with Marxism-Leninism, Maoism, and Deng Xiaoping's theory about constructing a socialism with Chinese characteristics, disseminate knowledge about science and culture, and cultivate new socialist people with "four qualities" (i.e. idealistic, moral, educated, disciplined). Therefore, all forms of religious activities are prohibited, and no religious groups or individuals shall build or set up mosques, Buddhist temples or Daoism temples on school campuses, including school-run factories, farms, internship sites, etc., and those preexisting ones must be demolished or relocated within a certain time. No students shall be recruited to study religious texts. There shall be no interfering with school-conducted education about dialectical materialism, historical materialism, atheism, and scientific or cultural knowledge. There shall be no dissemination of religious ideas or practice of religious rituals on school campus or among students. There shall be no coercion of

registered students to join religious activities. Schools, teachers, students and other social groups ought to report such activities to the
local government or concerned government agencies and have them handle such activities according to the law and regulations.

III. Teachers of the people are the disseminators of knowledge about science and culture and carriers of the honorable duty of teaching knowledge and educating people. Therefore, they must carefully implement the Party's and our country's guidelines for education, adhere to educating students about Marxism-Leninism and Maoism, impart knowledge about the scientific worldview and outlooks on life, atheism, and educate students about defending national unification and ethnic unity. Teachers shall not participate in religious activities, spread religious ideas among students, or coerce and organize students to join religious activities. Those who violate this regulation will be subject to school's criticism and education and those who refuse to mend their ways will lose their teaching qualifications. Those who commit severe violations shall be removed from the faculty team.

IV. As the future constructors and successors of the socialist cause, students must voluntarily accept the patriotic, collectivist and socialist education and adopt scientific worldviews and outlooks on life. They shall not participate in religious activities, join classes to study religious texts, join choirs to sing worship songs, observe fasting, or wear religious logos. Students' parents and other people shall not force students to convert to religion or join religious activities. Students who participate in religious activities will be criticized and educated by schools. Those who refuse to mend their ways are subject to discipline and penalty.

V. Faculty, staff and students who are members of the Communist Party or Youth League should be Marxists and atheists who strictly abide by the regulations of the Communist Party Charter and the Youth League Charter. They should champion Marxism-Leninism and Maoism, study knowledge about science and culture, adopt the worldviews of dialectical materialism and historical materialism, and abstain from converting to religion or joining any religious activities. Violators who are Party members or Youth League members are subject to criticism and education, and those who refuse to mend their ways shall be persuaded to renounce their membership or expelled from the Party or Youth League.

VI. Schools of all levels and all kinds shall further reinforce ideological and political education, maintaining a certain number of hours of atheistic education in the curriculum of ideological and moral lessons taught in colleges, middles schools and elementary schools, and mixing the atheistic education in the teaching of all the school subjects. On-campus Party and Youth League organizations, Worker's Union, Women's Federation, and the League of Young Pioneers shall often organize faculty and students in studying current political affairs, conduct education about dialectical materialism, develop a great variety of cultural, athletic, scientific and technological activities, turn schools into heathy and progressive platforms where students pursue truths and study science, and increase the youth's ability to resist idealism and religious thoughts.

VII. The educational administrations of all levels and schools shall further reinforce management, perfect various rules and regulations, and make the performance reviews of officials and faculty, certification of teaching credentials, and the rating and promotion of faculty contingent on how well they have implemented the Party's guidelines for education, how correctly they have carried out the Party's policy on religion, and how effectively they have conducted the education about patriotism, ethnic unity, and atheism on students. In the meanwhile, students' moral evaluation shall include content regarding whether they treat the problem of religion in the right way.

VIII. Schools, society and families are to work together closely to implement the above regulations carefully, oppose religious infiltration and its interference with education, and protect the healthy development of young students.
VIIII. This regulation is applicable to schools of all levels and all types except religious schools.

Xinjiang Uygur Autonomous Region's Education Commission
2/2/1996

The Ministry of Education's Opinions about How to Properly Handle Religion's Disruption of School Education in Ethnic Minority Regions

Forwarded by:
The General Office of the Central Committee of the Communist Party of China and the General Office of the State Council

February 27, 1983

The Ministry of Education's Opinions about How to Properly Handle Religion's Disruption of School Education in Ethnic Minority Regions[1] has been approved by the Secretariat of the Central Committee and the State Council. It is now being forwarded to you to be implemented in conjunction with your specific reality and circumstances.

In recent years, it has occurred in some ethnic minority regions that religion interfered with education and attacked schools. Although these are spotty occurrences that happened in the context of remarkable success in implementing the Party's religious policy, Party and political officials of all levels still need to attach great importance to them. Local governments nationwide ought to review and implement The Basic Viewpoint and Policy on the Religious Question during Our Country's Socialist Period issued by the Secretariat of the Central Committee, and craft necessary administrative rules and local regulations through the democratic process to carefully handle this problem on the basis of thoroughly, patiently and meticulously conduct ideological education among religious believers, patriotic religious clergy, and leaders of religious communities. Those counterrevolutionaries who use religion as a disguise to instigate the sabotage of the socialist education cause and engage in other counterrevolutionary activities must be relentlessly exposed and suppressed.

Developing the education of ethnic minority groups is a key component of constructing the material civilization and socialist spiritual civilization in ethnic minority regions, and crucial to reinforcing ethnic unity as well as safeguarding and defending the interests of ethnic minority people. Therefore, while focusing on developing economy in these regions, great efforts shall be made to promote the education of ethnic minority people to significantly improve their standard of education in a short period of time and make it gradually adapt to the demands of the construction of socialist modernization in these regions.

The Ministry of Education's Opinions about How to Properly Handle Religion's Disruption of School Education in Ethnic Minority Regions

Jan. 15, 1983

The Secretariat of the Central Committee and the State Council:

Since the Third Plenary Session of the Eleventh Central Committee of the CPC, CPC's religious policy has been gradually implemented and people's normal religious activities have been restored, which has played an important part in improving CPC's and the government's relationship with people, increasing ethnic unity, and promoting political stability and unity. Nevertheless, research in some provinces and autonomous regions, such as Xinjiang, Gansu, Ningxia, Qinghai, Yunnan and Sichuan, revealed that in recent years, religion's interference with education, fighting over students, and raiding schools occurred in some ethnic minority regions that endorse Islam, Theravada Buddhism and Lamaism. In some regions, there even occurred the interference with education by Catholicism and Christianity. Such circumstances even prevail in certain.religions. For example, imams were invited to schools to chant scriptures and perform religious services, and they indoctrinated youth and children with religious ideas and seduced them to join religious activities. Some imams tell students they won't be able to go to heaven upon death unless they study religious texts. An official in Lufeng county, Chuxiong Autonomous Prefecture,
Yunnan, who is a Catholic, dared to make such rules as 1) children who don't believe in God cannot attend school; 2) the Bible must be studied at school; 3) teachers who don't believe in God cannot

teach any more. Some imams used religion to undermine ethic unity, calling on students to "fight for religion and drown the Han people in water", and falsely labeling the red scarf worn by Young Pioneers as "the lasso to drag people to hell", which caused some students to burn the red scarves and the textbooks for Politics and the Chinese Language classes.

In Xinjiang, Gansu, Ningxia and some other regions where Islam is the dominant religion, some people run unauthorized scripture schools, mostly in mosques though some in believers' homes, and some of these are boarding schools, causing a large number of school-age children to drop out of public schools and enter these schools to study scriptures. By March 1981, 6,000 children dropped out of public schools for this reason in Guanghe county, Linxia Autonomous Prefecture, Gansu, which accounted for 38.8% of the population of school-age children. In Linxia, 12,000 children received education in public schools whereas as many as 14,000 children attended religious schools. During only six months after March 1981, the number of students who dropped out of public schools to attend scripture schools increased from 4,000 to 18, 000 in Xinjiang's Kashgar. In some areas of Yunnan, Sichuan, Qinghai and Gansu inhabited with Dai and Tibetan people who believe
Theravada Buddhism or Lamaism, numerous youths and children dropped out of school to become lamas and monks. In the past two years, about 2,000 students dropped out of schools to become monks in temples in Xishuangbanna Dai Autonomous Prefecture's Menghai county, which accounts for 30% of the total number of Dai students in public schools. In the rural areas of Sichuan province's Ganzi inhabited with Tibetans, some lamas who returned to laity recruited Tibetan students to teach them scriptures in "private schools" and rejected teachers sent by the government. After the reform of the religious system in 1958 and during the 10-year Cultural Revolution, some temples were appropriated by public schools. In recent years, some religious believers used this as an excuse to forcibly take over school properties and demolish schools to build temples, causing some schools to close down and leaving students with nowhere to go for education.
The problems listed above should not be attributed to the proper implementation of religious policies. What we should examine is

the influence of religion and the effectiveness of our work. As far as religion is concerned, Islam, Lamaism and Theravada Buddhism have a long history and powerful influence in some ethnic minority regions. People who are very devoted to these religious beliefs will pass them on to their children, which gives some religious clergy the opportunity to violate religious policies, run religious schools without permission and spread the influence of their religion. As far as the effectiveness of our work goes, some officials without a comprehensive understanding of religious policies feel reluctant or lack the courage to handle the problems that arise in the implementation of religious policies, or they leave the problems unattended because they are too tricky. In the meanwhile, not enough importance is attached to education in some areas, causing the underdevelopment of education, science and technology. In some rural areas particularly, schools are few, poorly equipped, and providing poor-quality education, causing people to lose confidence in schools and lose motivation to send their children to schools. In areas inhabited with the Mongolians and Dai people, the study of people's ethnic languages has long been underrated due to the influence of the Leftist ideology, and even forbidden by the government at one point. As a result, some people choose to send their children to temples to learn their ethnic language. In addition to the reasons above, it is undeniable that a small number of counter-revolutionaries use religion as a disguise for instigation and sabotage. In 1981, a counter-revolutionary revolt fanned by religion broke out in Xinjiang's Yecheng county and many youths, mostly students of scripture schools, were lured to join in.

The problems we face now are mostly within the realm of people's internal conflicts and the solution is mainly to rely on CPC's policies in combination with patient and thorough ideological and political work as well as making necessary administrative regulations. To properly and fully implement CPC's religious policies and correctly handle religion's interference with education and schools, the opinions below shall be considered:

I. Adhere to the separation of religion from education.

This principle doesn't necessarily conflict with our country's current policy about the freedom of religious belief. Before 1949, the Buddhist temples among the Tibetan and Dai people were both religious entities and cultural/educational entities in the feudal society because religion and education were blended together, while the circumstance with Uygur and Hui people was slightly different because there were both religious schools and secular schools among these two ethnic groups. After 1949, we practiced the principle of separating education from religion, and after making great efforts, the majority of religious schools have gradually dissolved and the religious class in some secular schools has long been canceled, which is a great achievement of education reform. Today, we must continue to reinforce and perfect our country's socialist education system and never waver from the principle of separating religion and education that we have adhered to.

II. Adhere to the principle that religion shall not interfere with education.

This has been written into Resolution on Certain Questions in the History of Our Party unanimously passed at the 6th plenary session of CPC's Central Committee. The Constitution of People's Republic of China also clearly prescribes that no one shall use religion to engage in activities that interfere with the state's education system. This is also a principle supported by the mass of religious believers and patriotic clergymen. To prevent and prohibit religion's interference with education and the state's education system from happening again, we hold that, besides the policies and regulations regarding religious schools prescribed in The Basic Viewpoint and Policy on the Religious Question during Our Country's Socialist Period issued by the Central Committee (Document No. 19), we expect public schools to comply with the following regulations: 1) No spread of religion or religious ideas to students in schools; 2) Schools shall not cancel classes for the sake of religious activities; 3) No one shall force students to believe in religion or become monks, lamas or manlas; 4) No religious classes of any form shall be offered in schools; 5) No one shall use religion to disrupt or interrupt school's normal teaching activities; 6) No one shall in any way interfere with or resist school's teachings about Marxism-Leninism, Maoist ideology, science and culture.

III. Properly handle unauthorized scripture schools or classes.

The fundamental task in front of all the Chinese people nowadays is to turn China into a highly civilized and highly democratic socialist country. Every place in China, including ethnic minority regions, shall further develop scientific and cultural education, gradually make elementary school education accessible to every person, cultivate all kinds of talents, and constantly improve people's knowledge of science of culture. The emergence of numerous scripture schools which cause many school-age children to drop out of schools to study scriptures runs against the arduous task of constructing socialism and modernization and the request of building "two civilizations." It is detrimental to the next generation's healthy growth, to the development of ethnic education, and to the advance of the ethnic minority people's knowledge of science and culture. Therefore, it shall not be left unattended. Towards privately-run scripture schools unauthorized by the government, relevant government agencies must collaborate their efforts in actively channeling and gradually resolve them.

IV. No consent shall be given to the request of offering Arabic language class in elementary schools in some areas inhabited with Muslims.

Historically, Arabic was never a common language used by any ethnic group in China, and it was only used as a classic religious language by a small number of people. It was pointed out in the Report about the Founding of the Islamic Society of China by the Central Commission of Ethnic Affairs' Party Committee forwarded by CPC's Central Committee, "Arabic is not the Hui people's common language, but rather the classic language of Islam. Therefore, learning and using Arabic in the religious field is acceptable, but attempting to popularize it as a common language for the Hui people is a grave mistake and it will undermine the Hui people's political, economic and cultural development." Therefore, it is not necessary to offer Arabic language class in schools and this shall never be used as an excuse to restore religious classes.

V. Regarding schools' appropriation of temples' estates in the past, the local government ought to follow government policies,

differentiate various cases, negotiate with all parties involved, and resolve them properly.

In the future, no one is allowed to forcibly take over schools, demolish school buildings, damage school equipment, or for any reason force a school to stop running or close down.

VI. It was pointed out at CPC's 12th Annual Conference, "Making education accessible to all is the precondition of material civilization and spiritual civilization."

We must follow this instruction to steadily reinforce the elementary and middle school education in ethnic minority regions and take various
effective measures to admit more school-age children into schools. In the long term, this is a key to solve the problem of religion interfering with school education. First and foremost, strengthen the ideological and political education at schools, expose students to education about patriotism and ethnic unity and provide lively education to popularize science and culture. To that end, we shall reform the textbooks for political class and make the content lively and interesting. Make great efforts to improve the condition of schools, improve teaching, promote the quality of education, and actively promote recreational, athletic and various other beneficial extracurricular activities. In elementary and middle schools for ethnic minority people with their own ethnic languages, efforts should be made to quickly restore the teaching of ethnic languages so that students can learn their ethnic language well and then learn Chinese if needed. Actively train ethnic teachers and reinforce the development of teaching materials in ethnic languages.

VII. The key to successfully handling religion's impact on and interference with school education lies in strong leadership.

The Party committee and government of all levels shall consider the big picture and mobilize all relevant agencies to cooperate closely and deal with this issue effectively. To that end, first study carefully and then implement firmly Document No. 19. Be united in your understanding of this important document and the implementation of policies. All relevant government agencies shall take on their responsibilities, bravely work with officials, people, and religious clergy, explain to them our policies, clearly communicate our messages, educate the mass of religious believers and patriotic clergy to love our country and abide by the law, and make them voluntarily safeguard school education and comply with the principle of separating religion from education. Document No. 19 pointed out, "The basic starting point and firm foundation for our handling of the religious question and for the implementation of our policy and freedom of religious belief lies in our desire to unite the mass of believers and nonbelievers and enable them to center all their will and strength on the common goal of building a modernized, powerful socialist state. Any action or speech that deviates in the least from this basic line is completely erroneous and must be firmly resisted and opposed by both Party and people." This is the fundamental principle we must carry out steadily and resolutely when we handle the problem of religion's interference with school education.

If the opinions above are seen as proper, please send them out for implementation.

Note: This document is an abridged version of the original.
Source: CPC News:
http://cpc.people.com.cn/GB/64184/64186/66704/4495671.html.

Discrimination on the Basis of Religion or Belief in Education

Edited by Katherine Capps

Note: This article contains excerpts from the extensive research conducted by Christian Solidarity Worldwide (CSW). For their full and in-depth report pertaining to this topic and to their countries of focus, please refer to: "Discrimination on the Basis of Religion or Belief in Education – Faith and a Future",
http://faithandafuture.com/wp-content/uploads/2018/02/Faith_and_a_Future_HR.pdf.

Introduction

A child's right to freedom of religion or belief (FoRB) is guaranteed under Article 18 of the Universal Declaration of Human Rights (UDHR) and the International Covenant on Civil and Political Rights (ICCPR), as well as under Article 14 of the United Nations Convention on the Rights of the Child (CRC). All UN Member States (except for the United States) have ratified the CRC. And yet, in practice, children and young adults across the world face varying degrees of discrimination because of their religion or belief, including in educational settings.

Education can either create a culture of tolerance or fuel stereotyping, animosity and extremism. It can provide opportunities for social mobility or entrench disadvantage.

FoRB violations in the educational setting can take a number of forms:

1. Bias

Biased education, including intolerance from teachers and discrimination in school textbooks, creates a toxic mix, leaving students from minority religious communities isolated and reviled. Curriculum reform must be an urgent priority in countries where religious bigotry is fostered through bias in textbooks and stereotypes, and teachers should receive training to enable them to understand and promote respect for other religious traditions.

2. Discrimination

CSW found that discrimination and intolerance on the basis of religion or belief is a significant factor undermining the right to education, including in Rakhine State, Burma, where Rohingya children are unable to access education on account of their religion and ethnicity. Effective action must be taken to protect the rights of children in countries or communities where they are barred from attending school because of their religious beliefs or those of their parents.

3. Abuse

The psychological impact of abuse received by children at school cannot be overstated. Many interviewees told CSW of the 'mental torture' they have suffered as a result of religious discrimination and intolerance in educational settings. Rejected by their peers and teachers, this suffering can have lasting consequences.

Governments must address and end these violations, ensuring that perpetrators are held to account for their actions. For the sake of the children who suffer the consequences of religious discrimination in educational settings, the international community must act immediately to address violations and invest resources into examining further the interaction between FoRB and the right to education.

The importance of the right to education has been acknowledged for some time in national and international legislation, and in many countries great progress has been made towards achieving universal primary education and increased secondary and tertiary attendance. However, despite significant focus by the international community on the right to education, millions of children are still not able to enjoy this right fully. The UN Secretary General's report of 2016 on the progress towards the Sustainable Development Goals (SDGs) highlighted that 'In 2013, the latest year for which data are available, 59 million children of primary-school age were out of school. Estimates show that, among those 59 million children, 1 in 5 of those children had dropped out and recent trends suggest that 2 in 5 of out-of-school children will never set foot in a classroom.'[37] An even larger number of children are denied access to the quality of education that would provide them with greater opportunities later in life.

International Legal Framework: the right to Education and the right to Freedom of Religion of Belief (FoRB)

The right of the child to education has received considerable attention both in human rights treaties and monitoring bodies, and in the work of United Nations (UN) bodies. For example, education features prominently in the Sustainable Development Goals (SDGs), adopted in 2015. Comparatively, the right of the child to FoRB has received far less attention. The reduced attention to this right has been recognized by relevant UN Human Rights Council (HRC) Special Procedures mandate holders. Consequently, successive Special Rapporteurs on FoRB have focused increasingly on the rights of the child, providing essential guidance on the intersection between FoRB and other rights, including the right to education.

In addition, the intersection between FoRB violations and violations of the right to education has received limited attention in the international human rights system. FoRB violations in educational settings, discrimination on the basis of religion or belief, and the violation of the right to education because of the religious identity of the child or their parents or legal guardians, all have a detrimental impact on the development of the child. The immediate impact of such violations is obvious; however, the possible long-term consequences as children move into adulthood are incalculable. It is therefore vital that these restrictions are recognized and systematically addressed at the international, regional, national and local levels.

UNESCO Convention against Discrimination in Education

The Convention against Discrimination in Education was adopted at the General Conference of the United Nations Educational,

---

[37] UN ECOSOC, 'Report of the Secretary General: Progress towards the Sustainable Development Goals', 2016 E/2016/75, p. 7 https://unstats.un.org/sdgs/files/report/2016/secretary-general-sdg-report-2016--EN.pdf

Scientific and Cultural Organization (UNESCO) in 1960. The Convention, which came into effect in 1962, asserted the principle of non-discrimination and the right to education. In Article 1, discrimination is defined as 'distinction, exclusion, limitation or preference' which is based on a number of protected characteristics, including religion, and which has the 'purpose, or effect of nullifying or impairing equality of treatment in education', including depriving a person or persons from accessing education, limiting a person or persons to accessing education of an inferior standard, or maintaining separate systems of education. The Convention does allow for the existence of separate education in three specific circumstances:[38] in establishing or maintaining separate educational institutions for boys and girls; in establishing or maintaining separate education systems for religious or linguistic reasons; or in establishing or maintaining private education institutions. Where schools are created to separate genders, the quality and standard of education must be equitable or equivalent. The kind of education offered to religious or linguistic groups should be in keeping with the wishes of parents or legal guardians, while private institutions should not be created 'to secure the exclusion of any group, but to provide educational facilities in addition to those provided by the public.'

Article 3 places a duty on States to eliminate and prevent discrimination by ensuring that legislation and administrative practices, in schools and public authorities, do not discriminate against or restrict a particular group from accessing education. Additionally, unlike other international instruments, Article 9 prevents States from placing reservations on any part of the Convention. Possibly as a consequence of this, acceptance and ratification of the Convention is low in comparison with the ICCPR, ICESCR and similar instruments.[39]

The significance of school education

---

[38] Article 2 articulates situations that would not be deemed to constitute discrimination.

[39] United Nations Treaty Collection, 'International Covenant on Economic, Social and Cultural Rights' https://treaties.un.org/Pages/ViewDetails.aspx?src=IND&mtdsg_no=IV-3&chapter=4&lang=en.

International human rights instruments articulating the right to education provide a binary understanding of the right; either a child has access to primary, secondary or tertiary education, or they do not. Compared to FoRB, which often requires a deeper analysis of the facts of a particular case in order to make an assessment of a violation, the right to education on a prima facie basis is easier to assess.

Within the school environment, former Special Rapporteur Bielefeldt emphasized that a distinction should be made between religious instruction and religious information in education:[40]

> "Whereas religious instruction aims at familiarizing students with their own religious tradition, i.e. with theological doctrines and norms of their particular faith, information about religions, by contrast, serves the purpose of broadening the students' general knowledge about different religions and beliefs, in particular those religions and beliefs they may encounter in the society in which they live."

The forceful exposure of a child to religious instruction that is not in conformity with their own conviction is a contravention of the character of Article 18, which articulates the freedom 'to have or to adopt' a religion as an intrinsic right (forum internum) that cannot be derogated under any circumstances, including during public emergency.[41] Limitations on the right 'to have or to adopt' a religion or belief that are imposed through coercive practices, laws or policies are also invalid under international human rights law. In fact, Article 18(2) states that 'no one shall be subject to coercion which would impair his freedom to have or to adopt a religion of belief of his choice.'

Countries that are facing Discrimination on the basis of Religion or Belief in Education

BURMA (MYANMAR)

---

[40] United Nations General Assembly, 'Report of the Special Rapporteur on freedom of religion or belief, Heiner Bielefeldt', 15 December 2010 www.undocs.org/A/HRC/16/53.
[41] International Covenant on Civil and Political rights, Article 4; also Human Rights Committee, General Comment 22, para 1.

Constitutional commitments: Although Article 34 appears to protect freedom of religion or belief (FoRB) for all, it is undermined by a set of qualifying conditions: religious freedom is guaranteed as long as religion does not undermine 'public order', 'morality', 'health' or 'other provisions of this constitution'. Article 361 states that 'The Union recognizes the special position of Buddhism as the faith professed by the great majority of the citizens of the Union'. Writing the special status of Buddhism into the constitution legitimizes policies that discriminate against religious minorities in the name of the protection of Buddhism. The result is that a vaguely defined idea of 'public welfare' takes precedence over full FoRB.

Destruction of schools: Religious nationalists have destroyed Muslim schools in acts of communal violence in which officials have sometimes been complicit. The government has not repaired these schools.

IRAN

Constitutional commitments: Article 13 states that 'Zoroastrian, Jewish, and Christian Iranians are the only recognized religious minorities, who, within the limits of the law, are free to perform their religious rites and ceremonies, and to act according to their own canon in matters of personal affairs and religious education.' Article 14 states that the rights of these non-Muslims must be respected, provided they are not engaging in activities against Islam or Iran.

Abuse: Some Baha'i children have suffered physical abuse in school, while others have been incarcerated with their parents.

MEXICO

Constitutional commitments: Referring specifically to the relationship between education and religious observance, Article 3(1) states: 'Freedom of religious beliefs being guaranteed by Article 24, the standard which shall guide such education shall be maintained entirely apart from any religious doctrine and, based on the results of scientific progress, shall strive against ignorance and its effects, servitudes, fanaticism, and prejudices.'

Forced participation: Children are sometimes forced to participate in overtly religious activities against their will under the guise of 'cultural education.' In some areas of the country, members of a religious minority are often pressured by local authorities either to convert to the majority faith, or to participate actively in activities such as religious festivals linked to the majority faith, through financial support or physical involvement. When they refuse to participate, the local leaders often strip them of basic services including education, by barring their children from school.

NIGERIA

Constitutional commitments: Article 38.2 states, 'No person attending any place of education shall be required to receive religious instruction or to take part in or attend any religious ceremony or observance if such instruction, ceremony or observance relates to a religion other than his own, or religion not approved by his parent or guardian.'
Forced conversion: The education of Christian schoolgirls is frequently shortened by abduction, forcible conversion and underage marriage without parental consent.

Report of the Special Rapporteur on freedom of religion or belief

Heiner Bielefeldt

December 15, 2010

III. Freedom of religion or belief and school education

A. Introductory remarks

20. The school constitutes by far the most important formal institution for the implementation of the right to education as it has been enshrined in international human rights documents, such as the Universal Declaration of Human Rights (art. 26), the International Covenant on Economic, Social and Cultural Rights (art. 13), the Convention on the Rights of the Child (art. 28) and the Convention on the Rights of Persons with Disabilities (art. 24). The right to education is also anchored in basic documents of regional human rights protection systems.[42] There seems to be worldwide consensus that the right to education is of strategic importance for the effective enjoyment of human rights in general. Not least for this reason, article 28 of the Convention on the Rights of the Child demands that primary education be made compulsory and available free to all, whereas secondary education should be made available and accessible to every child.

21. Besides providing students with the necessary knowledge and information in different disciplines, school education can facilitate a daily exchange between people from different ethnic, economic, social, cultural and religious backgrounds. The possibility of having face-to-face interaction of students on a regular basis is not less important than the development of intellectual skills, because such regular interaction can promote a sense of communality that

---

[42] See for example the first Protocol to the Convention for the Protection of Human Rights and Fundamental Freedoms (art. 2); the African Charter on Human and Peoples' Rights (art. 17, para. 1); the African Charter on the Rights and Welfare of the Child (art. 11); and the Additional Protocol to the American Convention on Human Rights in the Area of Economic, Social and Cultural Rights (art. 13).

goes hand in hand with the appreciation of diversity, including diversity in questions of religion or belief. Experiencing the combination of communality and diversity is also a main purpose of interreligious and intercultural dialogue projects. Thus, the school provides unique possibilities for such a dialogue to take place on a daily basis, at a grass-roots level and during the formative years of a young person's development.

22. The Durban Declaration and Programme of Action (2001) promotes the purpose of an "inclusive society"[43] in which people from different ethnic or social backgrounds can participate on the basis of equality. From a different angle, this goal has recently been taken up in the Convention on the Rights of Persons with Disabilities, in which the principle of inclusion features as a key concept closely related to other principles, such as respect for personal autonomy and appreciation of diverse life situations. It is in such a complex understanding that the Convention on the Rights of Persons with Disabilities lays down the right to inclusive education.[44] Although this right explicitly relates to students with disabilities, it is at least worth discussing whether and how the principle of inclusive education could also be applied to other contexts, including diversity in religion or belief in the school life. Inclusive education pertaining to the issue of religious diversity would make use of the school as a place in which students of different religious or non-religious orientations get to know each other in a natural way.

23. Freedom of religion or belief and school education, however, require very careful handling. The main reason is that the school, besides providing a place of learning and social development, is also a place in which authority is exercised. It is during their school education that young people receive, or fail to receive, crucial diplomas on which their future life and work opportunities may depend to a large extent. Moreover, especially for young

---

[43] See A/CONF.189/12 and Corr. 1, chap. I, paras. 6 and 96.
[44] See art. 24, para. 1: "States Parties recognize the right of persons with disabilities to education. With a view to realizing this right without discrimination and on the basis of equal opportunity, States Parties shall ensure an inclusive education system at all levels and life long learning directed to: (a) The full development of human potential and sense of dignity and self-worth, and the strengthening of respect for human rights, fundamental freedoms and human diversity; (b) The development by persons with disabilities of their personality, talents and creativity, as well as their mental and physical abilities, to their fullest potential; (c) Enabling persons with disabilities to participate effectively in a free society."

children, the teacher may represent an authority with an enormous influence, coming close to, and sometimes even superseding, the authority of parents and other adult family members. Hence school life can put persons in situations of unilateral dependency or particular vulnerability. Students may feel exposed to pressure exercised by fellow students, teachers or the school administration. Parents may fear that the school could alienate their children from the family tradition. At any rate, more so than other societal institutions the school can trigger a host of contradictory emotions ranging from hopes and high expectations to scepticism and various fears.

24. For members of minorities, including religious or belief minorities, such ambivalent feelings are typically more pronounced. On the one hand, they may hope that school education can contribute to dispelling negative stereotypes and prejudices from which they may personally suffer. On the other hand, members of religious minorities – students as well as parents – may fear discrimination, mobbing or pressure in the school, perhaps even with the intention of urging them to assimilate into mainstream society by abandoning their faith. Such fears, be they justified or not, must always be taken seriously.

25. According to article 18, paragraph 4, of the International Covenant on Civil and Political Rights, States "undertake to have respect for the liberty of parents and, when applicable, legal guardians to ensure the religious and moral education of their children in conformity with their own convictions". This has been reaffirmed by article 5, paragraph 1, of the Declaration on the Elimination of All Forms of Intolerance and of Discrimination Based on Religion or Belief which states: "The parents or, as the case may be, the legal guardians of the child have the right to organize the life within the family in accordance with their religion or belief and bearing in mind the moral education in which they believe the child should be brought up". The Convention on the Rights of the Child connects respect for parents' rights with the principle of respecting also the evolving capacities of the child. Its article 14, paragraph 2, requires States to "respect the rights and duties of the parents and, when applicable, legal guardians, to provide direction to the child in the exercise of his or her right in a manner consistent with the evolving capacities of the child".

26. In view of this legal background, fundamental questions of school education related to issues of religion or belief – including the definition of educational principles, the compilation of the topics of the school curriculum, basic institutional and organizational arrangements, etc. – require a high degree of sensitivity. Whenever possible, these questions should not be decided without due consultation of all parties involved, including members of religious or belief communities, while taking care that international human rights standards are respected. In this context, the Special Rapporteur would like to refer to a study prepared under the guidance of his predecessor, which states:

> "Again, the main focus being human rights, what is relevant is that education on religious trends, tradition and movements as well as convictions, be provided in a fair and objective way, stimulating the curiosity of the audience, encouraging it to question their bias and stereotypes about cultures, religions and views other than the one which they see as being part of their own identity. Succeeding in portraying the others so that they can recognize themselves provides not only a valuable and inspiring educational experience; it also helps create understanding and mutual respect between different communities or world-views."[45]

B. Elimination of stereotypes and prejudices

27. Under international human rights law, States are obliged not merely to respect freedom of religion or belief but also to protect such freedom against undue interference from third parties. In addition, States should promote an atmosphere of tolerance and appreciation of religious diversity. The child should "be brought up in a spirit of understanding, tolerance, friendship among peoples, peace and universal brotherhood, respect for freedom of religion or belief of others, and in full consciousness that his energy and

---

[45] "The role of religious education in the pursuit of tolerance and non-discrimination", study prepared
under the guidance of Abdelfattah Amor, published in La libertad religiosa en la educación escolar, Alberto de la Hera and Rosa María Martínez de Codes, eds. (Madrid, Ministry of Justice, 2002), pp. 55-56.

talents should be devoted to the service of his fellow men."[46] Moreover, article 29, paragraph 1 (d), of the Convention on the Rights of the Child indicates that States parties agree that the education of the child shall be directed to "the preparation of the child for responsible life in a free society, in the spirit of understanding, peace, tolerance, equality of sexes, and friendship among all peoples, ethnic, national and religious groups and persons of indigenous origin".

28. Given the enormous significance and potential of school education, such efforts necessarily also involve the school in all its curricular, social and organizational aspects. In this context, the Special Rapporteur would like to recommend the study of the final document adopted at the International Consultative Conference on School Education in relation to Freedom of Religion or Belief, Tolerance and Non-discrimination. This Consultative Conference took place in Madrid from 23 to 25 November 2001. It was initiated, among others, by the second mandate holder on freedom of religion or belief, Mr. Amor, who in his 2002 report to the Commission on Human Rights reproduced the full text of the Madrid final document and presented important findings (E/CN.4/2002/73, annex, appendix). In 2007, the third mandate holder, Ms. Jahangir, contributed comments during the development of the Toledo Guiding Principles on Teaching about Religions and Beliefs in Public Schools. [47] The following observations and recommendations should be read together with the Madrid final document and the Toledo Guiding Principles, which need to be recalled and further implemented.

29. School education can and should contribute to the elimination of negative stereotypes which frequently poison the relationship between different communities and have particularly detrimental effects on minorities. This is also true with regard to religious or belief communities of different – theistic, non-theistic or atheistic – orientations. Indeed, in many countries members of religious or belief minorities experience a shocking degree of public resentment or even hatred which is often nourished by a

---

[46] Declaration on the Elimination of All Forms of Intolerance and of Discrimination Based on Religion or Belief, art. 5, para. 3.
[47] Prepared by the Advisory Council of Experts on Freedom of Religion or Belief of the OSCE Office for Democratic Institutions and Human Rights. Available from www.osce.org/publications/odihr/2007/11/28314_993_en.pdf.

paradoxical combination of fear and contempt. Even tiny groups are sometimes portrayed as "dangerous" because they are alleged to undermine the social cohesion of the nation, due to some mysteriously "infectious" effects attributed to them. Such allegations can escalate into fully fledged conspiracy theories fabricated by competing groups, the media or even State authorities. At the same time, members of religious or belief minorities are often exposed to public contempt based for instance on rumours that they allegedly lack any moral values. It is exactly this combination of demonizing conspiracy projections and public contempt that typically triggers violence either directed against members of minorities or occurring between different communities. Hence the eradication of stereotypes and prejudices that constitute the root causes of fear, resentment and hatred is the most important contribution to preventing violence and concomitant human rights abuses.

30. School education has a complex role to play in this endeavour. On the one hand, school education should provide fair information about different religions and beliefs. On the other hand, the school offers unique possibilities for face-to-face communication between members of different communities. Both avenues are equally important in the attempt to overcome prejudices and should, wherever possible, be pursued in conjunction.

31. Information about religions and beliefs provided in school education must be distinguished conceptually from religious instruction based on a particular faith (see also paras. 47-56 below). Whereas religious instruction aims at familiarizing students with their own religious tradition, i.e. with theological doctrines and norms of their particular faith, information about religions, by contrast, serves the purpose of broadening the students' general knowledge about different religions and beliefs, in particular those religions and beliefs they may encounter in the society in which they live. In this sense, providing other disciplines, such as history or social sciences.

32. If information about religions and beliefs is to have a positive effect on the elimination of stereotypes and prejudices, however, it must be given in a non-biased and neutral way. Moreover, such forms of information about religion, given in the context of the public school, which either intentionally or in effect would amount to State propaganda in questions of religion or belief, could run

counter to the right of parents and legal guardians "to ensure the religious and moral education of their children in conformity with their own convictions".[48] According to information received from various sources, however, in many countries textbooks used for providing information about religions in school education actually fall far behind the requirement of neutrality, sometimes even reinforcing existing stereotypes against minorities.[49] It is incumbent upon States to take appropriate measures to rectify this unfortunate situation.

33. Providing information about religions and beliefs in a neutral fashion is not an easy task. It may even be argued that, strictly speaking, no one can have a completely "neutral" standpoint that would be above the different horizons of meaning which competing religions or belief systems provide. Yet, without at least the aspiration to overcome biases – and to be neutral in this sense – information about religions could not unfold its beneficial effects on students' minds. One way of overcoming existing biases is to consult with members of the various communities to actively include their understanding of their own tradition and practice into school education. Such consultations are particularly useful in the process of designing textbooks and other teaching materials. They may also be part of regular trainings for teachers and other target groups on their task to provide fair and accurate information about religions and beliefs in the context of school education.

34. Information about religions and beliefs should always include the crucial insight that religions – as a social reality – are not monolithic; the same applies to non-religious belief systems. This message is particularly important, because it helps to deconstruct existing notions of a collective mentality that is stereotypically, and often negatively, ascribed to all followers of various religions or beliefs. In extreme cases, such ascription of a collective mentality may amount to "de-personalized" perceptions of human beings, possibly with devastating dehumanizing repercussions. Rather than being respected as irreplaceable individuals with their own personal faces as well as their own personal characters,

---

[48] International Covenant on Civil and Political Rights, art. 18, para. 4; International Convention on the Protection of the Rights of All Migrant Workers and Members of Their Families, art. 12, para. 4.
[49] See, for example, the Special Rapporteur's reports A/54/386, para. 49; A/55/280/Add.1, para. 112; A/55/280/Add.2, para. 105; A/58/296, paras. 51-52; A/CONF.189/PC.2/22, para. 86; A/HRC/4/21, para. 50; E/CN.4/1996/95/Add.1, para. 59; E/CN.4/2002/73/Add.1, para. 80.

opinions, life plans, etc., the followers of a particular religion or belief then are simply portrayed as a "faceless mass" whose members appear to be all more or less exchangeable. Needless to say, from such a point of view any serious communicative interaction is doomed to fail from the outset.

35. From the crucial insight that religions or beliefs – in social reality – are never monolithic it follows that they may also change over time. Interpretations of basic doctrines can adapt, and have in fact adapted, to different societal circumstances. Moreover, traditional practices can and have been challenged time and again by some of their adherents. When it comes to such practices that may have a negative bearing on the situation of women or girls, for example, some women have called for reforms by advocating and pursuing innovative interpretations of the respective sources, doctrines and norms.

36. Even though public schools, when informing about religions and beliefs, have no authority to decide on controversial theological issues, it is important that textbooks and other materials draw a sufficiently complex picture of the various religions or beliefs and their internal pluralism. Furthermore, existing alternative voices within religious traditions, including voices of women, should always have their appropriate and fair share of attention. [50] In general, respect for difference should not be confined to differences between various religions but should always include an awareness of internal differences as they may exist within various religious or belief communities. Only by overcoming monolithic perceptions can we become aware of the real diversity among human beings who are the rights holders in the context of human rights.

37. Not less significant than the dissemination of fair and accurate information on religions is the day-to-day interaction of students of different religious or belief backgrounds. This is the second avenue available for dispelling adverse stereotypes and prejudices. Teachers and the school administration bear a particular responsibility to ensure that students' interaction can take place in a spirit of open-mindedness, respect and fairness. Through voluntary meetings and school exchanges, teachers and students

---

[50] See also E/CN.4/2002/73, annex, appendix, para. 5.

may have the opportunity to meet with counterparts of different religions or beliefs, either at a domestic level or abroad. The goal should be to promote behaviour patterns which recognize difference, including differences in questions of religion or belief, as something "normal" in modern pluralistic societies.

38. Diversity in questions of religion and belief should be taken up in the school context in a spirit of respect and fairness. Against a typical misunderstanding, the Special Rapporteur would also like to emphasize that a respectful attitude does not require avoiding sensitive issues – for instance the situation of women – or even putting a taboo around such issues. It can be more respectful, as long as this is done in a spirit of fairness, to frankly speak about sensitive religious or belief issues, to raise questions, to open up a debate and possibly to agree to disagree. In this regard, the concepts of respect and fairness are closely intertwined.

39. With regard to the treatment of religious or belief diversity in school it is worth reiterating that from the perspective of freedom of religion or belief, the starting point must always be the self-understanding of human beings, who are the only rights holders in the context of human rights. Furthermore, freedom of religion or belief has a "positive" as well as a "negative" component, both of which equally derive from due respect for the dignity of all human beings as it is enshrined as an axiomatic principle in all basic human rights documents. The first component of freedom of religion or belief is freedom to positively express and manifest one's own religion or belief, while its (negative) flip side is freedom not to be exposed to any pressure, especially from the State or in State institutions, to perform religious or belief activities against one's own will. Given the ambivalence of the school as both a place of communication and social encounter as well as a place in which situations of particular vulnerability can occur, the positive and the negative components within freedom of religion or belief should always be considered in conjunction. Neglecting one of the two interrelated components would ultimately undermine the human right of freedom of religion or belief in its entirety.

40. Thus from a human rights perspective, it should be left primarily to pupils (or their parents or guardians, respectively) to express their religious or non-religious conviction in the school

context in such a way which they themselves see fit, provided this does not conflict with the rights of others, etc. Teachers should neither play down existing religious diversity nor place undue emphasis on religious differences. Just as it would be wrong to ignore religious differences that may come up in the context of school education, it would be equally problematic to organize communication among students primarily under the auspices of inter-religious exchange between predefined groupings. Instead, respect for difference based on freedom of religion or belief requires an attitude of giving students (or their parents or guardians) the possibility to decide for themselves whether, to which degree and on which occasions they wish to manifest, or not manifest, their religion or belief. Such an atmosphere of relaxed openness provides a fertile ground for developing a sense of diversity as being a normal feature of modern pluralistic societies. It is the obligation of the State to provide an appropriate framework conducive to this goal, always bearing in mind the best interests of the child as an overarching principle laid down in article 3, paragraph 1, of the Convention on the Rights of the Child.

C. Religious symbols in the school context

41. The role of religious symbols, including wearing religious garments in school and displaying religious symbols in classrooms, has been, and continues to be, a matter of controversy in a number of countries. Students or teachers observing religious dress codes, including Islamic headscarves and Sikh turbans, have in some countries been expelled from schools, denied access to higher education or suspended from their jobs. [51] In addition, the compulsory display of religious symbols, such as the crucifix, in the exercise of public authority in relation to specific situations subject to governmental supervision, particularly in classrooms, has yielded numerous court decisions at national and regional

---

[51] See, for example, the Special Rapporteur's reports A/HRC/10/8, para. 51; A/HRC/10/8/Add.1, paras. 196-198; E/CN.4/2006/5, paras. 43-50; and E/CN.4/2006/5/Add.4, paras. 47-72 and 98-104.

levels.[52] Furthermore, cases of imposition of religious dress codes are also of concern.[53]

42. To do justice to the complexity of the topic, one has to bear in mind a number of important distinctions. For example, given the specific role and status of the teacher, it obviously makes a difference whether religious symbols are worn by teachers or by students, and there may be good reasons for such a difference to be reflected in respective legislation or court decisions. The age of pupils could possibly be a factor for having different regulations in primary schools and in institutions of higher education. It would again be different if the presence of a particular religious symbol in classrooms of public schools was prescribed by the authorities without any exceptions and if the State itself was perceived to express a religious belief. Moreover, an important factor to be taken into consideration is the general dynamics of majority and minority religious groupings in society at large or within a particular school situation. Thus, different constellations may require different solutions which should be precisely assessed on a case-by-case basis.

43. Without prejudice to contextual specificities, however, there are nevertheless good reasons to start with a general presumption of the students' right to wear religious symbols in the school. According to article 18, paragraph 1, of the International Covenant on Civil and Political Rights, the right to freedom of thought, conscience and religion includes freedom to manifest one's religion or belief in worship, observance, practice and teaching. There can be little doubt that observing and practicing one's religion or belief may also include the wearing of distinctive clothing or head coverings in conformity with the individual's faith.[54] Moreover, freedom of religion or belief can be exercised either individually or in community with others and in public or

---

[52] See references in E/CN.4/2006/5, para. 36 (endnote 1). See also the judgment of 3 November 2009 of the Second Section of the European Court of Human Rights in the case of Lautsi v. Italy, application No. 30814/06, which has been referred to the Grand Chamber (the final judgment was not yet published at the time of writing).

[53] See, for example, the Special Rapporteur's reports A/51/542/Add.2, para. 51; E/CN.4/1998/6, para.60; E/CN.4/2006/5, para. 38; A/HRC/7/10/Add.1, paras. 125-126.

[54] See Human Rights Committee, general comment No. 22 (1993) on the right to freedom of thought, conscience and religion, para. 4; Human Rights Committee, communication No. 931/2000, Hudoyberganova v. Uzbekistan, Views adopted on 5 November 2004, para. 6.2; E/CN.4/2006/5, paras. 40-41.

private. The possibility to wear religious symbols in the public sphere, including in the school context, thus appears to be a natural result of the freedom to manifest one's religion or belief. In addition, religious symbols in the school may also reflect the religious diversity as it exists in society at large.

44. On the other hand, the freedom to manifest one's religion or belief is not without limitations. According to the criteria set out in article 18, paragraph 3, of the International Covenant on Civil and Political Rights, limitations must be "prescribed by law and [be] necessary to protect public safety, order, health, or morals or the fundamental rights and freedoms of others". The application of the criteria for possible limitations of the freedom to manifest one's religion or belief, at any rate, requires diligence, precision and precaution. Given the ambivalence of the school situation in which students, in particular members of minorities, might at times experience situations of personal or structural vulnerability, the general presumption in favour of the possibility to wear religious symbols must thus be connected with a number of caveats. For instance, in some constellations restrictions on the freedom to manifest religion or belief by wearing religious symbols may be justifiable in order to protect minority students from pressure exercised by schoolmates or their community. Moreover, a teacher wearing religious symbols in the class may have an undue impact on students, depending on the general behaviour of the teacher, the age of students and other factors. In addition, it may be difficult to reconcile the compulsory display of a religious symbol in all classrooms with the State's duty to uphold confessional neutrality in public education in order to include students of different religions or beliefs on the basis of equality and non-discrimination.

45. Obviously, finding appropriate solutions for conflicts over religious symbols in the school is not an easy task, and there exists no general blueprint simply applicable to all constellations or situations. At the same time, it is clear that the goal must always be to equally protect the positive and the negative aspects of freedom of religion or belief, i.e. the freedom positively to manifest one's belief, for instance by wearing religious clothing, and the freedom not to be exposed to any pressure, especially from the State or within State institutions, to perform religious activities. Furthermore, any restrictions on the freedom to observe religious dress codes deemed necessary in that context must be formulated

in a non-discriminatory manner. It would not be legitimate, for instance, if restrictions were linked to exception clauses in favour only of the dominant religion of the country concerned.

46. In this context, the Special Rapporteur would like to draw attention to the observations made by the previous mandate holder in her last report to the Commission on Human Rights (E/CN.4/2006/5, paras. 51-60). In that report, Ms. Jahangir developed a number of general criteria on the assessment of conflicts over religious symbols, especially in a school situation. Inter alia, she draws a distinction between regulations addressed to all religious symbols in a neutral manner and regulations which – de jure or de facto – privilege the symbolic presence of some religions, at the expense of other religions or beliefs, a practice which may be in breach of the principle of non-discrimination. She also indicated that accommodating different situations according to the perceived vulnerability of the persons involved might in certain situations be considered legitimate, e.g. in order to protect underage schoolchildren and the parents' liberty to ensure the religious and moral education of their children in conformity with their own convictions. Furthermore, women's rights, and in particular the principle of equality between men and women and the individual's freedom to wear or not to wear religious symbols, should be duly taken into account.[55]

D. Religious instruction in schools

47. As elaborated above (see paras. 27-40), it is crucial to distinguish conceptually between information about religions or beliefs on the one hand and religious instruction on the other. On a practical level there are a number of overlaps which pose problems in the actual application of that distinction.[56] In addition, different pedagogical approaches may add nuances, for example if teaching methods encourage pupils to "learn about religions"[57] or to "learn

---

[55] See A/HRC/15/53, para. 60; A/65/207, para. 34.

[56] One example would be a school subject that "combines education on religious knowledge with practising a particular religious belief, e.g. learning by heart of prayers, singing religious hymns or attendance at religious services". See Human Rights Committee, communication No. 1155/2003, Leirvåg v. Norway, Views adopted on 3 November 2004, para. 14.6.

[57] "'Learning about religion' includes enquiry into, and investigation of, the nature of religions, their beliefs, teachings and ways of life, sources, practices and forms of expression. It covers students' knowledge and understanding of individual religions and how they relate to each other as well as

from religion".[58] At any rate, on a normative level conceptual clarity remains of strategic importance to pursue a human rights approach and to do justice to the ambivalence of the school being a place of learning, social development and communicative interaction but also a place in which situations of particular vulnerability can occur.

48. Religious instruction, i.e. instruction in a particular religion or belief based on its tenets, can take place in different constellations. The following paragraphs will primarily focus on religious instruction given in the public-school system, i.e. the system of public education provided by the State. While the role of private schools, including denominational schools, will also be mentioned, the Special Rapporteur will leave aside in this chapter those forms of religious instruction that are organized in religious institutions – such as churches, mosques, pagodas, synagogues or temples – and attended by students outside of school.

49. In many countries religious instruction in the above defined sense constitutes an integral part of public school teaching and maybe even of the mandatory school curriculum. Such practice may reflect the interests and demands of large parts of the population. Many parents may wish that their children be familiarized with the basic doctrines and rules of their own religion or belief and that the school take an active role in that endeavour. In the understanding of many parents, the development of knowledge and social skills of their children through school education would be incomplete unless it includes a sense of religious awareness and familiarity with their own religion or belief. Hence the provision of religious instruction in the public-school system may be based on the explicit or implicit wishes of considerable currents within the country's population.

50. However, given the ambivalence of the school situation – including possible situations of particular vulnerability for some

---

the study of the nature and characteristics of religion. It includes the skills of interpretation, analysis and
explanation. Pupils learn to communicate their knowledge and understanding using specialist vocabulary." (Toledo Guiding Principles on Teaching about Religions and Beliefs in Public Schools, pp. 45-46, footnote 52).
[58] "'Learning from religion' is concerned with developing students' reflection on and response to their
own and others' experiences in the light of their learning about religion. It develops pupils' skills of application, interpretation and evaluation of what they learn about religion." (Ibid.).

persons or groups – religious instruction in the public-school system must always go hand in hand with specific safeguards on behalf of members of religious or belief minorities. The Human Rights Committee has also emphasized that instruction in a religious context should "respect the convictions of parents and guardians who do not believe in any religion". [59] A minimum requirement would be that members of minorities have the possibility of "opting out" of a religious instruction that goes against their own convictions. Such exemptions should also be available for persons adhering to the very same faith on which instruction is given, whenever they feel that their personal convictions – including maybe dissenting convictions – are not respected. Moreover, the possibility of opting out should not be linked to onerous bureaucratic procedures and must never carry with it de jure or de facto penalties. Finally, wherever possible, students not participating in religious instruction due to their different faith should have access to alternative courses provided by the school.

51. The decision whether or not to opt out of religious instruction must be left to students or their parents or guardians who are the decisive rights holders in that respect. With regard to article 18, paragraph 4, of the International Covenant on Civil and Political Rights, the Human Rights Committee has noted that "public education that includes instruction in a particular religion or belief is inconsistent with article 18.4 unless provision is made for non-discriminatory exemptions or alternatives that would accommodate the wishes of parents and guardians".[60] Moreover, attention must be given to the rights and duties of the parents and, when applicable, legal guardians, to provide direction to the child in the exercise of his or her right to freedom of thought, conscience and religion in a manner consistent with the evolving capacities of the child.[61] The concept of "evolving capacities" is crucial since it acknowledges that the child at some point "comes of age" and should be able to make personal choices in matters of religion or belief. Due weight should be given to the views of the child in

---

[59] See Human Rights Committee, communications No. 40/1978, Hartikainen v. Finland, Views adopted on 9 April 1981, para. 10.4, and Leirvåg v. Norway, para. 14.2.
[60] Human Rights Committee, general comment No. 22, para. 6. See also Committee on Economic, Social and Cultural Rights, general comment No. 13 (1999) on the right to education, para. 28.
[61] Art. 14, para. 2, of the Convention on the Rights of the Child.

accordance with his or her age and maturity, which need to be assessed on a case-by-case basis.[62]

52. Unfortunately, however, reports from various countries indicate that the above-mentioned principles – which constitute an integral part of freedom of religion or belief – are not always respected. In some countries students belonging to minorities allegedly experience formal or informal pressure to attend religious instruction given on the sole basis of the country's dominant religious tradition. The same can happen to adherents of alternative interpretation of, or dissenting views on, the dominant religion on which school instruction is based. Even worse, incidents have been reported that in some school's members of minorities or persons with dissenting views have to express criticism of their own conviction as a precondition to take their school examinations. Exemptions for students adhering to religions or beliefs other than those instructed in school, if available at all, are sometimes linked to onerous application procedures or stigmatizing practices, with the result that students and parents often refrain from making use of them.

53. In this context, it is worth emphasizing that practices which forcibly expose students to religious instruction against their own will violate article 18, paragraph 2, of the International Covenant on Civil and Political Rights which states that "no one shall be subject to coercion which would impair his freedom to have or adopt a religion or belief of his choice". This forum internum component of freedom of religion or belief enjoys particularly strong protection under international human rights law as no derogation from article 18 of the Covenant may be made, not even in a time of public emergency which threatens the life of the nation.[63] In addition, coercive practices may also violate the rights of parents "to ensure the religious and moral education of their children in conformity with their own convictions" (art. 18, para. 4, of the Covenant).

54. The situation of religious instruction in private schools warrants a distinct assessment. The reason is that private schools,

---

[62] See Committee on the Rights of the Child, general comment No. 12 (2009) on the right of the child to be heard, para. 29. With regard to the concept of "evolving capacities" in the context of the child's
right to freedom of religion or belief see A/64/159, paras. 26-28.
[63] International Covenant on Civil and Political Rights, art. 4; see also Human Rights Committee, general comment No. 22, para. 1.

depending on their particular rationale and curriculum, might accommodate the more specific educational interests or needs of parents and children, including in questions of religion or belief. Indeed, many private schools have a specific denominational profile which can make them particularly attractive to adherents of the respective denomination, but frequently also for parents and children of other religious or belief orientation. In this sense, private schools constitute a part of the institutionalized diversity within a modern pluralistic society. States are not obliged under international human rights law to fund schools which are established on a religious basis, however, if the State chooses to provide public funding to religious schools, it should make this funding available without any discrimination.[64]

55. Furthermore, the existence of private denominational schools – or the possibility of their establishment – cannot serve as an excuse for the State not to pay sufficient attention to religious and belief diversity in public school education. Even though private denominational schools may be one way for parents to ensure a religious and moral education of their children in conformity with their own convictions, the public-school system must also respect religious and belief diversity. In this context, the inaugural session of the Forum on Minority Issues, held in December 2008, recommended that "where separate educational institutions are established for minorities for linguistic, religious or cultural reasons, no barriers should be erected to prevent members of minority groups from studying at general educational institutions, should they or their families so wish".[65]

IV. Conclusions and recommendations

57. Freedom of religion or belief and school education is a multifaceted issue that entails significant opportunities and far-reaching challenges. The school is the most important formal institution for the realization of the right to education. It provides a place of learning, social development and social encounter. At the same time, the school is also a place in which authority is exercised and some persons, including members of religious or

---

[64] Human Rights Committee, communication No. 694/1996, Waldman v. Canada, Views adopted on 3 November 1999, para. 10.6.
[65] See the report of the independent expert on minority issues (A/HRC/10/11/Add.1), para. 27.

belief minorities, may find themselves in situations of vulnerability. Given this ambivalence of the school situation, safeguards to protect the individual's right to freedom of religion or belief are necessary. Special attention must be given to the forum internum component of freedom of religion or belief which enjoys the status of an absolute guarantee under international human rights law. With regard to the freedom to manifest one's religion or belief, both the positive and the negative aspects of that freedom must be equally ensured, i.e. the freedom to express one's conviction as well the freedom not to be exposed to any pressure, especially from State authorities or in the State institution, to practice religious or belief activities against one's will.

58. Schools may offer unique possibilities for constructive dialogue among all parts of society and human rights education in particular can contribute to the elimination of negative stereotypes that often adversely affect members of religious minorities. However, freedom of religion or belief and school education has also sparked controversy in many societies, particularly with regard to contentious issues such as religious symbols in the school context and religious instruction (see paras. 20-56 above).

59. With regard to religious symbols, especially in public schools, the Special Rapporteur would like to reiterate that each case has to be decided according to its own circumstances. If restrictions on the wearing of religious symbols are deemed necessary, these restrictions should not be applied in a discriminatory manner and they must be directly related and proportionate to the specific need on which the restrictions are predicated. At the same time, for example, the rights of the child and their parents or legal guardians may justify limiting the freedom of teachers who wish to manifest their religion or belief by wearing a religious symbol. In all actions concerning children, the "best interests" of the child shall be a primary consideration. With regard to the State-prescribed mandatory display of religious symbols in classrooms, States should uphold confessional neutrality in public education in order to include students of different religions or beliefs on the basis of equality and nondiscrimination.

60. In general, educational policies should aim to strengthen the promotion and protection of human rights, eradicating prejudices and conceptions incompatible with freedom of religion or belief and ensuring respect for and acceptance of pluralism and diversity

in the field of religion or belief as well as the right not to receive religious instruction inconsistent with one's conviction. Efforts should be made to establish advisory bodies at different levels that take an inclusive approach to involving different stakeholders in the preparation and implementation of school curricula related to issues of religion or belief and in the training of teachers.

61. The Special Rapporteur would like to refer to his predecessors' reports on these issues and to their involvement in the elaboration of the final document of the International Consultative Conference on School Education in relation to Freedom of Religion or Belief, Tolerance and Non-discrimination and the Toledo Guiding Principles on Teaching about Religions and Beliefs in Public Schools. In this context, the Special Rapporteur reiterates that States, at the appropriate level of Government and in accordance with their educational systems, should favourably consider:

(a) Providing teachers and students with voluntary opportunities for meetings and exchanges with their counterparts of different religions or beliefs;

(b) Encouraging exchanges of teachers and students and facilitating educational study abroad;

(c) Strengthening a non-discriminatory perspective in education and of knowledge in relation to freedom of religion or belief at the appropriate levels; A/HRC/16/53 19

(d) Ensuring equal rights to women and men in the field of education and freedom of religion or belief, and in particular reinforcing the protection of the right of girls to education, especially for those coming from vulnerable groups;

(e) Taking appropriate measures against all forms of intolerance and discrimination based on religion or belief which manifest themselves in school curricula, textbooks and teaching methods;

(f) Evaluating existing curricula being used in public schools that touch upon teaching about religions and beliefs with a view to determining whether they promote respect for freedom of religion or belief and whether they are impartial, balanced, inclusive, age appropriate, free of bias and meet professional standards;

(g) Assessing the process that leads to the development of curricula on teaching about religions and beliefs to make sure that this process is sensitive to the needs of various religious and belief communities and that all relevant stakeholders have an opportunity to have their voices heard;

(h) Examining to what extent existing teacher-training institutions are capable of providing the necessary professional training for teaching about religions and beliefs in a way that promotes respect for human rights and, in particular, for freedom of religion or belief;

(i) Determining the extent to which teacher-training institutions provide sufficient knowledge of human rights issues, an understanding of the diversity of religious and non-religious views in society, a firm grasp of various teaching methodologies (with particular attention to those founded on an intercultural approach) and significant insight into ways that one can teach about religions and beliefs in a respectful, impartial and professional way.

62. Finally, the Special Rapporteur would like to reiterate that the role of parents, families and legal guardians is an essential factor in the education of children in the field of religion or belief. Consequently, special attention should be paid to encouraging positive attitudes and, in view of the best interest of the child, to supporting parents to exercise their rights and fully play their role in education in the field of tolerance and non-discrimination, taking into account the relevant provisions of the Universal Declaration of Human Rights, the International Covenant on Civil and Political Rights, the International Covenant on Economic, Social and Cultural Rights, the Declaration on the Elimination of All Forms of Intolerance and Discrimination Based on Religion or Belief and the Convention on the Rights of the Child.

Editor's Note: The above report in its entirety can be found at: *Report of the Special Rapporteur on freedom of religion or belief, Heiner Bielefeldt,* United Nations General Assembly (Dec. 15, 2010), www.undocs.org/A/HRC/16/53.
Or in the book Heiner Bielefeldt, *Freedom of Religion or Belief: Thematic Reports of the UN Special Rapporteur 2010-2016* 27 (2nd ed. 2017).

目录

本刊编委会：

- 傅希秋, 总编辑
- 利百加•艾萨克斯, 发行经理
- 凯瑟琳•卡普斯, 客座英文编辑, Waterbrooks 研究所
- 凯文•卡普斯, 客座助理英文编辑, Waterbrooks 研究所
- 孟元新, 客座中文编辑
- 郑乐国, 中文编辑
- 万英豪, 出版主任

本刊顾问委员会：

- 亚瑟•沃尔德伦，宾夕法尼亚大学历史系国际关系教授
- 大卫•艾克曼，帕特里克亨利学院教授，前时代杂志驻北京记者
- 大卫•泰勒，大卫•泰勒律师事务所，对华援助协会法律顾问
- 大卫•克雷默，前自由之家执行主任，前美国国务院民主、人权与劳工助理国务卿
- 黛博拉•菲克斯，世界福音联盟驻联合国代表
- 唐•阿格，护航希望无任所大使，美国国际宗教自由委员会前任专员和副主席。
- 杨宪宏博士，台湾关怀中国人权联盟主席
- 爱德华•麦克米兰•史考特，前欧洲议会人权与民主事务副主席，人权与民主网络创始人；
- 费斯•麦克唐纳尔，宗教与民主研究所宗教自由项目总监
- 弗兰克•沃尔夫，威伯福斯研究所高级研究员，前国会汤姆兰托斯人权委员会创始人及主席
- 卡特里娜•兰托斯•斯韦特，兰托斯人权与公义基金会主席兼首席执行官
- 斯格特•弗利普斯，美国国会-行政中国事物委员会传媒与政策主任;前美国国际宗教自由委员会政策副主任
- 威廉•英博登，德克萨斯大学克莱门特历史、战略和政策中心执行主任，前白宫国家安全委员会战略规划高级主任。

《中国法律与宗教观察》系对华援助协会刊物。

本刊版权归对华援助协会所有，未经许可，严禁以各种形式翻印。

本期国际书号：
ISBN-13: 978-1721828340 ISBN-10: 1721828346

《中国法律与宗教观察》内含中国颁布、发行的涉及法律、政治、政府的政策文件、学术作品及其完整的英文译本。

本刊地址：1300 Pennsylvania Ave. NW, Suite 700
　　　　　 Washington, DC 20004

本刊电话: 202-213-0506

访问对华援助协会网站： **www.chinaaid.net**

编者的话

Bob Fu (傅希秋)

正如全世界所看到的那样，今年 2 月，中国通过了新"宗教事务条例"。新规定对中国人民增加了进一步的限制，包括对中国儿童教育方面的限制。一些国际和区域法律文书都承认受教育的权利，这些文书包括条约（公约、契约、章程）和软性法律文件，后者指一般性意见、建议，声明和行动框架等。

此外，2018 年 3 月 11 日，中国在北京召开全国人民代表大会通过了中华人民共和国宪法修正案，其中一项修正出现在序言中，提出 "建立人类命运共同体"的口号。在最新的人权理事会提议中，中国继续攻击联合国人权框架[https://chinachange.org/2018/04/09/with-its-latest-human-rights-council]，对此，美国表示："很明显，中国正试图通过这项提议削弱联合国人权体系及其得以构建的规范。关于"互利合作"的"花言巧语"旨在使专制国家受益，而牺牲那些我们都有义务尊重其人权和基本自由的人。因此，美国要求投票，并将投票反对该提议。我们鼓励其他国家不要支持这项提议。"。看到中国提议坚持应该尊重政府，美国表示了明确的异议："一个致力于尊重和保护个人人权和基本自由的论坛与呼吁侵犯本国公民权利的政府受到尊重的言论互不相容。"。美国将该提议描述为中国"试图通过要求尊重来使自己免于人权记录批评"。美国进一步确认："任何政府获得尊重的唯一途径是该政府尊重人权和基本自由。"

鉴于这种情况，"中国法律与宗教观察 2018 年秋冬刊"将分析中国儿童教育的现状。需要认识到教育是一项人权，这意味着：1）所有人都受到法律保障，不受任何歧视；2）国家有义务保护，尊重并实现受教育的权利；3）国家要对侵犯或剥夺受教育权的现象负责。

本期内容包含以下文章和报告：

1. 在"儿童的宗教教育权与宗教教育"一文中，国际法与宗教教授、国际法专家 Jeroen Temperman 对国际社会儿童的宗教教育权和宗教教育相关阐述有深刻的理解，这种理解正好与当今中国存在的情况形成了鲜明的对比。

2. 在"教育要有宗教自由？"一文中，查尔斯·格兰挑战了一种假设，即基于信仰的教育往往使学生不适合成为憧憬自由民主的公民。

3. 王怡的文章"教会学校合法吗？"表明：在当代中国经营教会学校和经营家庭教会都是非法的。他的结论是：中国人民正面临着基督教信仰与中国宪法的冲突。

4. 在"覆巢之下、完卵何存？中国儿童宗教教育状况观察"一文中，孟元新向读者指出，根据联合国有关人权公约，宗教教育自由是宗教自由的一个组成部分。该文详细介绍了中国共产党迫使教育与宗教分离的历史，以及中国儿童的宗教教育如何逐渐从公立学校体系中消亡。

5. 日本作家佐藤千岁的文章"基督教信仰和残障儿童教育 — 面对弱势群体主内草根机构的挑战和可能性"，调研了未在政府登记的基督教的"家庭教会"和天主教的"地下教会"常年从事孤残儿童抚养和教育的情况，从福利教育政策及宗教政策的角度分析了他们所面临的困难处境，辨析了在残障儿童抚养教育中基督徒的角色及其社会意义。该文指出，中国共产党政权的宗教管理制度已成为儿童福利教育事业中侵害儿童基本人权的原因。

6. "八福公学事件原始材料"，披露了北京爱加倍教会租赁北京市昌平区北七家镇王府牧场燕园 2 号办学遭到警察逼迫和房东骚扰的情况。

7. 凯瑟琳·卡普斯（Katherine A. Capps）撰写的"中国在校儿童的宗教自由岌岌可危"一文分析了中国如何明显违反了多项国际公约以及这些侵权行为如何最终影响到中国儿童的宗教教育权利。该文进一步探讨了中国政府应该采取哪些措施来保障儿童宗教教育权利，以及如果中国政府不遵守有关国际公约，国际社会应该如何做出反应。

8. "厦门市思明区教育局对"麦种学堂"告知书"显示，厦门市思明区教育局对"麦种学堂"进行了调查并告知他们要纠正所谓违法行为，包括向儿童提供教育。

9. "河南省天主教爱国会，河南省天主教教务委员会通知"明确表示禁止儿童进入礼拜场所。

10. 在"新疆当局监禁送儿子到未经批准的宗教学校的维吾尔族伊玛目"报道中披露了中国共产党意图控制中国人民的心灵，但宗教自由是一项普遍人权，即使它不是你所信仰的宗教。

11. 在"维吾尔族学生、父母在斋月期间被迫放弃禁食"报道中详细介绍了中共对家庭宗教自由权的侵犯。

12. "新疆维吾尔自治区教委关于在学校禁止宗教活动的规定"，在 2018 年新宗教事务条例出台之前即有，该文件显示了关于中国宗教自由的官方立场，甚至规定了学校要保证一定小时的无神论教育时间。

13. "中共中央办公厅、国务院办公厅转发教育部《关于正确处理少数民族地区宗教干扰学校教育问题的意见》"，这是一份中国共产党（CCP）中央的文件，清楚地表明了对儿童宗教教育权强硬和持续的限制政策。

14. "学校里基于宗教或信仰的歧视" 节选自"全球基督教团结阵线"所做的研究，报告了世界上许多国家在教育环境中侵犯宗教或信仰自由的情况。

15. "宗教或信仰自由及学校教育——宗教或信仰自由问题 2010 年 12 月份报告（节录）"，来自特别报告员海纳比勒费尔特关于宗教或信仰自由问题特别报告的第三部分。比勒费尔特先生的报告清楚地表明 "学校"是迄今为止实施受教育权的最重要的正式机构，认同教师/学生关系所应该发挥的作用，并强调家庭和父母的角色是宗教或信仰领域儿童教育的重要因素。

总而言之，"中国法律与宗教观察 2018 年秋冬刊"针对此特定主题，精心挑选的系列文章和报告表明中国共产党政府明显无视与中国儿童宗教教育有关的国际人权。

一如既往，对华援助协会将继续致力于推动中国的宗教自由，人权和法治。

儿童的宗教教育权与宗教教育

Jeroen Temperman

伊拉斯姆斯大学鹿特丹伊拉斯姆斯学院国际法与宗教教授

1. 引言

无论是在全球还是地区层面，都应充分保障儿童的教育和宗教权利。对此，"联合国儿童权利公约"（CRC）在全球范围内明确要求"*缔约国应尊重儿童享有思想，良心和宗教自由的权利*"[1]，同时针对教育的权利，该公约还特别做出以下规定：

1. 缔约国确认儿童有受教育的权利，为在机会均等的基础上逐步实现此项权利，缔约国尤应：

（A）实现全面的免费义务小学教育；

（B）鼓励发展不同形式的中学教育，包括普通和职业教育，使所有儿童均能享有和接受这种教育，并采取适当措施，诸如实行免费教育和对有需要的人提供津贴；

（C）根据能力以一切适当方式使所有人均有受高等教育的机会；

（D）使所有儿童均能得到教育和职业方面的资料和指导；

（E）采取措施鼓励学生按时出勤和降低辍学率。

2. 缔约国应采取一切适当措施，确保学校执行纪律的方式符合儿童的人格尊严及本公约的规定。

3. 缔约国应促进和鼓励有关教育事项方面的国际合作，特别着眼于在全世界消灭愚昧与文盲，并能够便利地获得科技知识和现代教学方法。在这方面，应特别考虑到发展中国家的

---

[1] 儿童权利公约（CRC）第 14 条第（1）段；联合国大会决议 44/25 附件；第 44 届联合国大会正式纪录补编（第 49 号）第 167 页；联合国文件编号：A／44/49（1989），1990 年 9 月 2 日生效。

需要。 2

因此，综合以上，很容易得出结论：儿童的宗教自由权和儿童受教育权使"儿童的宗教教育权"得以自动产生。 这一结论将产生一个认为这种权利是一项可规范的权利的观念；其次，根据国际法，正在形成一种替代/补充性的概念，即"关于宗教的教育"，这一概念可能成为法定权利也可能不成为法定权利。 后者（能否成为法定权利）取决于国际法律基准和各国的实践进程。

2．宗教教育权：儿童还是父母的权利？

国际法肯定了"宗教教育权"的存在，但对这种权利有许多方面的规范和独特的要求。首先，国际法认可父母或法定监护人作为中间人（如果不是临时权利人）的重要作用。 也就是说，有关宗教自由和受教育权利的相关国际条款规定，父母对于他们子女所涉及的宗教和教育的所有事项有重要的发言权。

相应的，联合国"公民权利和政治权利国际公约"（"ICCPR"）的宗教自由条款规定，"*本公约缔约各国承担，尊重父母和法定监护人（如适用时）保证他们的孩子能按照他们自己的信仰接受宗教和道德教育的自由。*" 3。 "欧洲人权公约"（ECHR）虽然只在教育权条款中涉及该内容，但同样规定"*在行使其有关教育和教学的任何职能时，国家应尊重父母有权确保这种教育和教学符合自己的宗教和哲学信念*" 4。 儿童

---

2 联合国儿童权利公约第 28 条。

3 "公民权利和政治权利国际公约"（ ICCPR）第 18 条第 4 段，联合国大会决议 2200A (XXI)，第 21 届联合国大会正式纪录补编（第 16 号）52 页，联合国文件编号：A/6316(1966)，《联合国条约汇编》第 999 卷，页 171，1976 年 3 月 23 日生效。

4 "欧洲人权公约"（ ECHR）议定书第 2 条（第二句）；"保护人权和基本自由公约"，《联合国条约汇编》第 213 卷，页 222，1953 年 9 月 3 日生效；"保护人权和基本自由公约议定书"，《联合国条约汇编》第 213 卷，页 262，1954 年 5 月 18 日生效。

权利委员会一方面规定了上文引用的儿童自主的宗教自由权利，另一方面强调了父母所有的相应权利："*缔约国应尊重父母和法定监护人（如适用时）的权利和义务，指导儿童以符合自己不断发展的能力的方式行使[宗教或信仰自由]的权利*"[5]。

　　因此，这一切都要求我们回答一个问题：宗教教育权利到底是儿童还是父母的权利？ 国际法的回答模棱两可：两者都有，儿童自主享有宗教自由和教育的权利，以及父母监督和保证儿童享有上述权利的权利，两者同时存在。 严格地讲，我们可以说前者（儿童自主享有宗教教育权利）占主导地位，因为儿童权利公约出现在后（相比公民权利和政治权利国际公约而言），还特别针对儿童权利（相比公民权利和政治权利国际公约，以更专业化的方式看待儿童的权利）。 也就是说，儿童权利公约本身在儿童享有宗教权利方面，为父母保留了重要的作用。[6]

　　因此，解决这一难题的关键在于国际法所规定的"儿童的最大利益"[7]和"儿童不断发展的能力"等调解性概念。后者在"儿童权利公约"第 5 条中被强调："*缔约国应尊重父母或当地习俗认定的大家庭或社会成员、法定监护人或其他对儿童负有法律责任的人（如适用时）的责任、权利和义务，以符合儿童不同阶段接受能力的方式适当指导和指引儿童行使本公约所确认的权利。*"[8]。重要的是，它分别重申了宗教自由条款："*缔约国应尊重父母和法定监护人（如适用时）的权利和义务，以符合儿童不同阶段接受能力的方式适当指导和指引儿童行使本公约所确认的权利。*"[9]。因此，对儿童行使宗教自由，父母有重要的发言权，但父母指导子女的权利会随着儿童认知能力的

---

[5]儿童权利公约（CRC）第 14 条第（2）段。

[6]儿童权利公约（CRC）第 14 条第（2）段。

[7]儿童权利公约（CRC）第 3 条（主要原则），并在整个"CRC"中重复出现。

[8]儿童权利公约（CRC）第 5 条。

[9]儿童权利公约（CRC）第 14 条第（2）段，强调补充。

发展而消减。换句话说，随着儿童成长并逐渐能够对此表述自己某种选择的意见或看法，父母的权利就应减少。

尽管目前还没有办法确定这一时刻（父母权利减少）的绝对年龄（毕竟每个孩子都不一样），但监督国家遵守"儿童权利公约"的儿童权利委员会要求缔约国把此项内容作为国别报告的一部分[10]。一些国家颁布立法，确保儿童完全自主行使宗教和教育权利的年龄在达到一般法定年龄之前几年开始[11]，从而在法律上强化"不断发展的儿童能力"这一法律概念的重要性。

总之，不言而喻，根据国际法，宗教教育的权利在很大程度上取决于父母，包括他们如何选择、以及积极性和主动性。值得注意的是，各国没有义务组织（包括资助，见下一节）宗教教育。组织和运作选择性教育的负担超出了国家教育体系的范围，依赖于个人而不是国家。首先，最重要的是，国家教育的责任范围仅限于国家组织的教育。其次，我们也可以从宗教自治的角度找出一个理由：强烈的国家干预或控制私立教育会自然而然地使在国家组织的教育体系之外组织某种事情的目的难以达成。

因此，在建立希望满足宗教教育者需求的私立机构时，国际法明确规定父母也可以自己组织私立机构满足这方面的需求[12]。例如，联合国经济、社会和文化权利国际公约（ICESCR）规定，"*本公约缔约各国承担，尊重父母和法定监*

---

[10]关于缔约国提交的定期报告的格式和内容的一般准则，1996年10月11日通过，联合国大会正式纪录，儿童权利委员会第13次会议，联合国文件编号：CRC/C/58 (1996),第24段。

[11]例如 德国1985年关于儿童宗教教育的联邦法律（BGBl 1985/155），规定年龄14岁。

[12]这也适用于欧洲区域性人权公约。它早在欧洲人权法院具有里程碑意义的关于比利时语言学案的判例中就已经确立，即个人不能从"欧洲人权公约"（ECHR）议定书第2条中得出公共机构具有举办特定类型的教育机构的权利。关于比利时教育语言使用法律某些方面的案例，申请号：1474/62; 1677/62; 1691/62; 1769/63; 1994/63; 2126/64,1968年7月23日判决书B节9段。

护人（如适用时）的下列自由：为他们的孩子选择非公立的但系符合于国家所可能规定或批准的最低教育标准的学校，并保证他们的孩子能按照他们自己的信仰接受宗教和道德教育。" [13]。儿童权利委员会同样规定，*"本条或第 28 条不能解释为干涉个人和机构设立、指导教育机构的自由，但始终遵守在本条第 1 款中规定所阐明的原则，并且要求这些机构的教育应符合国家规定的可能的最低标准。"* [14]。

很显然，父母的确有权通过建立学校来为他们的孩子开展宗教教育。 虽然这样的父母自由权利预设了相当程度的机构自治，但所有相关条款确实规定了各国执行最低标准的可能性。 这些最低标准涉及课程和教学的内容、质量。

国际人权法没有规定父母在公立学校领域为其子女开展宗教教育的具体权利。 如果国家决定不允许在公立学校进行宗教教育，这并不一定意味着违反父母权利，因为父母替代学校的权利恰恰是保证父母宗教需求的补充权利。

3．资助

宗教教育的权利也有其它方面的限制。 值得注意的是，与公立教育不同的是[15]，国家没有义务资助私立学校，包括私立宗教学校。 例如，联合国人权事务委员会指出，"公民权利和政治权利国际公约"并没有规定缔约国要资助建立在宗教基础上的学校[16]。

---

[13] "经济，社会，文化权利国际公约"（ICESCR）第 13 条，联合国大会决议 2200A (XXI)，第 21 届联合国大会正式纪录补编（第 16 号）49 页，联合国文件编号：A/6316(1966)，《联合国条约汇编》第 993 卷，页 3，1976 年 1 月 3 日生效.

[14] 儿童权利公约（CRC）第 29 条（2）款， 另见"反对教育歧视公约"第 5 条第 1 款（b），1960 年 12 月 14 日，教科文组织第 11 届会议，《联合国条约汇编》第 429 卷，页 93。

[15] 初等教育必须是"义务性的，并免费提供给所有人"，儿童权利公约（CRC）第 28 条（1）款（a）节。

[16] Waldman 诉加拿大，第 694/1996 号来文，人权事务委员会的意见，1999 年 11 月 5 日通过，段：10.6。

也就是说，如果国家决定资助宗教教育，必须不得基于宗教或信仰的歧视。 例如，在瓦尔德曼诉加拿大案中，关于加拿大罗马天主教学校在财政上享有特权地位的案件，人权委员会认为，"*如果一个缔约国选择向宗教学校提供公共资金，它应该没有歧视。 这意味着为一个宗教团体的学校提供资金，而不为另一个宗教团体的学校提供资金，必须基于合理和客观的标准*"[17]。 在这个特殊案例中，委员会认为根据"公民权利和政治权利国际公约"，资助罗马天主教学校，实际上对基于其它信仰的学校构成了歧视。

在其它地方已经表明，实际上监督机构往往难以处理资金领域的平等问题，因为在财政上各国都有一些非常复杂和隐蔽、行之有效的诸多政策做法，使得该国主导或传统宗教拥有特权[18]。

4．宗教教育：新兴的儿童权利？

尽管积极的国际人权法并不严格规定儿童接受有关宗教教育的权利，但这种权利可能间接以国际法所刊载的一些法律概念为依据。 值得注意的是，儿童权利委员会要求学校体系旨在 "*培养儿童本着各国人民、族裔、民族和宗教群体以及原为土著居民的人之间谅解、和平、宽容、男女平等和友好的精神，在自由社会里过有责任感的生活*"[19]。 可以说，一个国家对不同宗教的认知有助于实现这一目标。

自然而然，"宗教教学"不同于传统的基于一种特定的宗教的教学。国际社会存在一些有关"宗教教学"的最佳做法指引， 包括欧安组织托莱多公立学校宗教和信仰教学指导原则[20]

---

[17]同上。

[18]Jeroen Temperman， "欧洲人权公约涉及家长关于宗派教育的权利"，宗教与人权：国际期刊（2017 年 11：2-3），第 142-152 页。

[19]儿童权利公约（CRC）第 29 条（d）款。

[20]欧安组织（OSCE），托莱多公立学校宗教和信仰教学指导原则（2007 年）。

和欧洲委员会路标教学指导原则[21]，其他重要例子包括欧盟的 REDCo 项目[22]以及联合国特别报告员关于宗教或信仰自由的工作[23]。

由欧洲委员会民主制度和人权办公室（ODIHR）完成的托莱多指导原则，强烈呼吁尊重儿童的权利，将有关宗教和信仰的课程纳入（公立）学校。总而言之，为了也许还不熟悉本主题的意义的读者，很有必要将一些关键原则摘录如下：

1.关于宗教和信仰的知识可以强化以下观念：尊重每个人的宗教或信仰自由权利，培养公民对民主的重要性的认识，促进对社会多样性的理解，同时增强社会凝聚力。

2. 冲突常常基于对他人的信仰缺乏了解，关于宗教和信仰的知识具有减少冲突的宝贵潜力，并促进相互尊重。

3.有关宗教和信仰的知识是优质教育的重要组成部分。需要了解许多历史、文学和艺术，并有助于拓宽自己的文化视野，深化对过去和现在复杂性的洞察力。

4.当与尊重他人权利的努力相结合时，即使在对宗教或信仰存在分歧的情况下，关于宗教和信仰的教学也是最有效的。宗教或信仰自由权尊重所有人的尊严，是一项普遍权利，并承担保护他人权利的义务。

5.不能因为个人宗教信仰（或非宗教信仰）不让其参与有关宗教和信仰的教学。这方面最重要的考虑因素应是专业知识，以及对一般人权、宗教或信仰自由的基本态度和认知。

6.为了避免侵犯宗教或信仰自由的权利，可能需要对政策做出合理的调整以回应独特的宗教需求。即使法律上没有严格要求，这种适应性和灵活性也将有助于建立宽容和相互尊重的气氛。

7.涉及宗教和信仰教学的必修课程应该非常中立和客观，

---

[21]路标 - 在跨文化教育中教授宗教和非宗教世界观的政策和实践（2014 年）；宗教与学校世界观的包容性研究：欧洲理事会的路标（2016）。

[22]欧洲范围内涉及 10 所大学的宗教教育研究。

[23]联合国宗教或信仰自由问题特别报告员，宗教或信仰自由与学校教育（A／HRC／16／53,2011 年）。

政府要求参加这样的课程并不违反宗教和信仰自由（当然各国应该自由地允许儿童/家长选择部分或全部退出）[24]。

---

[24]托莱多指导原则，第 13-14 页。

教育要有宗教自由？

查尔斯·格兰
2012 年 12 月

在不违反家长和信仰群体的自由的前提下,国家应该有, 或者实际能有多大权力决定儿童教育的内容和目标?

国家对国民教育的介入始于两百年前,但在世界大部分地区, 政府的介入都是更晚才出现。我在之前的几项历史研究里曾经提到（格兰,1988, 1995, 2011）,国家的介入首先是出于管控社会的目的,其次才是为了促进个体的成功。

国民教育的有效普及始于法国,是在 1830 年的七月革命之后产生,也是因这场革命而起。和其他国家一样,国民教育在法国的扩展首先是出于政治原因,而非经济原因。革命清楚地表明越来越多的人身不由己地地卷入政治,若非通过选举,就是通过反政府的暴力革命。因此,为了保护社会秩序和财产安全,亟需教导普通民众正确的行事习惯和人生态度。教育改良的负责人弗朗索瓦·基佐是这样定义公立学校的角色的:"国家明显需要一个巨大的世俗机构,既与社会休戚相关,了解社会的运作,也与国家密切团结,接受国家的授权和指引。这个机构将负责塑造未成年人的价值观,把他们栽培成遵纪守法的人。" 他写道,在每个村庄,政府都是通过武装警察治理人们的身体,通过教师治理人们的思想。

在 19 世纪 80 年代,朱尔·费里为共和国的学校奠定了明确的根基,直到今天还时不时被法国的政客引用。朱尔和他的同道都认同一位法国历史学家的话:"共和国的建立离不开一个属灵的权柄",因此学校有责任给学生灌输某位教育官员所说的"世俗宗教"。正是这种信念,即公立学校不可在对立的信仰体系中保持中立,而是要传达和强化有利于国家政治的信仰体系,导致了近来有关穆斯林女孩是否可以在学校蒙头,或者犹太男孩是否可以戴着小圆帽去上学的激烈争论。

就在 2012 年 10 月,弗朗索瓦·奥朗德政府指定的委员会发表了名为"我们要重建共和国的学校"的报告,大声疾呼公民身份是基于"一套共同的价值观,深入人心,并且为国家这个共同体提供秩序和核心参照;这套价值观中首当其冲的就是世俗主义。"法国的政教分离不是简单的拒绝宗教,而是用另一个信仰系统取代宗教。时任法国教育部长的文森特·培尔隆曾经写了一本有关朱尔的同道的书,名为《共和国所需的宗教:斐迪南·比松的世俗宗教》。

同样,我在《平民学校的迷思》(1988)中也指出,贺拉斯·曼和他的同道们在全美国推动一个应者甚众的观点:公立学校在塑造国家公民方面有着独特和不可推卸的责任。随着1840 年末欧洲移民潮涌入美国,这个观点被直接拿来针对当时人们感受到的一个威胁,即天主教学校会妨碍这些移民的后代效忠美国。有关平民公立学校的迷思持续影响着政治辩论,虽然毫无证据表明私立学校和有宗教背景的私立学校的毕业生在公民素质方面比公立学校的毕业生要差。

我认为让国家来塑造未来的公民是对自由的一个严重威胁,不仅是对宗教自由本身和家长的宗教自由,从长远看,它对自由民主也是一个威胁。我认为国家对保护正义有着毋庸置疑的责任,包括确保每个儿童得到最好的教育,长大以后可以胜任生活,但这并不代表国家要亲自参与教育,塑造儿童的品格和价值观,这应该是家庭的责任,是接受家长托付的学校的责任。

我的这个观点其实与国际法的有关规定是一致的。1948年通过的《世界人权宣言》26 条第 3 款指出:"父母对其子女所应受的教育的种类,有优先选择的权利"。1966 年通过的《经济、社会及文化权利国际公约》指出:

"本公约缔约各国承担,尊重父母……的下列自由:为他们的孩 子选择非公立的但系符合于国家所可能规定或批准的最低教育标准的学校,并保证他们的孩子能按照他们自己的信仰接受宗教和道德教育。"

同样的,《欧洲保护人权与基本自由公约第一议定书》也规定:国家在行使任何有关教育和教导的职能时,都必须尊重家长的权利，确保国家提供的教育和教导与家长自身的宗教和哲学信念保持一致。

这一原则也被若干后共产主义时期的东欧国家写入了本国宪法。例如， 保加利亚 1991 年通过的《宪法》规定：抚养和教育未成年的孩子是家长的权利和义务，国家在旁提供协助（第 47 条第 1 款）。爱沙尼亚 1992 年通过的《宪法》规定：家长在孩子接受怎样的教育上，有最终决定权（第 37 条）。克罗地亚 1990 年通过的《宪法》规定：家长有责任抚养、扶持和教育孩子，也有权利和自由自行决定怎样抚养孩子（第 63 条）。匈牙利 1989 年通过的《宪法》规定：家长有权利决定自己的孩子将接受怎样的教育（第 67 条第 2 款）。。

这些国际公约和后共产主义国家的宪法条款的产生是为了预防以前的极权政府对教育的摧残。为了消灭一切与政府的想法有分歧的"思想罪"，极权政府对孩子和青少年进行全方位的洗脑教育。

我可以谈一点我的背景，来说明为什么我对这个话题感兴趣，以及我对这个话题的看法。我曾担任马赛诸塞州的政府官员二十多年，负责执行有关教育机会平等的法案，也负责管理给少数族裔、移民和城市青少年的教育拨款，因此我对州政府权力的运作非常熟悉，特别是在十几个城市推行种族融合和起草有关双语教育和性别平权的规章制度之后。这些实践经验促使我总是在互相冲突的权利和社会目标中寻找平衡点，这也在我与简·德·格罗夫合编的最新著作《教育中的自由、自主与责任的平衡》（奈梅亨：沃尔夫法律出版社）中反映出来。这本书一共四册，包括了对 65 个国家从幼儿园到 12 年级的教育政策的调查结果。我们提出的主要观点是：公共政策要平衡家长为孩子选择教育的自由权、教育工作者创造有特色学校的自主权、以及学校（包括让孩子在家上学的家长）面向政府承担的责任，即提供合格的、达到考核标准的课堂教学。

这里也许应该强调一个在其他几种语言里很清晰，但在英语语言中却常被忽略的一个区别：教学是教授技能和知识，教育是培养品格和人生定位。对孩子而言， 缺一不可。我认为前者可以让国家予以规范，以确保每个孩子都能继续升学，成人后也能学以致用；而后者，我认为应该由家长和家长选择的教育工作者去负责。

我在我的第一本著作《平民学校的迷思》中探究了法国、荷兰和美国政府与宗教团体之间有关教育的争端的历史渊源。在之后的的十几本著作中，我持续思考这个问题，从历史的角度和文化比较的角度探究何以，用迈克尔·麦康奈尔的话说，"世俗政权的倡导者，遵循贺拉斯·曼和约翰·杜威的传统，认为政府应当通过对教育的控制向学生灌输一套与政府原则一致的民主理念（106）……而这种做法何以遭到公民个体和信仰群体的拒斥。其中一本书探究了在美国和几个欧洲国家，政府拨款和规定对有信仰背景的学校和机构产生的影响。书名《暧昧的拥抱》就已经透露了我的结论。

过去几年在欧洲参加的几次会议给了我新的紧迫感，会议是关于教育系统要如何回应伊斯兰教的挑战，以及好几个国家的基督新教和天主教学校，在力图保持自身特色时遭遇到越来越严重的威胁。作为"全国宗教信仰学校委员会"的成员，我们几周前在"正教以色列世界组织"的纽约总部召开了第一次会议，出席会议的也包括一位伊斯兰教学校的代表。

与美国正相反，除意大利以外的每个西欧国家的宪法或法律中都有对家长选择的非公立学校（大部分是，但不全是宗教学校）拨款的规定。虽然这类学校不断增加的"市场份额"已经说明了它们的受欢迎程度，但也有人对伊斯兰教的不断扩大以及很多人认为它对社会和人民和睦产生的威胁表示担忧，因为由家长选择教育已经变成了一个国家负担不起的奢侈品。这样的辩论在荷兰显得尤其尖锐，因为荷兰 70%的小学生都在非公立学校上学，而这些学校中 50%是伊斯兰教学校。

说到底，问题就变成：为了社会安定和人民团结，是否有必要让国家动用自己的权力和资源来确保所有的儿童，不管出自什么宗教和文化背景，一律接受同一种教育，透过这种教育获得同样的心态和公民身份认同，并且远离父母的信仰和传统？目前这种观点往往是跟政治上的左派挂钩，虽然常常是从右派的嘴里说出来。在 19 世纪的大部分时间里，左派都在反对保守派政府利用学校教育推广自己的利益，而现今这两者的角色对调了。公平的讲，左右两派都尽力推动自己拥戴的政府的教育目标，一旦对方掌权，就反对政府对教育的干预。我个人的立场，你很快就会看出，是非左非右，用我自己的话说，是"极端的中间派。"我支持个体和少数派人群的自由诉求，认为他们有权根据自己的信念养育孩子，但我也反对托克维尔曾经警告过的"多数人的集权"。

不可避免的是，国家运用自己的权力和资源把自己拟定的品格和价值培养模式强加给儿童的任何做法都会推翻很多笃信宗教的家长对孩子的期待和设想。就如罗布·赖克所说："自由主义对公民的要求和定义绝不是中立的，而是偏向特定的文化群体。自由主义有意识、有目的的让公民向某一种人格看齐，敦促人们成为那样的人，但这种做法会影响文化群体塑造自己的群体人格的方式（38）"。这些群体中的家长原本享有的按照自己的信念养育孩子的自由，如今受到了国家的干涉，实则是国家夺走了这些家长的职分。

当然，这种做法和认为孩子先属于国家，才属于父母的观点并非初来乍到。自从柏拉图和亚里士多德提议把孩子从父母身边拿走，交由公共托儿所来抚养以来，上述做法和观点就一直是乌托邦式社会政治改革的一个核心要件。试图用教育来塑造道德高尚的民众的做法在历史上不断改头换面、打着各种政治旗号出现。奇怪的是，很多坚信个体自由的自由派竟然忘记了约翰·斯图尔特·密尔曾经发出的警告，反而支持国家对教育的主导。

我不反对国家的权柄，也不反对国家的强势行动，只要行动是恰切合理的。作为一个加尔文主义者，我相信政府是神设立的，用来惩恶扬善，保护公义。当有证据表明孩子正受到虐待或者父母未尽养护之职，我赞同政府的适当介入，即使介入的对象是有宗教背景的学校，甚至家庭。

在另一方面，我也赞同阿布纳·格林尼对霍布斯主义和黑格尔主义意义上的国家绝对主权提出的挑战。他说：

"主权是可渗透的，不是绝对的。作为公民，我们首先是承诺要遵守诸多规范的人，这其中只有一部分规范是对国家的承诺。我们没有充分的理由把国家视为规范的源头……国家有时候应当准许我们按照信仰的光照，而非国家的法律过生活，所以才要有立法上的调整适应和司法豁免（282）。我特别要挑战柏拉图、卢梭和很多当代自由派推崇的一个理念，即社会必须建立在共享的信念之上，而国家有权运用自己的权柄和资源来推动这些共享信念。我认为这在本质上是极权主义的做法。

朱尔·斯坦伯格在他对洛克和卢梭的研究中指出：

"当代民主社会的成员不是'一个信仰共同体'，也不具备共同的道德承诺，而这两点恰恰是'许可'作为道德责任和道德合法性之源头得以适用的必要条件。反之，我们面对的社会是由'各种信仰共同体'分裂而成，'离同质性相去甚远，所持价值观常常互相冲突，甚至截然相反'（124）"。

"有鉴于此，国家在如何定义'美好生活'的各种理念上严格持守中立，就变得至关重要了。实际上，'中立'一词常被滥用，用来为一种排斥宗教视角、却任由环保主义者、女权主义者、自由主义者或其他'包罗万象的'视角大行其道的教育立场提供正当性。再次引用麦康奈尔的话，'所谓的'中立'，从多元主义者的角度看，实际上是一种根深蒂固的对某些思维方式和生活方式的意识形态偏好，实际上它偏向理性主义和个人选择，却排斥传统和良知（104）。"

我们要留意阿布纳·格林尼发出的警告：一味追求一致性向来不足以成为一个有号召力的国家利益诉求；对于将法律适用于宗教和其他根深蒂固的规范性观点，使之合理化的家长式做法，我们要谨慎对待（118）。诚然，我们经历过的高度多元化并且普遍很成功的社会，证明了尼古拉斯·雷彻的正确性：只要人们准备好接受和运用已有的机制来解决共同体的问题，（不管是出于怎样形形色色乃至于水火不容的理由），有建设性的管理社会事务所需的稳定和宁静并不需要建立在'观点一致'的基础上，甚至不需要建立在为解决第一序列的冲突而建立的第二序列的'观点一致'的基础上。

借用琳达·麦克莱恩发明的概念，我是一个"公民社会复兴主义者"，赞同玛丽·安·格兰顿和比尔·盖尔斯顿等人推崇的社会多元主义。我认为守法不是道德责任，而是一个理性的决定。哈罗德·拉斯基在一百多年前就写下了这样的话：

"每个政府都声明违法是不对的。在多元主义者看来，这个声明的前提必须是知道在什么情况下，违反了什么法律。有一些个体和群体的行为领域，在特定情况下，政府是无权进行干涉的（215）"。

就在半个世纪以前，我在北卡罗来纳州坐了一阵子牢，还在阿拉巴马州的塞尔玛故意违法，以求被警察逮捕，因为我认为我当时触犯的是不公义的法律，而我遵从的是一个比国家更高的权柄。一直有人前赴后继像我这么做，也常常受到自由派的赞美，因为自由派也承认，国家并不总是对的。然而，为什么这些自由派却毫不犹豫的认为代表国家的政府官员比家长更有智慧，更知道怎样做才对孩子有最大的益处？当然只要不是他们自己的孩子……

容我重申我的观点：国家在教育工作中有自己的职分，而且是很重要的职分。国家的角色是确保每个儿童都能得到充分的教育，但国家自己不应当成为教育者，以防僭越自己本来的职分。一旦国家成为教育者，开始插手孩子和青少年的信仰内容和效忠对象，就是对自由的巨大威胁。我们身后有这样一个漫长而有毒的政治思想传统，即国家成为一个大一统社会的良善的塑造者，如苏格拉底在《共和国》里指出的：观点的分歧是最大的罪恶。拉斯基曾经指出过这种观点的普遍性：

"国家在今天是一种强制性的联合会，而在长达两千多年的历史里，我们总被告知，国家的目的是缔造完美的生活，而这个目的具有其他机构的目的所不具备的宽泛性。这样一个可以放之四海的利益诉求，好像是其他任何联合会都不能准确认领的。国家的主权似乎因此就代表了对广泛意义上的人的保护，即卢梭所说的集体利益，保护其不受更个人化的利益的侵犯……至少今天看来，人们无从逃避国家的这个主权及其要求，它的良知高于任何个体对善的理解和概念……这个领域一直不断扩大，直到今日，你几乎找不出任何一个人类活动的领域是或多或少没有受到它的影响的（185）"。

与这种政治思想传统相反的，是出自天主教的社会教导的一个理念："辅助"。这个理念也出现在欧盟的奠基性文件《马斯特里赫特条约》里。这个词的拉丁词根是 subsidium（意为

帮助或协助），意思是权柄应当尽可能地贴近受到影响的人们，而国家承担的是一个帮助者的角色。我更喜欢

一个出自荷兰的新加尔文主义传统的相关概念，即"领域主权"。亚伯拉罕·库珀认为有三层泾渭分明的"创造秩序"，每一层有其直接源于上帝的权柄和责任。 他说："家庭、生意、科学和艺术之类都属社会领域，该领域不依附国家而存在，管辖该领域的法律也不是出自国家，而是出自人心中的至高权柄；这权柄和国家的主权一样，直接受到上帝恩典的管辖（90）"。

当然，这其中有一个领域是国家，而国家"拥有三重权利和责任：1）每当不同的领域之间发生冲突，国家要强制冲突双方尊重彼此的界限；2）国家要保护这些领域中的个体和弱者，不受其他领域里权力滥用的侵害；3）强制所有人为维护国家的自然统一担负起人身责任和经济责任"。

但是国家绝不能伺机侵占或篡夺其他领域的职责功能。就如赫尔曼·杜伊威尔不断强调的，领域主权不仅仅是一个"后退放手"的政策，更重要的是，分割开各个领域的边界才是一切的本质核心。无论是国家还是教会，都不应当认为自己高过其他的领域。

教育在所有的层面上都是这样一个领域：一方面，学校和教育工作者要与家庭配合，有时也要与教会密切同工；另一方面，教育要遵守国家设立的法制法规，却不能成为国家下属的一个部门……或是教会下属的一个部门。这也是为什么荷兰的基督新教学校虽然吸收了全国 1/3 的小学生，却并不"属于"教会，而是属于独立的委员会。这个模式正在被越来越多的天主教乃至城市学校效法，而这两者对半平分了了剩下的 2/3 的小学生。

那么就教育而言，政府到底扮演怎样的角色呢？当然不是为我们提供"完美生活"的定义，那是我们必须去宗教和哲学传统当中寻找，或者从和我们共享生活彼此信任的小群体中，亦或从我们夜深人静的沉思默想中寻找答案。不管我们称之为良知，上帝，还是至高的忠诚，这是令我们"深入自己内心"的声音，帮助我们判断国家对我们提出的要求是否公义，我们是应当遵从，还是不惜一切代价反对。

不，国家的角色不是决定我们应该成为怎样的人，而是为学校设立课堂教学必须达到的、可以测量的目标，并且确保学校（和在家里自己教孩子的父母）实现所定的教学目标。教学目标应当包括找工作和日常生活所需的技能，以及对法律框架、程序、权利和义务的理解，后者是公民生活的基础。教学目标不应当包括信仰、价值观和忠诚，虽然良好的教育必须包括这些内容，但这些是公民社会的责任，由家人、家长委托的教育工作者、青少年团体、体育项目、娱乐和艺术中心，以及宗教团体组成。这些群体和活动都承担重要的角色，是政府应该尊重和支持的，例如通过免税和提供公用设施，但是政府不能参与指导。我们难道忘了"希特勒青年团"和"少先队"，和极权政府用来"动员"青少年的前车之鉴吗？

也许你已经注意到我在上文中用了"教导"，而非"教育"一词。这两个词在很多语言中都有明确的区分，但在日常英语中却并非如此。"教导"是教人如何做一件事，是讲解事实和事物之间的关系；而"教育"却是塑造人，是一个长达一生的过程，可以发生在各种场景和关系当中，也就是德文中的"Bildung"，即按照某种理想的形象进行教化和陶冶。

自由的民主社会政府不应该想要成为"教育者"，也不应该告诉学校（包括公立和私立学校）该教导什么价值观。不幸的是，许多当代的自由主义者似乎很难拒绝这个诱惑，总是呼吁政府这样做，但在其他领域，这些人又强烈反对政府对信仰和态度的把控。罗布·赖克在其著作《教育对自由主义和多元文化的联结》（2002）中的观点就是这样一个典型却并不极端的例子。赖克的一个核心观点也是艾米·哥特曼和其他自由主义者的观点，认为每个儿童都应该"自主"，自行决定要怎样生活和遵循哪些规范；否则的话，赖克等人认为，自由的民主社会就难以蓬勃发展。赖克承认"自主性""在文化上不是一个中立的概念，是有潜在的可能性去改变某些个体忠于或从属的价值观，并且并非所有的文化都崇尚或者倡导自主性（42）"。也就是说，这些人活该！赖克并不介意这种公民教育产生的震荡会波及到国家不具备管辖权的领域。

"为了打造自由平等的公民品格和能力，自由的国家要求其公民在公共生活中运用政治美德、技能和习惯，这会对那些在私生活中持非主流生活方式的公民产生影响。栽培有自主性的公民对本来就强调和培养自主性的文化群体是锦上添花，对不崇尚自主性的文化群体则有可能具有腐蚀性（46-7）。

赖克的核心观点是："强调自主性和政治智慧的教育是为了对抗阿米什人和原教旨主义父母追求他们自己以为的善（48）"。可是我们在宪法和道德上对宗教自由、多元文化和社会多元主义做出的承诺不就是要保障这些人能够按照自己的宗教信念生活的权利吗？赖克可不这样想，因为他觉得"栽培自主性的能力和实际操作必须先于我们对自主性的尊重。国家必须打破对自主性的尊重才能栽培公民的自主性（108）"。毕竟，一个"推动最小化自主性的国家将会限制和减少有可能蓬勃发展的生活形态（117）"，所以必须这样做。

至于公立学校在执行他所赋予的加强公民自主性和独立思考能力的使命时，成效究竟如何，赖克并没有心存幻想。他大度的同意"有证据表明在某些情况下，在家里自己教孩子的家长(家中教育)比公立和私立学校更好地完成了国家和孩子的教育目标"，他又说："一些学校，甚至可能很多学校，都没能有效抵御孩子们常常会遇到的同侪压力（159）"。实际上，研究表明家长和青少年选择在家上学的首要原因就包括想要逃离公立学校里大行其道的同侪压力，即随大流才能被接纳。

实际上，赖克准备接受家中教育，但前提是国家不仅要控制"教学"的效果，还要控制"教育"的目标和方法：

> "国家应当要求家长使用能够让孩子接触和参与多元文化的教学大纲。换句话说，家长必须向政府官员证明，家里的教育环境是与自由化和多元文化的教育方向契合的（169）。"

毋庸置疑，这就意味着那些不遵照自由化教育模式，继续坚持宗教传统之权威的家长们和有宗教背景的学校的教师将会遭遇到一些尚不明确的强制措施，以防止他们继续破坏国家的良善目标。"某些类型的家中教育和原教旨主义宗教学校如果故意不让孩子接触多元文化国家的价值观多元性，将会被取缔。"

琳达·麦克莱恩在她有关家庭的著作中做出的一个区分很有帮助。她是这样说的：

"我接受政治自由主义的这个信条：政府可以用游说来推广好公民应当具备的美德（或价值观），譬如宽容、礼貌、互惠、合作。我也接受附属于这个信条的条件：政府不应该推广以某种生活方式为标志的个人美德，而这种生活方式是出自于某一套道德教义（或是关于好人的理念）（47）。"

这似乎是一个很恰当的区分，而且很明显，赖克和其同道定义的"自主性"实际上是一种"个人美德"，并且是自由主义这"一套道德教义"中的一个关键教义。赖克说的很清楚，自主性是他所认为的好人的一个固有特征。

这就意味着，正如政府也许不会说服人们有关宗教的事情（麦克莱恩 43），政府同样也不应该说服人们有关一套世俗生活的理念。正如赖克自己也承认的，这套理念可能损害多元社会中很多文化群体和宗教群体的生活方式，而这些群体构成了麦克莱恩所刻画的"话语和行动被保护起来的小群体"。在这些群体中，"与大众背道而驰"并不是一个困扰，反倒培育出与外界大众不同的自我认知、社群和公义观。

那要拿"自主性"怎么办呢？哈南·亚历山大最近提议：

"自由民主的公民特质自身所需的自主性道德……并不在康德的普遍理性和罗尔斯主义的公共理性里，而是存在于厚重而活泼的伦理和宗教传统里。这种传统藉着人们之间主体对主体的关系，例如父母与孩子，教师与学生，孩子与孩子，以及学生和他们即将进入的传统之间的关系，为"好人"和"正义的社会"提供了清晰具体的愿景……(因此)，宗教教育和其他形式的道德和伦理教育在自由民主社会中不仅要被宽容对待，它更是培育道德自主的民主公民所需的核心要件（160）。"

相仿的，南茜·罗森布鲁姆也警告说："利维坦国家不应该自行扩大、毁灭或者吸收（宗教）群体本身能够以更强的道德权威、活力和合法性天然行使的功能（17）"。她还对这种功能提出了建议：

"获得公共支持的、与宗教融合的教育实际上是一种比公立学校提供的世俗教育更可靠、更有效的民主教育。因为公共教育通常躲避任何一种有争议的、包罗万象的价值观，导致它提供的公民教育就很'单薄'。相反的，宗教群体用自己的信仰故事和神圣历史来支持民主，从自己的角度宣扬公民美德和民主制度，反而加深了人们对民主的委身。"

随后她敦促国家不要干预这些群体用什么方式推动公民建设（162）。

赖克和其同道的观点中有一个奇怪的悖论：年轻人的自主性需要国家用强制的教学方法和教学目标进行培养，最好是在国家经营的公立学校里。因此，他警告说："脱离学校和免受学校教育的权利……可能会潜在地危害公民美德的发展，譬如自主性和互相尊重，而这些美德对自由国家的合法性和稳定是非常关键的（7）"。所以，为了加强孩子的自主性就必须限制家庭和学校的自主性吗？这让我想起卢梭不断强调的"必须强迫公民接受自由"！通过观察成年人，包括父母和老师，在孩子的教育问题上做出符合本心的决定，难道不是会更激发儿童和青少年的能力和自信，在行事为人上也更有自主性吗？在官僚管理的学校里，按照定好的教学内容照本宣科，一举一动都要按照工作合同照章办事的教师，能够怎样为学生示范自主性呢？

东欧的共产党政府纷纷垮台时，我受美国教育部委托撰写一份政治变革给学校教育带来变化的报告，于是有了后来出版的《东欧的教育自由》（1995）让我印象最深刻的是看到教师和家长们被释放出来的热情，因为终于可以创立各种新学校去服务不同特色的人群。在这个过程中，我也看到人们发展出信任和配合，而这恰恰是因极权政府长期压制，不给人们从事公民活动的空间时极度缺乏的。如今在波士顿和全国其他地方生机勃勃的特许学校里，我们也看到同样的情景，特许学校正是围绕某个共同的、强烈的、极具地方特色的愿景兴建起来的。

我的波士顿大学同事斯科特·赛德在他的新著《品格的指南针：强有力的校园文化如何引领学生走向成功》中对这个过程及其生命力给出了生动的描述。赛德详细讲述了波士顿的三所特许学校如何通过教导、礼仪和学校里的人际关系规范来培养学生的品格。在每个案例研究里，他都指出（学校领导也同意）品格发展是这些学校成功的关键因素，不但令学生在标准化考试里成绩斐然，而且帮助非裔和拉丁裔学生的成绩达到、甚至高于来自富裕郊区家庭的孩子的成绩。最明显的是，每所学校都有一套清晰的品格培养目标，与其他的学校大不相同。这三所学校都是公立学校，在教学方面都遵照政府为所有公立学校设立的要求，但它们都有效利用自己的自由，设立了自己独特的育人目标。

相反的，正如社会学家艾伦·裴氏金指出的，"公立学校在财力上的优势常常被它们的缺乏管教、社会问题、无敬业精神的教师和无所谓的家长，以及它们在品格培养和真理教导上的无能为力给抵消了（84）"。詹姆士·科尔曼、安东尼·布里克和其他著名的社会学学者的研究也表明，大力注重校园文化是千千万万有宗教背景的学校的一个关键特色，使这些学校在每个学生身上能够用远低于公立学校的财政投入获得更好的学习成绩。就如科尔曼指出的，"现如今，（一个）出勤率基于寄宿制的公立学校的校长本人并不推崇任何成体系的社区价值观。相反，这种学校里倒是有一堆互不相容的价值观，每个都认为自己有合法性，还动不动就闹上法庭以求胜出"（11-12）。

就连坚持认为"公立学校，而非私立学校，才是对孩子最有益的福利，也是对未来的公民进行道德教育的主要渠道"（70）的艾米·哥特曼也不得不同意说，"虽然证据寥寥……但是平均看来，私立学校在提高学生的学习成绩，用更挑战智力的方式教导美国历史和公民课方面，比公立学校做得更好，即便在多种族混合的课堂里也是如此"。（65）裴氏金通过研究伊利诺伊州的基督教原教旨主义学校发现，那里的学生比当地公立学校的学生"融入相处的更好。"（189）

而在当地的公立学校里，

"有 75%的学生……说学校应该强调品格培养，但是只有 39%的学生说学校做到了（325）…… 其中有 59%的学生说'挣大钱'对自己很重要，而伯大尼私立学校只有 10%的学生这么想（329）…… 93%的伯大尼学校的学生和 80%的公立学校学生愿意和黑人家庭做邻居（332）…… 93%的伯大尼学校的学生和 95%的公立学校学生认为'不信上帝的人应该和其他人一样拥有言论自由（333）…… 83%的伯大尼学校的学生和 84%的公立学校学生不赞同'只有信上帝的人才是美国的好公民'（334）……72%的公立学校学生和仅有 33%的伯大尼学校的学生赞同'不违规的人在社会上很难成功'"（335）。

　　我在这里不是要为有宗教背景的学校摇旗呐喊，而是挑战一个普遍存在的假定，即这种学校会培养出狭隘偏执的学生，不适合作为自由民主社会里的公民。最近一项对美国（2011）和加拿大（2012）好几千名不同学校的毕业生所做的调查表明（网站：https://www.cardus.ca/store/publications/），事实正好与这个假定相反。实际上，谁能自信的宣称：一个典型的基督教福音派学校对同性婚姻的态度会比一个地处波士顿郊区富人区的典型公立学校对原教旨主义基督教的态度更加敌对和缺乏宽容？

　　对有宗教背景的学校的研究和最近对特许学校的研究表明，在具有清晰和共同价值取向的学校里，学生的表现最好，也更具备好公民的特质。史蒂文·弗里霍夫认为：

　　"生活在一个碎片化和社区匮乏的世界里，孩子们既需要文化记忆（他/她们的故事，他/她们的身份认同，他/她们的避风港），也需要文化愿景（想象中的未来，世界观和生活观），为他/她们的一生提供目标和意义。学校要承担的一个角色就是保存、并把社区的记忆和未来的愿景传递给学生。然而记忆和愿景都和信仰有关，并且深植于社区当中。"（48）

这样的社区为高质量的教育提供了沃土，也是青少年得以扎根并以此抵御往往有害的媒体和青少年文化的地方。弗里霍夫接着指出：

"针对政府经营的学校的道德观的一个关键假设是：去除掉单一的、指导一切的世界观的学校是年轻人能够进行探索、发问和选择的最佳环境。然而一个提供各种选择的自助餐真的是最好的吗？学校不是都应该有其鲜明独特的价值观，不管是传统宗教信仰还是世俗信仰吗？针对紧迫而严肃的议题产生的思考和探究才是最有效率的。出自于沉稳的信念和强烈身份认同的教学活动会更有激情、更个人化、也更深入。（51）"

伯克利法学院的教授约翰·昆斯和史蒂文·舒格曼在其 1978 年赞同教育优惠券的经典辩论中提出了相同的观点：

"孩子在自己选择的学校里最重要的体验莫过于发现自己信任的成年人也持守这个孩子的家人所推崇的道德关怀。这种道德关怀的内容不必和道德关怀在学校生活的核心地位一样重要。虽然某些价值观似乎狭隘偏颇，但是孩子在个人成长的关键阶段跟价值观的互动也许会加固他对人们应当礼尚往来这个观念的认同，而这个观念正是公民自主性不可缺少的一部分。（83）"

我们需要为故意与当下盛行的文化作对的宗教群体感到担忧吗？荷兰的政策制定者已经在想办法只让愿意接受裸体海滩和其他文化放任行为的人移民到荷兰。可是，美国社会和美国流行文化中有很多东西也是我不能接受的，我敢说我们大多数人也都有一个类似的清单，可这并不会使我们失去作公民的资格。莫莉莎·威廉姆斯提出了以下建议：

"一些人，也许是虔诚的宗教徒，会对个体自由或自主性的原则心存疑窦，是因为他们看见这个原则被用来为自我放纵和为所欲为找借口，而不是出于强烈的道德责任感。还有一部分人会排斥公民身份这个理念，因为马塞多和费恩伯格之类的人告诉他们，公民身份要求人们要首先效忠一个政治团体，可这些人不愿意在政治团体和他们自己的文化团体之间优先选择前者，"

（只要一个受到质疑的群体没有计划或者发起对公共安全的威胁），为什么要将其对主流文化的排斥视为对社会秩序和成功运行的威胁呢？毕竟"这些个人并非一定是民主的敌人。其实，他们也许很渴望能够加入到民主对话当中，只要获得入门卷的代价不是必须遵从某种特定的公民身份认同"（234）。诚然，一个自由多元的民主国家本来就不该向他们提出这样的要求！

一个自由多元的民主国家也不应该运用国家的权柄和资源要求所有负责儿童教育的人，包括家长和教师，按照政府规定地单一模式培养孩子……。

参考文献

1. 哈南·亚历山大，2012. "有关真实性的争鸣：开放社会中宗教教育的后果"，选自《委身、品格和公民素质：自由民主社会中的宗教教育》。纽约：劳特利奇出版社

2. 詹姆士·科尔曼，托马斯·郝佛尔，1987. 《公立中学和私立中学：社区的影响力》，纽约：基础图书出版社

3. 约翰·昆斯，史蒂文·舒格曼，1978.《自主选择的教育：家庭做主》，伯克利：加州大学出版社

4. 查尔斯·格兰，1988.《平民学校的迷思》。 阿姆赫斯特：马萨诸塞大学出版社

5. 查尔斯·格兰，1995.《东欧的教育自由》，华盛顿特区：卡托研究所出版社

6. 查尔斯·格兰，2000.《暧昧的拥抱：政府与基于信仰的学校和社会机构》，普林斯顿大学出版社

7. 查尔斯·格兰，2011.《国家和学校的对比模式》，纽约：康提纽姆出版社

8. 阿布纳·格林尼，2012. 《反对义务：自由化民主社会中权柄的多重源头》，哈佛大学出版社

9. 艾米·哥特曼, 1987.《民主教育》，普林斯顿大学出版社。

10. 亚伯拉罕·库珀, 1931.《有关加尔文主义的演讲》，大激流城：伊尔德曼斯

11. 哈罗德·拉斯基, 1989. "摘自《主权的基础和其他文章》（1921）"， 选自《国家的多元主义理论》。编辑：保罗·赫斯特。 伦敦：劳特利奇出版社

12. 琳达·麦克莱恩, 2006. 《家庭的职分：缔造能力、平等和责任》，剑桥：哈佛大学出版社

13. 迈克尔·麦康奈尔, 2000. "享有同等公民权的信众"，选自《公民的责任和信仰的要求：多元民主社会中的宗教调试》。编辑：南希·罗森布鲁姆；普林斯顿大学出版社，第 90-110 页

14. 艾伦·裴氏金, 1986.《上帝的选择：一个基督教原教旨主义学校的前生今世》，芝加哥：芝加哥大学出版社

15. 罗布·赖克, 2002. 《教育对自由主义和多元文化的联结》，芝加哥大学出版社

16. 尼古拉斯·雷彻, 1993. 《多元主义：反对共识的要求》，牛津：柯莱瑞登出版社

17. 南希·罗森布鲁姆, 2000. "简介"，选自《公民的责任和信仰的要求：多元民主社会中的宗教调试》。编辑：南希·罗森布鲁姆；普林斯顿大学出版社，第 3-31 页

18. 南希·罗森布鲁姆, 2000. "阿摩司：宗教自治和多元主义的道德用途"，选自《公民的责任和信仰的要求：多元民主社会中的宗教调试》。编辑：南希·罗森布鲁姆；普林斯顿大学出版社

19. 斯科特·赛德, 2012. 《品格的指南针》，剑桥：哈佛教育出版社

20. 朱尔·斯坦伯格, 1978. 《洛克、卢梭和"许可"的理念：探究有关政治责任的自由民主理念》，康涅狄格州韦斯特泊特：格林伍德出版社

21. 史蒂文·弗里霍夫, 2012. "记忆和愿景之间：作为意义群体的学校"。出自《承诺、品格和公民身份：自由民主治下的宗教教育》。编辑：哈南·亚历山大,阿曼·艾格巴瑞。纽约：劳特利奇出版社

22. 莫莉莎·威廉姆, 2007. "公民身份的非地域界限"，出自《身份、归属与忠诚》。编者：塞拉·本哈比布，伊恩·沙皮罗，德尼罗·皮查诺威。剑桥大学出版社，226-256 页

本 文 转 载 于 *http://www.champion.org/pacape-drupal/ReligiousFreedominEducation.pdf.*

办教会学校合法吗？

王怡

各位"追求公义、寻求耶和华的"（赛 51:1）神的儿女，平安。

陆续听到一些同工和家长，询问或讨论归正学堂的法律问题。学堂有无可能注册？兴办教会学校是否违背《义务教育法》？校长和教师们有什么风险？家长们又有什么风险？

在新疆，有许多清真寺举办穆斯林学校。最近，当地防爆警察强攻一间穆斯林学校，引发暴力反抗，当场炸死数名儿童。一份政府文件指出，有阿訇在礼拜中宣称，"只学文化、不读经文，将来不能进天堂。导致很多孩子离开公办教育，转入地下的穆斯林学校"。

在西藏，也有许多寺庙举办宗教教育。今年以来，一批藏族年轻僧人，前赴后继地自焚，抗议政府对宗教的控制，死难者已达数十人。最近，在印度的噶玛巴"活佛"发出呼吁，恳请西藏的僧人停止自焚。

在香港，约有 25% 的中小学是教会学校。今年 6-9 月，也爆发了反对香港政府推行"国民教育课"的社会运动，维护教育内容独立于政府的自由。其中，率先拒绝"政治思想课"进入学校的，是天主教、圣公会和路德宗等几个主要的基督教宗派。直到 13 万香港居民走上街头，全港大学生宣布罢课，香港政府被迫收回了今年 9 月在中小学实施"国民教育课"的措施。

我诚然向主祷告，期望教会中的每个基督徒家庭，都立志将小学和初中阶段的子女，送到归正学堂，接受"基督教教育"。但我也要诚实地对你们说，万事开头难，我们的法律风险，与我们的地理位置相当，都介于新疆、西藏和香港之间。

在有宗教自由的地方，香港社会以"非暴力"的方式，拒绝政府"不合法"的教育要求。在没有宗教自由的地方，阿訇和喇嘛们孤注一掷，以死相抗。如果，我们信奉的是真神，我们传扬的是真理；但我们为下一代的灵魂而付的代价，却不如大发热心的异教徒。试问，我们怎么可能向那些决绝的藏人，和那些信奉上帝却拒绝主基督的穆斯林，传扬福音？

如果，你是一个冒死也要为儿女提供宗教教育的穆斯林；一个从成都来的、将自己儿女送在无神论者手中受教育的人向你传福音，说他所信的真是"福音"，你信吗？

又如果，你是一个走上街头抗议"政治思想课"的香港妈妈；一个从成都来到，儿女从小接受辩证唯物主义教育的基督徒向你传福音，说她所信的真是"福音"，你信吗？

不，他们多半不会信的。他们会回答，如果你说的真是"福音"，你为什么任凭自己的儿女留在"祸音"中？我们虽然不好，儿女求饼，也不至于给他们石头；儿女求鱼，也不至于给他们蛇。但如果你说的真是"福音"，你尽了全力来帮助你的儿女脱离世上的凶恶吗？我们至少抗争过，我们以自己的前途、职业，甚至性命来追求过，但你们自称信耶稣的，从哪里显明你们真信呢。你们可以给儿女吃有三聚氰胺的奶粉，上帝会保佑你们的儿女；但你们怎么可以给儿女提供有三聚氰胺的教育呢？

因此，我有两个回答，供你们参考：

第一，在当代中国，办教会学校，和办家庭教会一样，都是非法的。在基督教教育的议题上，我们的困境，与但以理和他的三个朋友的困境是类似的。也就是说，我们面对的不是行政的审批、注册的层面上的难题；我们面对的，是基督教信仰与中国《宪法》的直接冲突。

《宪法》第 36 条，对"中华人民共和国公民有宗教信仰自由"，加了一个重要的，关于教育的限制，"任何人不得利用宗教进行妨碍国家教育制度的活动"。宗教信仰怎么会妨碍"国家教育制度"呢？除非这个"国家教育制度"具有特定的宗教和思想立场。这个立场就是《宪法》第 24 条所说的，"国家提倡爱祖国、爱人民、爱劳动、爱科学、爱社会主义的公德，在人民中进行爱国主义、集体主义和国际主义、共产主义的教育，进行辩证唯物主义和历史唯物主义的教育，反对资本主义的、封建主义的和其他的腐朽思想"。

换言之，这两个《宪法》条款表明，中国迄今为止，仍然是一个以"无神论"为国教的、政教合一的国家。所以，我必须告诉你们，秋雨之福归正教会要举办"圣约归正学堂"这件事，不但违法，而且直接违背宪法。说到底，在当代中国，基督教信仰就是一种违宪的信仰。各位从受洗那一天开始，就走上了"违宪"的不归路。保罗说，忘记背后，努力面前。表明"归正"之路，就是不归之路。要么是宪法将来被修改，要么是你将来被修改。

接着，《教育法》第 8 条的规定，是根据《宪法》第 36 条来的，"国家实行教育与宗教相分离。任何组织和个人不得利用宗教进行妨碍国家教育制度的活动"。第 3 条和第 6 条的规定，则是根据《宪法》第 24 条来的，"国家坚持以马克思列宁主义、毛泽东思想和建设有中国特色社会主义理论为指导，遵循宪法确定的基本原则，发展社会主义的教育事业。……国家在受教育者中进行爱国主义、集体主义、社会主义的教育，进行理想、道德、纪律、法制、国防和民族团结的教育"。

因着这间教会的信条，和我所蒙的呼召；我必须告诉你们，我和众长老、及在我们之后担任牧师和长老的弟兄们，直到主基督再来之日，都一心反对"教育与宗教相分离"。主若以为美，求主帮助我们，愿意付出比香港人、西藏人和新疆人更大的代价。我对着你们，也对着你们的后代说，在我们之后，谁若没有这样的心志，没有显出这信心的恩赐，就不要选立他成为这间教会的长老。

最后，《义务教育法》第 62 条规定，可以由"社会组织或者个人依法举办的民办学校实施义务教育"。因此，义务的主要意思，是指国家应当提供免费教育，而不是指公民必须接受公立教育。不过，《民办教育促进法》又再次根据《宪法》和《教育法》的规定，重申如下："第四条，民办学校应当贯彻教育与宗教相分离的原则。任何组织和个人不得利用宗教进行妨碍国家教育制度的活动"。这相当于是一个无神论教育的"申命记"，从《宪法》到《民办教育法》，一以贯之。因此，我们的违法，也是一以贯之。你们看出这一政策的邪恶了吗？如果"公民有宗教信仰自由"和"教育与宗教相分离"这两个命题能够同时成立，那就意味着我们的子女都不是公民。换言之，"十八岁以下的公民没有宗教信仰自由"。这也是"三自会"的政策不为十八岁以下的人施洗的原因。耶稣说，"你们要去使万民作我的门徒，奉父、子、圣灵的名，给他们施洗"（太28:19），但这一政策却说，"十八岁以下的"，不但不是公民，而且根本就不是人，因为是人就要施洗，"凡我所吩咐你们的，都教训他们遵守"（太28:20）。

如果说，基督徒在今天的宪法上是"二等公民"。那么，基督徒的未成年子女就相当于"三等公民"。因为这一"教育与宗教相分离"的原则，不但剥夺了教会，也剥夺了家长，更直接剥夺了孩子们。主的教会别无选择，必须拒绝"教育与宗教相分离"的公立教育体制，必须在"国家教育制度"以外，重建教会学校，恢复基督教教育。我在微博上曾说，"坐牢也要办学校"。因为"顺从神，不顺从人，是应当的"（徒5:29）。家庭教会的前辈，曾为自己的信仰付过代价；那么，现在到了为孩子们付代价的时代了。家庭教会的成员，都曾为教会的今天付过代价；那么，现在是到了为教会的未来付代价的时候了。

耶稣说，"时间将到，如今就是了，那真正拜父的，要用心灵和真理拜他，因为父要这样的人拜他"（约4:23）。亲爱的弟兄姊妹，让我们记得，基督徒的孩子是人，而且是"这样的人"。

第二，在当今世界，办教会学校，和办家庭教会一样，都是合法的。

首先，基督徒和教会的"宪法"，乃是《圣经》。当我们思考一件事是否"合法"时，首先是指这件事是否合乎《圣经》。在无神论控制的国家教育之外，不但办教会学校合法，而且不办教会学校就不合法。换言之，"教养孩童，使他走当行的道"（箴22:6），对父母和教会来说，不是一项可以放弃的权利，而是一项不可放弃的责任。"教养"的意思，不是指一个由父母自由作主的过程。这个词的原意，是指"奉献"。所罗门王和众民修好圣殿，行"奉献之礼"（代下7:5），就是用这个词。教养孩童的意思，就是在教育中将孩童如同神的殿奉献给神。"教育"是一个奉献的过程，或一个敬拜的过程。没有敬拜和奉献的教育，就不是教育，而是"反教育"，或者是"非法的教育"。在没有选择的环境下，我们只能仰望上帝的怜悯，在"非法的教育"中施超然的恩典；但在有选择的环境下，如果我们继续让下一代接受"非法的教育"，就是公开地、以子女的命运来试探神。

其次，在《圣经》与中国的现行宪法和法律之间，还有一个世俗的、教会学校的"合法"空间，就是中国政府参加或签署的一系列国际公约。如果说，《圣经》不能在世俗法律上约束中国政府，也暂时不能在世俗法律上定国家的罪。那么，这些国际公约，在效力上是高于国内法的。在政府不守信诺的前提下，教会对君王的顺服的责任，便体现为遵循和顺从联合国的人权公约。

1、《世界人权宣言》，第 18 条规定，"人人有思想、良心和宗教自由的权利；此项权利包括改变他的宗教或信仰的自由，以及单独或集体、公开或秘密地以教义、实践、礼拜和戒律表示他的宗教或信仰的自由"。第 26 条，针对教育作出规定，"父母对其子女所应受的教育的种类，有优先选择的权利"。换言之，是父母，而不是国家，有权替子女决定他们应该接受什么样的教育。

2、《公民权利和政治权利公约》，第18条，采用了《世界人权宣言》对宗教自由的表述。但第 4 条在论述父母对子女教育的选择权时，特别指出教育选择权包括了宗教教育："本公约缔约各国承诺，尊重父母和法定监护人保证他们的孩子能按照他们自己的信仰接受宗教和道德教育的自由"。

3、《儿童权利公约》第 14 条，更加明确了儿童也是人，也享有宗教自由："缔约国应遵守儿童享有思想、信仰和宗教自由的权利"。

4、《经济、社会、文化权利国际公约》，第 13 条，对宗教教育和儿童教育有更综合的表述，"本公约缔约各国承担，尊重父母和法定监护人的下列自由：为他们的孩子选择非公立的但系符合于国家所可能规定或批准的最低教育标准的学校，并保证他们的孩子能按照他们自己的信仰接受宗教和道德教育"。

最后，尽管中国的《教育法》确立了"教育与宗教相分离"的原则，但《教育法》第 82 条仍然提到了"宗教学校"：宗教学校教育由国务院另行规定。

　　这一规定表明，其一，《教育法》承认，"宗教学校"是一个合法的法律概念；其二，《教育法》承认，宗教学校的存在不一定与"不得利用宗教妨碍国家教育制度"相冲突；其三，《教育法》承认，它不适用于对宗教学校的管理；其四，宗教学校的设立和登记，是目前教育法治的一块空白，因为迄今为止，国务院尚未出台关于宗教学校的条例。

　　因此，让我们勇敢地宣告，归正学堂的法律身份，就是《教育法》所说的"宗教学校"。为此，我们向全能全智、掌管历史人心的主祈祷，如同家庭教会等待着、有一天能在民政部门独立登记一样；归正学堂也将等待着、有一天能在教育部门独立登记。因为归正学堂的合法性，远超过一切世俗教育的合法性；既出自中国政府不承认的万军之耶和华的命令，也合乎中国政府承认的普世的人权公约。

　　因此，在"教育与宗教相分离"的立场被修改之前，学堂和教会一样，以基督为唯一的元首，持定身份，不寻求第三条道路。因为我们的立场，是"政教分立"的立场，这是我们信仰告白的内容。在教育上，这一立场意味着"国家与教育相分离"，而不是"教育与宗教相分离"。意思是说，教育的内容，应由公民的良心和信仰自由来决定，而不是由政府来决定。一些家长误以为，自己在决定孩子接受什么样的教育。这是一种自欺欺人的假相。事实上，在教会学校出现之前，我们根本没有决定权。你决定送孩子上归正学堂，是你在决定。你决定送孩子上公立学校，这根本就不是一个决定，而是国家在替你决定。

　　我们的主啊，求真相，求智慧，求信心。我们的神啊，帮孩子，帮教会，也帮我们的政府。

　　　　　　　　为教会学校在中国的复兴而俯伏的仆人

　　　　　　　　王怡

　　　　　　　　2012 年 10 月 18 日

覆巢之下、完卵何存？

----中国儿童宗教教育状况观察

孟元新

依据联合国系列人权公约，宗教教育自由是宗教自由的一部分。何为宗教教育 (religious education)？在胡森(T.Hu-sen)等人所编的《教育国际百科全书》 (The International Encyclopedia of Education)中， 认为宗教教育包括两种类型：一是宗教教导 (religious instruction)，另一是关于宗教的教导 (instruction about religions)(Husen,T.& Postlethwaite T.N.,1994,4996)。台湾《教育百科辞典》以教育内容来定义宗教教育："以宗教教义、教规为内容的教育"(释恒清，2002)。本文儿童宗教教育界定为对儿童进行教义、教规为内容的有关宗教的知识性教导。根据中国《未成年人保护法》，"未成年人"指"未满十八周岁的公民"，因此中国法律上"未成年人"的概念与联合国公约对儿童的定义完全一致，本文所引述相关文献，"未成年人"、"未满十八周岁的公民"和"儿童"的涵义一致。事实上，中国共产党、中国政府至今根本就不承认"儿童宗教教育"这个概念。经笔者不完全的检索，还未能发现有关中国大陆儿童宗教教育主题的中文学术文章，仅有少量的讨论意见和新闻报道之类，反而反对儿童宗教教育，倡导反宗教的无神论宣传教育的中共官方文章倒是不少。本文主要通过全景式的概述中国大陆自中共 1949 年建政至今的涉及儿童宗教教育的政策，包括有关宗教和教育的政策法规以及被曝光的可能只是冰山一角的案例，重点是邓小平时代和习近平成为中共领导人以来的内容，试图较全面地反应中国儿童宗教教育的政策演变和实际发展状况，还与联合国相关人权公约和国际社会绝大多数国家的政策措施进行了简单比较。本文认为中国在所谓的习近平新时代，中国儿童宗教教育正在经历、而且即将面临日益更为严酷的类似毛泽东时代的黑暗期。

一、毛泽东时期：皮之不存，毛将焉附，政治消灭宗

教、统领教育，勿论儿童宗教教育

　　1954 年中国颁布的《中华人民共和国宪法》中，没有任何涉及宗教教育的条款，1949 -1978 年 30 年间，中国没有制定出台任何有关教育的法律法规。所以在此时期，关于中国宗教教育，不存在任何法治甚或法制因素，只有中共政策管制。毛泽东《在莫斯科共产党和工人党代表会议上的讲话》（ 1957 年 11 月 18 日）中说:"*要用唯物论代替唯心论，用无神论代替有神论。*" 1958 年 9 月 19 日，中共中央、国务院《关于教育工作的指示》，提出 "*党的教育工作方针，是教育为无产阶级的政治服务...*"。教育完全由中国共产党控制，中国儿童完全被迫接受中共以唯物主义、共产主义为核心的反宗教无神论教育。文革期间全国寺观教堂全部关闭，宗教界人士全部转业还俗，在公共场合，全国没有任何宗教活动。政治上消灭宗教，各类宗教都面临灭顶之灾，政治统领教育，何谈宗教教育，更勿论儿童宗教教育。

　　（一）针对天主教、基督教：教会学校被"接管、接收、改造"

　　早在 1949 年之前的清朝时期，中国就出现了教会学校。中国共产党 1949 年建政伊始，即开始接管教会学校，导致教会学校、基督化教育被中断。虽然 1950 年 8 月 19 日出台的《中共中央关于天主教、基督教问题的指示》还规定:"*关于教会学校...应视为私营事业，政府本公私兼顾原则，一视同仁。教会学校应遵守政府法令设政治课为必修课，同时在教会办的高等学校中亦得设宗教课为选修课，教会学校内不举行宣传宗教的或反对宗教的展览会、群众集会等。*" 但同年 11 月 30 日，属于中国天主教成都教区的四川省广元县王良佐神父等人向全国发表《自立革新宣言》，中国政府随即将天主教会举办的学校收归国有。1950 年 12 月 29 日，政务院第 65 次政务会议通过了《关于处理接受美国津贴的文化教育救济机关及宗教团体的方针的决定》，由此接收了接受美国津贴的学校。1951 年 1 月 14 日，政务院文教委员会发布《接受外国津贴及外资文化教育救济机关及宗教团体登记条例》，对各地接收外资津贴及外资经营的学校按当地规定期限进行登记。1951 年 6 月 15 日，上海《解放日报》宣称，"教会学校"这个名词已送进了历史博物馆。按照 1952 年 8 月 10 日教育部《关于接办私立中小学的指示》，包括不完全统计的 200 多所教会中学、1700 多所教会小学在内的私立中小学全部被政府接办，改为公立。从此教会学校都被中共政府接管、接收和改造。

（二）对少数民族宗教教育

1949 年前，藏、傣族中的佛教寺院，宗教和文化教育合一。维吾尔、回等民族中，既有专设的宗教学校，也有普通学校。1949 年后，宗教学校被逐步解散，一般学校中的宗教课被取消。

从 1958 年至 1960 年的宗教制度"民主"改革，主要针对伊斯兰教回民、藏传佛教。回民主要涉及宁夏回族自治区、甘肃、青海、陕西的穆斯林聚居区。藏传佛教主要涉及滇、川、甘、青等藏族聚居区。1958 年 8 月 10 日，中央统战部发布《关于在回族中改革宗教制度的意见》，同年 12 月 7 日，中央统战部批转了《民委党组关于当前伊斯兰教、喇嘛教工作问题报告》。提出："*寺院不得强迫...儿童学经文，当满拉(学习伊斯兰教知识的学生)*"，对"*阿訇等宗教职业者...使他们不要干涉...国家教育*"。由此在信仰伊斯兰教的各少数民族居住地区，废除了穆斯林少年儿童到清真寺学经、当满拉的制度。

1. 新疆：经文学校被禁止

20 世纪中共建政之初，新疆的学校教育仍分国民教育和经堂教育两种，公立和会（即各民族文化促进会）立小学也上经文课。1950 年，新疆教育部门对小学进行接管和改革，明令取缔经文学校，但并没有得到有效实施。1952 年，中共新疆分局根据宗教界的要求，在小学恢复了一周两节经文课，规定由学校老师教授，学生学习与否自愿。1953 年，新疆经文学校发展超过了 1949 年，因此在同年底新疆作出宗教不得干涉学校的决定。1956 年随着社会主义改造基本完成，新疆一些初级经文学校停办。1958 年新疆自治区再次明令取消经文学校和经文课。"文革"时期，新疆所有伊斯兰经文学校被禁止。

2. 藏区：藏传佛教寺院所剩无几，宗教教育被彻底取消

寺院教育是藏区传统教育的最主要形式之一，至今已有一千二百多年的历史，藏传佛教的寺院教育与宗教教育密切相连。1958 年的宗教改革以来，针对藏区开展了一系列有步骤的摧毁行动，不少藏传佛教寺院被政府学校占用，仅青海省 618 座藏传佛教寺院中，就有 597 处被解体。文化大革命之后，西藏自治区境内原有的 2713 座寺院仅剩下 8 座，全藏区包括青海、四川、甘肃、云南省藏区共计六千多座寺院仅剩下几十座。因此，在改革开放前，藏区藏传佛教寺院所剩无几，传统的包含儿童宗教教育的寺院教育被彻底取消。

二、邓小平时代："政策与法规、非法和合法"的纠结

邓小平时代起讫时间，没有定论。本文仅就宗教管理而言，认为邓小平时代包括邓小平正式实际成为最高领导人的 1978 年之后，按中共总书记职位更迭依次经过胡耀邦赵紫阳时期、江泽民时期、胡锦涛温家宝时期。中共延续改革开放前在国民教育中排除宗教教育的一贯方针政策，不同的是，将此内容纳入了相关教育立法条款，披上了一件法律、法制，甚至更加迷惑人的"法治"外衣。另外，对国民教育体制外的处于灰色状态的，合法与否，官方和民间存在完全不同解读的一些儿童宗教教育生态形式，中国政府的打压政策，在说法上有所缓和，在实际执行上，限于个别地区，只是选择性进行，各地执行政策法规力度和尺度把握有较大差别。

（一）国民教育：政策在后、法规在前，继续排除宗教教育

对此，2010 年 5 月，中华人民共和国外交部在《中华人

民共和国关于《儿童权利公约》执行情况的第三、四次合并报告》中也承认"*在中国国民教育体系中，不进行宗教教育。*"。

1. 教育与宗教两大原则涵义：政策和法规的细微差异

(1) "教育与宗教相分离原则"

"教育与宗教相分离原则"于中共而言可谓源远流长。早在1923 年 6 月，中国共产党第三次代表大会上通过的《中国共产党纲草案》第十二条就规定："*实行义务教育,教育与宗教相分离。*"。1995 年 3 月 18 日，第八届全国人民代表大会第三次会议通过的现行《中华人民共和国教育法》有 4 处提到宗教，其中第八条第二款规定"*...。国家实行教育与宗教相分离。任何组织和个人不得利用宗教进行妨碍国家教育制度的活动。*"。

何为"教育与宗教相分离原则"？

中国人大网 www.npc.gov.cn（2000-12-17）法律释义与问答，"为什么教育必须与宗教相分离？"中，直接涉及学校和宗教关系的回答完全采用禁止性语句，内容如下：

"*...宗教组织或者个人不得非法干预国民教育领域内的学校及其他教育机构的教育教学活动及管理事务。任何组织或者个人不得利用宗教进行妨碍国家教育制度的非法活动，不得干预学校进行自然科学知识教育和政治思想教育，不得在学校及其他教育机构内传播宗教、举行宗教仪式，也不得利用学校对在校学生灌输宗教思想，发展宗教教徒...。*"

中国宗教实际直接的领导部门中共中央统战部解释，禁止性语句和倡导性语句并重，见于"坚持宗教与国民教育相分离原则的规定"(2008-12-08 中央统战部网站)：

"*...任何组织和个人不得利用宗教干预国民教育，不得以任何形式在学校宣扬宗教；...对各族师生进一步加强无神论和唯物主义的教育，...不断增强各族师生自觉抵御封建迷信和邪教影响的能力。民办学校应当贯彻教育与宗教相分离的原则。任何组织和个人不得利用宗教进行妨碍国家教育制度的活动。*"

（2）"宗教不得干预教育"

中共中央决策文件中的表述和宪法以及系列教育法规中的表述略有差异，差异在于中共中央决策文件中有关教育概念的外延比宪法和系列教育法规中有关教育概念的外延更广泛。

中共中央决策文件中的表述

1981 年 6 月 27 日，中国共产党第十一届六中全会通过的《中国共产党中央委员会关于建国以来中国共产党的若干历史问题的决议》提出"......要求宗教不得干预......教育。"

随后的文件扩大了教育的含义，不仅指"学校教育"，还包括"社会公共教育"。1982 年 3 月 31 日，中共中央印发的《关于中国社会主义时期宗教问题的基本观点和基本政策》，即通常所说的 19 号文件指出："*社会主义的国家政权......绝不允许宗教......干预学校教育和社会公共教育，绝不允许强迫任何人特别是十八岁以下少年儿童入教、出家和到寺庙学经......*。"。1983 年 12 月 31 日，《中共中央关于在清除精神污染中正确对待宗教问题的指示》完全重复了 19 号文件的上述规定。

1990 年 7 月 14 日，《中共中央关于加强统一战线工作的通知》重申："*......宗教不得干预......学校教育和社会公共教育。*"

1994 年中共中央、国务院《关于进一步做好宗教工作若干问题的通知》中强调："*任何人不得利用宗教干预......学校教育和社会公共教育，不得利用宗教妨碍义务教育实施的活动*"。

宪法和系列教育法规中的表述

表述归纳为"任何组织/人（个人）不得利用宗教进行妨碍国家教育制度或义务教育实施的活动。"。分别出现在：1982年《中华人民共和国宪法》第三十六条第二款；自 1984 年 10 月 1 日起施行的《中华人民共和国民族区域自治法》第十一条；自 1986 年 7 月 1 日起施行的《中华人民共和国义务教育法》第十六条；自 1995 年 9 月 1 起施行的《中华人民共和国教育法》第八条 ；《宗教事务条例》（2004 年）第三条，《宗教事务条例》（2017 年）第四条。

2. 非政府办学校

一般民办学校：重申教育与宗教相分离的原则

2003 年 9 月 1 日起施行的《中华人民共和国民办教育促进法》第四条第二款规定"*民办学校应当贯彻教育与宗教相分离的原则。任何组织和个人不得利用宗教进行妨碍国家教育制度的活动*"。

涉外举办学校：特别禁止宗教参与，特别点名宗教教育

自 2003 年 9 月 1 日起施行的《中华人民共和国中外合作办学条例》第七条规定"*外国宗教组织、宗教机构、宗教院校和宗教教职人员不得在中国境内从事合作办学活动*"、"*中外合作办学机构不得进行宗教教育和开展宗教活动*"。

（二）针对基督教、天主教

1. 合法学校和非法宗教教育：基督徒社会办学遭遇"7 年之痒"

1997 年 10 月，中国开始实施《社会力量办学条例》，随后，包括基督徒在内的不同社会力量办学陆续出现。

第一批基督徒社会办学的先例中，较有社会影响的是许建一 2004 年开始举办的北京 "晨星"学校，实行走读制，从小学到高中共 12 个年级。2005 年 5 月 10 日，许建一拿到了办学许可证，2010 年 6 月，"晨星"被关闭。按许建一自己说法，主要原因是政府的过于谨慎和警惕，"我们曾经遇到过教委突然来查我们，说我们让学生读经背经，那其实是误传，只是因为我们墙上贴着很多品格教育的内容，其中有中英文圣经经

文。"

2009 年 7 月 30 日，由基督徒开办的华林外国语实验幼儿园获得广西壮族自治区柳州市鱼峰区教育局行政许可。据中新网 2015 年 7 月 17 日消息，因为被调查发现长期利用带有宗教内容的书刊进行教学，华林外国语实验幼儿园被鱼峰区教育局通报取缔。

2. 灰色的学校和非法的宗教：随时面临查处、关闭

中国基督化教育还有另外两类：父母主导的在家教育；主要由教会牧者推动，城市教会开办，以招收本教会信徒的孩子为主的没有注册为学校的教会学校。在家教育如快速基督化教育 ACE（Accelerated Christian Education）的课程，只是属于城市极少数中产精英基督徒家庭。教会主导开办基督化教育学校，不可能合法登记和许可，有的以"艺术学校"的名义注册，有的以"家教中心"或者"早教中心"的方式进行注册，有的根本就没有任何名义注册。属于灰色地带，基层政府大多默认，但常前来施加压力，随时面临查处、关闭。政府如果查处，所依据的理由往往是这些学校或中心存在超范围经营行为。这两类基督化教育与中国的公立教育无法对接，因此有家长虽然把孩子送到基督化教育的学校学习，但还保留公立学校的学籍，甚至为此给公立学校照常交费。

3. 教会儿童主日学宗教教育：基本默认和有限打压

中国教会对儿童实行宗教教育，为时很久。1940 年，中国主日学会成立，对中国儿童的早期宗教教育贡献很大。

在 20 世纪八十年代初，主要为了避免儿童吵闹而影响成人崇拜，中国大陆一些教会将成人和儿童分开，由此中国大陆开始重新出现了儿童主日学。但是，事实并非全如 2010 年《中华人民共和国关于《儿童权利公约》执行情况的第三、四次合并报告》所言："*中国法律未禁止父母和监护人向儿童进行宗教教育，政府部门对于这种行为也不予干预。信教的父母带着自己的孩子到宗教活动场所参加宗教活动，政府从未加以*

干涉。天主教、基督教举办要理班、主日学，分别对信徒子女进行宗教教育，有的宗教根据其传承特点对少数青少年进行特殊的宗教教育等，对此，政府既不鼓励，也不制止。"。

儿童主日学面临的外在困境，主要表现在个别地区的基层政府经常干涉儿童参加主日学聚会、剥夺儿童接触基督信仰权利。

（三）针对少数民族地区学校教育与宗教

针对普遍的少数民族地区学校教育与宗教问题，1983 年 2 月，中共中央办公厅、国务院办公厅转发教育部《关于正确处理少数民族地区宗教干扰学校教育问题的意见》（中办发[1983]16 号），提出 6 条规定：*(1)不得在学校向学生宣传宗教，灌输宗教思想；(2)学校不得停课集体进行宗教活动；(3)不得强迫学生信仰宗教，不得强迫他们当和尚、喇嘛或满拉等；(4)不得以任何形式在学校开设或讲授宗教课；(5)不得利用保教干扰或破坏学校的正常教学秩序；(6)不得以任何形式干扰或阻挠学校向学生进行马列主义、毛泽东思想教育和科学文化教育。*

1992 年 11 月 2 日，国家教委《关于加强民族散杂居地区少数民族教育工作的意见》提出*"坚持宗教不得干预教育的原则，并要坚持对学生进行唯物论和无神论教育，使学生树立科学的世界观和宗教观。"*。

1. 特别关注：新疆地区

（1）伊斯兰"地下"（民间）经文学校：政策内容和效果反复，矛盾升级

穆斯林传统的宗教教育形式为经堂教育（又称寺院教育），主要通过经文学校来实施。经文学校分高级、中级、初级三等；高级学校，专门培养上层宗教人士；中级学校针对成年穆斯林；初级学校，针对少年儿童。学习内容包括宗教仪式、阿拉伯文、《古兰经》、《圣训》以及伊斯兰哲学、法

学、文学等。本文所谈"地下"经文学校，指未经中国政府批准开办的初级经文学校，又称为私办经文班（点）、"民间"经文学校。因为中国政府禁止向未成年人传教，"地下"经文学校，都处于"非法"状态。从新疆针对"地下"经文学校的政策变化看，由开始的"疏导解散"变为一律"查禁取缔"；由主要关注宗教干预教育和影响儿童成长上升到了防范宗教极端势力传播和动员的高度。

改革开放后，20世纪70年代末，中共消灭宗教的政策有所缓和，新疆伊斯兰经文学校开始恢复。到了20世纪80年代，新疆很快出现了大量的"地下"经文学校。

1983年2月，中共中央办公厅、国务院办公厅转发教育部《关于正确处理少数民族地区宗教干扰学校教育问题的意见》（中办发[1983]16号），特别针对"地下"（民间）经文学校指出"*对未经政府批准擅自开办的经文学校，要逐步予以解决；某些地区民族中小学要求开设阿拉伯文课，不能同意，更不能借学习阿文之名，恢复宗教课。*"。

1984年，新疆自治区党委明令"*绝不允许私自开办经文学校*"，对于擅自开办经文学校（班），擅自在家中吸收儿童学经文的，要"积极做好疏导工作，予以解散"。

随着新疆各地穆斯林聚居的地方几乎都出现"地下"经文学校，"地下"经文学校的社会影响增大，政府的政策开始由"疏导解散"变为"查禁取缔"，开始将"地下"经文学校问题由人民内部矛盾向敌我矛盾转化。

1988年，新疆自治区专门规定，严禁地下经文学校，采取了一系列查禁取缔行动。自1990年起每年查禁"地下"经文学校1000余所，其中许多是在校学生。1994年颁布施行的《新疆维吾尔自治区宗教事务管理条例》规定：*未经批准，任何组织和个人不得私自开办宗教院校和经文班（点）。*

1997年后，新疆自治区连续多年在重点区域实行集中整治，但"地下"经文学校屡禁不止。1999年1至10月，新疆共查处"地下"经文学校118处；2004年1至10月，新疆共取缔"地下"经文学校420处；2006年1-5月，新疆共查处"地下"经文学校112处。中国人民公安大学硕士生丽扎在《新疆地区非法宗教活动现状浅析》一文中披露，"2008年，南疆三地州查处地下学经人员 1320 人。"

（2）合法学校:明令禁止宗教活动

在官方文件标题中出现"在学校禁止宗教活动"始于 1996
年的新疆地区。1996 年 2 月 2 日，新疆维吾尔自治区教育委
员会出台《关于在学校禁止宗教活动的规定》（适用于除宗教
学校以外的各级各类学校），提出："*社会主义的学校...禁止
任何形式的宗教活动，任何宗教组织和个人不得在学校内（包
括校办工厂、农场、实习基地等）和学校毗邻的地方修建和设
立清真寺及寺庙、道观，已经修建或成立的有限期拆除或搬
迁；不得招收在校学生学习经文；不得妨碍学校进行辨证唯物
主义、历史唯物主义、无神论和科学文化知识的教育；不得在
学校和学生中传播宗教思想，进行宗教仪式；不得胁迫、引诱
在校学生参加宗教活动。*"。要求教师"*...不得参加宗教活动，
不得向学生传播宗教思想，不得胁迫和带领学生参加宗教活
动*"，否则"*学校应进行批评教育，教育不改的，要取消教师资
格，情节严重的，要清除出教师队伍。*"。要求学生"*不得参与
宗教活动，不得到经文学校、唱诗班读经颂诗，不封斋，不佩
戴宗教标志*"，对参与宗教活动的学生，"*学校应进行批评教
育。教育不改者，要给予纪律处分。*"

（3）禁止未成年人进入清真寺

新疆乌鲁木齐、阿尔泰等地区清真寺门口长年累月用醒目
的告示张贴着："*禁止任何公务人员、未成年人进入*"的政府公
告。

2. 特别关注：藏区儿童宗教教育

1980 年 5 月，西藏自治区党委统战部出台的《关于继续
贯彻执行党的宗教信仰自由政策的几项具体规定》和西藏自治
区党委制定的《关于全面贯彻党的宗教信仰自由和加强对宗教
活动管理的意见》中，规定：父母愿意送子女入寺当僧尼者，
寺庙应搞好经典和文化学习，待本人年满十八岁后，当僧尼与

否听其自愿。由此，中国佛协西藏分会逐步恢复了念经班、学经班制度，在一些主要寺庙开办学经班。但随后 1980 年 11 月 22 日，西藏自治区发出《关于进一步全面贯彻落实党的宗教政策的指示》，规定"*对个别利用宗教影响干涉行政教育…要进行教育，加以制止*"。

1983 年 2 月，中共中央办公厅、国务院办公厅转发教育部《关于正确处理少数民族地区宗教干扰学校教育问题的意见》（中办发[1983]16 号），六条意见中" (3)不得强迫学生信仰宗教，不得强迫他们当…喇嘛…等"特别单独针对西藏地区。

从 1996 年起，西藏开始了所谓的"爱国教育运动"，官方报纸大力宣传对儿童进行无神论教育，并诋毁达赖喇嘛。

2010 年 9 月 30 日，国家宗教事务局发布，自 2010 年 11 月 1 日起施行的《藏传佛教寺庙管理办法》第二十七条第一款规定"寺庙学经班招收的学员，……*年龄一般应当在 18 周岁以上；*"，由此，几乎等于完全排除了儿童参加寺庙学经班的机会。

三、习近平主政以来：宗教本身和儿童宗教教育再次面临全面打压

从宗教管理的角度，习近平主政以来的时期，可以分为两阶段。第一阶段：自 2012 年 11 月中共 18 大到至 2017 年 10 月中共 19 大，在宗教政策方面经历了 2016 年 9 月中国国务院法制办，就国家宗教局递交的《宗教事务条例修订草案（送审稿）》在网站上公开征求意见，2017 年 8 月新《宗教事务条例》发布等重大事件。第二阶段：2017 年 10 月 24 日，中国共产党第十九次全国代表大会通过了《中国共产党章程（修正案）》，"习近平新时代中国特色社会主义思想"写入党章，从中共的代际传承来说，中共正式进入习近平新时代。在此期间，中共出台了系列违背中共自己制定的宪法法律的政策措施，不但打压儿童宗教教育，而且禁止儿童信仰宗教，全国各地相继爆发相关逼迫案例，可谓大倒退，甚至有回归改革开放前彻底消灭儿童宗教教育的趋势。

（一）风雨欲来：所谓"新时代"来临的前奏

1. 涉及宗教教育的改革和法律修改不进反退

（1）自由贸易试验区改革，宗教教育管控反而加强

自 2017 年 7 月 10 日起实施的《自由贸易试验区外商投资准入特别管理措施（负面清单）（2017 年版）》（国办发〔2017〕51 号），不仅重申《中华人民共和国中外合作办学条例》第七条"*外国宗教组织、宗教机构、宗教院校和宗教教职人员不得在中国境内从事合作办学活动，中外合作办学机构不得进行宗教教育和开展宗教活动；*"而且还增加一条"*不得在中国境内投资宗教教育机构*"。所谓的自由贸易试验区，对宗教教育的管控，不但没有进步，反而退步。

（2）新宗教事务条例，宣布国民教育、社会教育与宗教隔绝

2017 年 8 月份出台的新《宗 教 事 务 条 例》第四十四条规定"*禁止在宗教院校以外的学校及其他教育机构传教、举行宗教活动、成立宗教组织、设立宗教活动场所。*"，还特别把旧条例"宗教团体"中有关"宗教院校"的内容提出来单列"宗教院校"一章，再次专门规定宗教教育、培训脱离国民教育。非政府组织"自由之家"发布的《2018 年全球自由度报告》也指出：新规定进一步限制了宗教自由的范围，特别是对于儿童的"宗教教育"。

2. 新疆地区：由"禁止宗教进校园"上升到"抵御和防范宗教向校园渗透"

"禁止宗教进校园"主要针对公开、直接的宗教活动，"抵御和防范宗教向校园渗透"除了针对公开、直接的宗教活动之外，还针对潜在的、间接的宗教意义的表达等。

笔者查询到 2011 -2013 年间的三份文件（笔者费劲努力也

没有找到公开的原文）：中办发〔2011〕18 号文件、新疆自治区党委《关于抵御和防范宗教向校园渗透的意见》（新党厅字[2012]27 号）和《关于进一步依法治理非法宗教活动、遏制宗教极端思想渗透工作若干指导意见（试行）》（新党办发[2013]11 号）。笔者分析应该是通过以上三份文件，特别是后两份新疆本地区的文件，新疆地区形成了"抵御和防范宗教向校园渗透"的具体政策，并提出所谓"两个不得"（*任何人不得利用宗教进行妨碍国家教育制度的活动，任何组织和个人不得在学校进行宗教活动*）。"六个严禁"（笔者只找到 5 项：*严禁在学校传播宗教思想、发展教徒；严禁在学校设立宗教活动场所、举行宗教活动； 严禁师生建立宗教团体和组织；严禁师生在校内外参加或组织参加宗教活动； 严禁穿戴宗教服饰、佩戴宗教标志。*"）。另外，在一篇题为"阿克陶镇努克其小学"六个严禁"的措施"（落款为 2014 阿克陶镇努克其小学）的网络文章中，提到如下"六个禁止"：

1、禁止宗教活动进校园；2、禁止宗教行为进校园（师生不得在校园在家里有宗教行为的活动，一经发现造成不良后果的直接开除）；3、禁止宗教言论进校园； 4、禁止宗教服饰进校园（师生不得戴头巾，不得穿奇装异服）；5、禁止宗教思想进校园（师生不得有宗教思想，不能信教）；6、禁止宗教信仰进校园（师生不能参与宗教信仰的一切活动）。

2014 年 10 月 31 日，《兵团日报》披露：喀什地区教育系统开展"抵御宗教向校园渗透千名校长宣誓暨签名仪式"。

2016 年 5 月 6 日，亚心网题为"新疆喀什市第一中学：坚决不能让宗教走进学校的大门"披露：每天班主任都会在班里强调有关学生不能信教、不能参与宗教活动等方面的内容；在一中校门外的 4 个路口，每天上学前和放学后的半个小时，都有教师值班，观察学生是否有穿戴宗教服饰等不当行为。

2017 年 4 月 11 日，新疆维吾尔自治区教育厅"印发《围绕总目标做好学校安全稳定工作的指导意见》的通知"（新教维稳〔2017〕1 号）要求：坚决抵御和防范宗教向校园渗透，将"六个严禁"切实落实到学校规章制度、日常管理中。

3. 内地省份甘肃省严禁各种宗教活动进校园

2016 年 5 月初，一段名为"甘肃可爱的背经小女孩"的视频在网上流传，反映甘肃临夏某幼儿园孩子背诵古兰经。之后，甘肃省教育厅要求各级教育部门严禁各种宗教活动进校园，对除经政府批准设立的宗教院校外的各级各类学校提出 6 条要求：*（1）不得进行宗教活动；（2）不得开设宗教课或向学生传播宗教，不得组织学生到宗教活动场所开展教学和实践活动，干扰、阻挠学校向学生进行思想品德和科学文化教育；（3）不得强迫、诱使学生信仰宗教，更不得在学校内从事任何发展教徒、成立宗教团体和组织的活动；（4）中等和中等以下学校的教材不得有宣传宗教思想的内容；（5）学生不得参加非法的宗教组织和宗教聚会活动；（6）教师不得利用工作之便，在教学中进行宗教宣传和带领学生参加宗教活动，严禁外籍教师在学校从事传播宗教的活动。*

4. 多省区禁止儿童参加宗教场所内外所有活动

各地禁止儿童参加宗教场所内外所有活动，继歌舞厅和网吧之后，教会场所成为中国第三个禁止未成年人入内的场所。基督教新闻网站"世界守望观察站"2017 年 8 月曾报导，内蒙古、河南省、江苏省、浙江省和福建省等地，禁止儿童参与推广宗教信仰的夏令营等活动。

2016 年 6 月 15 日，贵州省遵义市桐梓县花秋镇家庭教会主日学被派出所公安警察和镇政法委书记骚扰，要求儿童不要参加聚会。6 月 23 日，花秋镇全镇的中小学校发给学生家长的"告知书"称：*根据上级会议精神及要求，严禁将未成年人带进有关教会组织的场所，并参加有关活动等。*花秋镇综合治理办公室和派出所还多次警告该教会，不得带未成年子女参加聚会，一旦发现，将取消他们高考或参军的资格。

2016 年 8 月 4 日，新疆维吾尔自治区伊犁地区新源县一个基督教会的负责人周燕华和信徒高敏，因为组织信徒的孩子出外旅游，参加夏令营活动，结果高敏、周燕华分别被拘留 15 天、10 天。拘留的理由是以宗教迷信思想教导未成年儿童。

2017 年 7 月 13 日，河南省政府控制下的基督教三自爱国运动委员会和省基督教协会，向下属各基督教两会发出一份通知称，各地两会及各堂点，均不得举办有在校生和青少年参加的夏令营活动。当地部分三自教会往年都会举行青少年夏令营活动，一般情况下，政府人员不会过问。

2017 年 8 月初，浙江省温州各县市及乡镇的政府工作人员和派出所公安，向各教会发出通知，警告信徒不得带自己的子女进入教堂参加主日学等宗教活动，更不准组织青少年夏令营活动。官员还到每个教堂监督和检查，派人在教堂"蹲点"。

5. 出现限制基督教会设立儿童学习班

2017 年 7 月，河南省商丘市夏邑县郭店乡朱庄村一家庭教会创办的一所为培养儿童品德所设立的神学班家庭式书院，被当地公安及宗教部门查封。

（二）似曾相识:习近平的新时代还是毛泽东的旧时代

1. 涉及宗教教育的改革和法律修改核心：中共直接管控

（1）党管宗教：名实合一

邓小平时代，中共对宗教的管理，虽然人所共知是共产党操控，但名义上的中央宗教事务管理部门国家宗教事务局还是隶属于政府国务院。2018 年两会后发布的中共中央《深化党和国家机构改革方案》，原属国务院的国家宗教事务局并入中央统战部，不再保留单设的国家宗教事务局。宗教事务部门脱离政府国务院，直接隶属中共中央统战部，信仰无神论的中共从以前的幕后间接管理宗教，抛开所谓的政府，走上前台，直接管控宗教，赤裸裸毫不掩饰党管宗教。

（2）民办学校：面临"党管民办"

2018 年 4 月 20 日，教育部发布关于《中华人民共和国民办教育促进法实施条例（修订草案）（征求意见稿）》公开征求意见的公告。核心修订在于增加的第四条 "*民办学校应当坚持中国共产党的领导，坚持社会主义办学方向，坚持教育公益性，落实立德树人根本任务。民办学校中的中国共产党基层组织贯彻党的方针政策，发挥政治核心作用，依据法律、本条例和国家有关规定参与学校重大决策并实施监督。*"，其它主要修订条款也无不围绕此进行。即将出台的新版民办教育促进法实施条例，相比 2004 年 4 月 1 日起施行的《中华人民共和国民办教育促进法实施条例》（国务院令第 399 号），出现根本性的倒退，中国的民办学校不但将与公办学校无异，而且面临更加严酷的监督，名为民办，实际上将沦为"党管民办"。

2. 禁止儿童参加宗教场所内外所有活动，从边疆少数民族地区向汉族省份扩大，有推向全国之势

2018 年 1 月 19 日，法新社引述中国官媒《环球时报》报道称，甘肃省临夏回族自治州广河县向幼儿园、中小学发通知，要求禁止学生寒假期间进入宗教场所参加活动，不得到经文学校、宗教场所学习诵读经文，并要求学校加强思想政治教育工作，做好宣传工作。

2018 年 4 月 8 日，河南省天主教爱国会、河南省天主教教务委员会发布《关于限制/不准未成年人进入教堂的通知》，声称"根据 4 月 3 日省宗教局关于"坚持宗教与教育相分离原则"，和落实《宗教事务条例》"宗教活动场所不得举行各种形式的培训班向未成年传播宗教教育"的要求，请各地市两会依照执行："一、全省宗教活动场所内不得举办未成年人宗教教育培训、或其它如冬令营、夏令营等形式的学习班。二、劝戒去教堂做礼拜望弥撒的教友把孩子交给别人托管，不要带进教堂。"，并说明"针对以上这些问题，过去是以宣传教育为主，现在却是红线高压线，不要不当回事。四、如果不听要求，会对场所负责人追究责任、取消教职人员备案资格、关闭活动场所。"事实上，这份通知的依据之一"宗教活动场所不得举行各种形式的培训班向未成年传播宗教教育"，在新《宗教事务条例》中完全不存在，属于无中生有、捏造妄称。

2018 年 4 月以来，杞县天主堂的门墙上和门头上挂着"宗

教活动场所不得向未成年人传教"等横幅标语。

2018 年 4 月 1 日复活节当天，河南郑州教区天主教堂正举行弥撒时，政府人员公然冲进驱赶孩子。此后每星期天，教堂门外都停着执法车，执法人员把守教堂大门，不准教友带孩子进入教堂，连怀抱的幼童也不允许。

2018 年 4 月初，政府在河南安阳教区主教座堂外强行挂着"未成年人不能进入教堂"的宣传牌，星期天，派执法人员把守教堂大门。安阳地区学校老师让学生报告父母是否信教，信什么教，并要求父母去学校登记自己的宗教信仰状况。2018 年 4 月 11 及 12 日，河南省安阳林州市第九小学和郑州荥阳市城关乡第一小学，分别发出《未成年人为什么不能进宗教场所——致全市中小学生家长的公开信》，称：*任何组织和个人引导、支持、允许、纵容未成年人信教，参加宗教活动均属违法行为；不论家长是否信教，都要教育孩子不进入宗教活动场所、不参与宗教活动及培训班*等。公开信需家长签名并写上学生姓名及班别。

2018 年 4 月初，河南商丘教区政府挨家挨户宣传，"*现在不让信教了，谁再信教，孩子不让上学，老人补助金扣除，再不听劝，开除公职，家有退休人员的工资也不发了。*"

2018 年 4 月 17 日，河南新乡教区焦作新区北西尚教堂中的儿童圣经和书籍被政府人员收走。

中共宁夏中宁县大战场镇"大战场镇党发（2018）2 号"标题为"中宁县宗教活动场所实施方案"的红头文件，提出了对宗教的八点排查意见，其中第四点规定"*18 岁以下的未成年人，不能进寺学习*"，第五点规定"*小学生寒暑假期，一律不能进寺*"。

2018 年 4 月 30 日，一份来自网络"中国教会的境遇和呼吁——为即将来到和已经来到的环境举手"，将全国各地不同程度遭遇的逼迫措施，总结归纳为十八条，与儿童宗教教育有关的有两条："*第一、青年聚会全部停掉，让学生回家撕掉家里的十字架纸画；第十六、未满 18 周岁以下不准进教堂，主日学全部取消，老师落实学生为什么要信耶稣？*"

3. 全国中小学校普遍开展抵御和防范宗教

教育部基础教育司《关于做好 2018 年中小学生安全教育工作的通知》，强调"防止宗教向学校渗透"，具体要求"*要加大国家宗教政策及相关法律法规宣传力度，加强学校教育管理工作，抓好学生德育工作和教职工思想政治工作，增强防范宗教向学校渗透的意识和能力。深入开展无神论和科学文化教育，组织开展丰富多彩的主题教育活动，引导学生树立科学正确的世界观、人生观和价值观。*"

2018 年 1 月 11 日，广西《贺州日报》报道：昭平县委政法委联合县委宣传部、县委统战部、县公安局、县教育局及民宗局开展"防范宗教进校园"活动，活动覆盖昭平中学、昭平一小等 8 所学校 900 余名教师。

2018 年 3 月份，网上流传一份据信是河南省教育部门发布的《校园宗教政策告知书》，内容包括：*学校是教育的地方*，"*是为党和国家培养社会主义建设者的阵地*"，任何组织不得在校内从事和开展传播宗教；"*个人、集体祷告、相互讨论宗教内容*"都属违法行为；学生，不得带校内同学及朋友参加校外宗教活动；班主任需把有关内容逐条告知学生，让学生遵守；学生需要写下传达人和被告知人的名字，及告知的时间和地点。

2018 年 4 月下旬，山东省济宁、邹城市各小学教师接到校方通知，称根据济宁、邹城市民宗局《关于贯彻落实上级要求开展宗教工作情况调研和报送宗教基础数据的通知》，要求填写《学生信教情况调查表》，《教师信教情况调查表》，《学校师生信教情况表》《学校抵御和防范校园传教渗透情况表》，并将四个表格纸质版各一份及电子版一并于 4 月 28 日上午 11 时前上报。该通知还要求教师"*根据自己的情况，认真做好调查，并填好相应表格，如实上报*"，并警告教师："*过期不候。如果不如实上报情况，后果自负*"。

4. 前所未有规模限制教会背景办学

河南安阳教区卫辉堂区纸坊教会天爱幼儿园于 2018 年 2 月 14 日和 3 月 14 日，以"证件不全"为由，两度遭中国公安查封，彻底不准再办。但各方面设施都不如天爱幼儿园的几个非教会幼儿园，都没有被查。

数月前，北京市昌平区政府不断向房东施压，催促与北京基督教爱加倍教会创办的八福公学解除租赁合同。在压力下，八福公学小学部于 2018 年 1 月搬迁。3 月 29 日清晨 5 点多，数十名保安员在警察的保护下，围堵八福公学幼儿园大门，并剪断大门上的铁锁，闯入园内强行将值班人员赶走，搬走幼儿的桌椅、书本等教学用品，并使用盾牌、铁叉等防暴器械威胁教师和学生家长，还驱逐教师，打伤家长信徒。

2018 年 4 月 16 日，约二十位宗教局和教育局的人员到厦门一教会创办的幼儿园，调查幼儿园的班级、教材及学生名单等情况，并登记宗教类印刷品。带头的人称，该学校未经登记，属于"非法办学"，称他们"接到群众举报"，因此前来调查。

四、纵横两方面比较

（一）纵向：从毛、邓到习，根本相同和不同

1. 根本相同：只许州官放火，"无神论"、"唯物主义"、"社会主义"为核心的反宗教官方信仰统领教育

中共建政以来的官方意识形态一直是唯物主义，唯物主义本身带有反宗教倾向。中国没有"学校宗教教育"概念，中小学作为义务教育，不管是有神论者，无论何种宗教家庭的孩子，还是无神论者家的孩子，都被强制性要求接受无神论教育。反对和批判宗教是中共教育系统无神论宣传的主要内容，污蔑宗教 是"精神鸦片"、"封建迷信"、"愚昧"等，教唆儿童仇视、蔑视、远离宗教。

《中华人民共和国教育法》第一章总则有 12 处提到"主义"，其中 9 处提到"社会主义"，"马克思列宁主义"、"爱国主义""集体主义"各 1 次，提到 "毛泽东思想"1 次。强调教育以"马克思列宁主义、毛泽东思想和建设有中国特色社会主义理论"为指导，发展社会主义的教育事业。"集体主义、爱国主

义、社会主义教育"，是教育的首要内容。《小学管理规程》（1996 年 3 月 9 日国家教育委员会令第 26 号发布），第六条规定小学的培养目标首要就是 "初步具有爱祖国、爱人民、爱劳动、爱科学、爱社会主义的思想感情…"。

2. 所谓不同：不许百姓点灯，排斥宗教的执行力度，略有不同

上述从毛泽东到习近平，中共在学校中禁止宗教，并且干涉儿童校外参与宗教活动的政策其实从来没有大的改变。只不过因为中国是人治社会，因领导人个性和要求不同而执行力度不同。笔者认为习近平似乎在各方面都在有意模仿效法毛泽东，毛泽东关于年轻人的名言"你们是早晨 8、9 点钟的太阳"，我想他更应是耳熟能详，因此习近平针对年轻人信教特别重视，也许与习近平对毛泽东成功利用年轻人（如红卫兵的作用）的认知有关。另外 2018 年两会后，依中共中央《深化党和国家机构改革方案》，宗教事务部门脱离政府国务院，直接隶属中共中央统战部，现在是赤裸裸毫不掩饰的党管宗教，都可能对政策执行力度的加强产生了影响。

（二）横向：国际比较

1. 完全违背联合国系列人权公约中涉及儿童宗教教育权利的条款

《世界人权宣言》第二十六条第三款规定"*父母对其子女所应受的教育的种类，有优先选择的权利*"。《消除基于宗教或信仰原因的一切形式的不容忍和歧视宣言》第五条规定"*1. 父母或法定监护人有权根据他们的宗教或信仰，并考虑到他们认为子女所应接受的道德教育来安排家庭生活。2. 所有儿童均应享有按照其父母或法定监护人意愿接受有关宗教或信仰方面的教育的权利；不得强迫他们接受违反其父母或法定监护人意愿之宗教或信仰的教育，关于这方面的指导原则应以最能符合儿童的利益为准。*"中国政府签署的《公民权利和政治权利国际公约》第十八条第四款，承认父母的教育主权："*本公约缔*

约各国承担，尊重父母和法定监护人保证他们的孩子能按照他们自己的信仰接受宗教和道德教育的自由"。中国政府批准的《经济、社会、文化权利国际公约》第三条规定，*"尊重父母和法定监护人的下列自由：为他们的孩子选择非公立的但符合于国家所可能规定或批准的最低教育标准的学校，并保证他们的孩子能按照他们自己的信仰接受宗教和道德教育"*。中国政府加入的联合国《儿童权利公约》第十四条，从儿童的角度阐明儿童应享有宗教教育的权利，*"缔约国应遵守儿童享有思想、信仰和宗教自由的权利。缔约国应尊重父母并于适用时尊重法定监护人以下的权利和义务，以符合儿童不同阶段接受能力的方式指导儿童行使其权利"*。

对照上述条款，不难得出结论：中国政府没有遵守任何一条国际社会有关儿童接受宗教教育自由权利的规定，长期以来中国政府完全无视并粗暴践踏中国亿万儿童接受宗教教育的权利，并且现在正在以更加明目张胆、肆无忌惮、触目惊心的政策使这一局面继续延续下去。

2. 与国际儿童宗教教育发展趋势背道而驰、渐行渐远

如果区分公立学校和私立学校，自现代民族国家形成与发展以来，国际儿童宗教教育发展有两种类型：第一种，宗教多元国家，公立学校不允许进行宗教教育，而私立学校则允许，例如美国、日本、韩国等；第二种，有国教的国家，国家推动以国教为主的宗教教育，公立学校必须进行宗教教育，私立学校自便，如许多伊斯兰教国家和泰国等佛教国家。

第一种类别，即将宗教内容排除在公共教育之外的国家，现在有重新考虑把宗教教育纳入公立学校的趋势。比如法国曾严格遵行宗教与公立学校分开，并且认为教派的教育(the denominational education)属于单纯私人性、教会事务，现在已经重新将宗教作为公立学校的教育内容。中国特别行政区《中华人民共和国香港特别行政区基本法》第一百三十七条、《中华人民共和国澳门特别行政区基本法》第一百二十八条，都有相同的规定："宗教组织所办的学校可继续提供宗教教育，包括开设宗教课程"。

因此，中国大陆现行钳制儿童宗教教育的政策与国际儿童宗教教育发展趋势也是背道而驰，且渐行渐远。

五、前瞻：覆巢之下、完卵何存？

凡事皆有迹可循！早在 2006 年，习近平在担任浙江省委书记时，就主导了当时堪称自文革结束以来规模最大、因而震惊中外的"萧山教案"：浙江省杭州市萧山区使用暴力强行拆毁萧山教会自己兴建的教堂，数十名教徒遭殴打，数十人被非法羁押，8 名基督徒被判处重刑。无独有偶，很难相信不是在习近平的授意下，在习近平曾经主政五年的浙江自 2014 年发生全省强拆十字架的运动（时任省委书记夏宝龙于 2018 年两会高升为全国政协副主席皆秘书长，位列中共所谓党和国家领导人，成为仅次于负责主管宗教事务的中共政治局常委政协主席汪洋的管理宗教的实权人物）。任何不带偏见的关注中国宗教迫害的人士都会承认，中共迫害宗教之暴虐，西藏为最。因 2011-2016 年 8 月主政西藏有功，2016 年 9 月开始，陈全国调职新疆，并于 19 大高升政治局委员，把迫害藏传佛教的所谓"治藏经验"全盘应用到了新疆伊斯兰教上。2017 年习近平在中共 19 大上，名字列入党章，在 2018 年中国两会上，又废除了宪法中自改革开放以来仅有的可视为政治意义上进步的国家主席任期限制条款。

没有最疯狂，只有更疯狂。2018 年 3 月底，中国各大网络电商接到通知：2018 年 3 月 30 日起，淘宝、京东及微店，禁止出售《圣经》。2018 年 4 月 23 日，习近平中共中央政治局就《共产党宣言》及其时代意义举行第五次集体学习。这是自 2002 年 12 月 26 日，十六届中共中央政治局集体学习，即中央政治局首次集体学习以来，合计 125 次中唯一、也是首次学习以共产主义"幽灵"信仰为中心的《共产党宣言》。笔者用"中共领导人学习《共产党宣言》"检索网络，没有发现完全相同的字样，只是在一篇"中共领导人与《共产党宣言》"（2017-12-01 中安在线-安徽日报农村版(合肥)）中提到，中共领导人毛泽东、刘少奇、周恩来、邓小平等读过《共产党宣言》。

当下习近平领导下的中国，无论何种宗教，都面临自文革结束以来最严峻的时期，最黑暗的文革时期、宗教在公开领域完全消失的噩梦，仿佛就在眼前。中国儿童宗教教育不但继续在公立教育系统绝迹，而且自改革开放至今在一些民办学校特别是教会信徒主办和涉外主办的民办学校中灰色存在的零星宗教教育，也几乎散失了任何存在的空间，更有甚者，儿童与父母一起到宗教场所体验宗教、以及相互一起参加学校和宗教场所之外的有关宗教机构组织的娱乐活动也被完全剥夺。

笔者将宗教面临的外在环境与儿童宗教教育，比拟为鸟巢和灵魂上需要遮风避雨生存成长的幼鸟。覆巢之下，焉有完卵。中国儿童宗教教育再次面临绝境，中国有宗教信仰的家庭再次面临代际传承的危机，中国各宗教再次面临在年轻一代中断的危机！虽然我们相信超越理性的宗教是任何包括中共及其党魁习近平的思维极限所不能够企及的，至高的主宰必不会使儿童宗教教育在中国就此销声匿迹。但我们也不得不担心：覆巢之下、完卵何存？也许更加需要我们回答的是，面对中国数以亿计的儿童遭受被剥夺接受宗教教育的自由权利，中国宗教自身和国际宗教团体以及享有儿童宗教教育自由的国际社会能够为此切实做些什么？！

参考文献

1. 方永泉（台湾）.從當代西方宗教教育理論看我國宗教教育的可能性

2. 靖东阁. "教育与宗教相分离"原则下藏区学校教育与寺院教育互补研究

3.何一平.大陆教會學校的消失
（
http://www.open.com.hk/content.php?id=953#.Wu57HaSFPIU）

4. 周泓. 民国时期新疆民族宗教教育与国民教育的并行《西北民族研究》 2001 年 02 期

5. 滕志妍. 西方国家公立学校中的宗教政策模式探析《外

国教育研究》2008 年第 9 期

6. 李 晓 霞 ． 新 疆 地 下 讲 经 的 前 世 今 生
http://blog.caijing.com.cn/expert_article-151687-68866.shtml

督教信仰和残障儿童教育

--面对弱势群体主内草根机构的挑战和可能性

佐藤千歳

弃婴，应该是人类社会中最弱势的特殊群体[25]。而在这些孩子 中更为弱势的，是有着维持生理功能障碍，比如呼吸器官障碍的残障弃婴。残障弃婴的小小生命之火，如果没有他人伸出手来帮助，会在一瞬间消失于黑暗中。

现在在中国，为保护弃婴的生命，以及支持他们的成长而设立的福利教育系统还在建设中。因此，福利院等福利单位不足，儿童福利制度不完善，教育制度地区间差距大，以及政府的不作为等多种因素，造成了在中国各地存在着得不到政府支持的弃婴孤儿问题。而代替父母或政府，承担这些从政策安全网中漏下的生命的养育责任，则是主内的民间团体。

本文，从常年从事孤残儿童的抚养和教育工作的主内民间团体中，分别列举出基督教和天主教的团体，考察在残障儿童抚养教育中的基督徒的特色以及其社会性意义。本文中所列举的都是和未在政府登记的非公认教会（基督教的"家庭教会"和天主教的"地下教会"）有着紧密的关系，受习近平政府宗教紧缩政策影响很大的团体。本文将从福利教育政策及宗教政策的角度来分析这两个团体所直面的困难处境，并指出，中国共产党政权的宗教管理制度已成为儿童福利教育事业中侵害儿童基本人权的原因这一事实。

1. 弃婴，中国社会的最弱势群体

（1）中国孤儿现状及宗教团体

---

[25]民政部、国家发展和改革委员会、公安部、司法部、财政部、国家卫生和计划生育委员会、国家宗教事务局[关于进一步做好弃婴相关工作的通知]民发〔2013〕83号

根据中国民政部的数字，截至 2015 年底、全国共有孤儿 50.2 万人，其中集中供养孤儿 9.2 万人，社会散居孤儿 41 万人[26]。

这里的"孤儿"是指，未满 14 岁且父母双亡或由人民法院宣告父母死亡的未成年人。在这 50 万孤儿中，被称为"社会散居"的，即在祖父母或亲戚，或养父母的家庭中生活的孤儿，占总体的 8 成以上。剩下的不到 20%的孤儿是"集中收养"的对象，在地方政府和民间的福利机构生活[27]。

集中收养的主流是各地方政府经营的"儿童福利院"。另一方面，全国有大约 1 万人的孤儿和弃婴在民间的福祉团体或个人经营的福利机构中生活。这里值得注意的是，集中收养孤儿和弃婴的民间机构中，教会和寺院等有宗教背景的机构占全体的 74%[28]。儿童福利机构全体的大多数为公营的福利院，但民间的福利机构的主流则是具有宗教背景的团体和个人。

中国民政部规定，发现弃婴的公民，需通报给居民委员会或村民委员会，经公安部门发放"弃婴证明"，由公营的儿童福利机构接收弃婴。但是现实情况是，基层政府的负责人或不熟悉弃婴接收手续；或制衡于计划生育政策，使得公安局发放"弃婴证明"很不顺畅；导致有的弃婴不能顺利进入福利机构。

接收这些在法律上不被承认为"孤儿"，且没有法律上的身份的这些弃婴的，是有宗教背景的福利机构和个人。除了天主教、基督教这些主内宗教团体以外，还有佛教和伊斯兰教的团体和个人也在收养弃婴和孤儿。但是，据业内人士指出，"佛教和伊斯兰教多接收健康儿童，对重度残障儿童的接收还是以

---

[26] ［让大龄孤儿更好融入社会（观点）］冯华朱峻仪《人民日报》（2017 年 06 月 09 日 17 版）

[27] 弃婴中，包含因为政府不承认人民法院宣布的父母死亡证明，或者用来证明被遗弃的证明文件，而导致在中国的法律上不被承认的"孤儿"。包含儿童福利院在内的儿童保育机构，收养的是弃婴和孤儿。

[28] 民政部等、民发〔2013〕83 号

主内宗教的团体和个人为中心"[29]。在残障儿童福利教育事业中，不论是否被公认，主内背景的团体的贡献都是不可小视的。

（2）中国的儿童福利政策中的"灰色空间"

联合国儿童基金会（UNICEF）将孤儿定义为 18 岁以下、其父母一方或双方因任何死因丧生的儿童[30]。

与上文的联合国儿童基金会的定义相比，中国政府对孤儿的定义范围要更窄。这导致，接受不到所需要的支持和保护的"事实孤儿"成为一个显着的社会问题[31]。"事实孤儿"是指，没有抚养人，生存有困难，但是在法律上不被承认为"孤儿"，接受不到适当的支持，被剥夺了受教育的机会的未成年人。

在这些事实孤儿当中，在第一节论述过的下述事例存在。①由于各种原因不具备父母的死亡证明或弃婴证明的孤儿；②父母一方未死亡，但由于服役或疾病以及精神或身体上的残障，不具备抚养儿童的能力或缺乏抚养意愿；③父母双方未死亡，但因为与②相同的理由而不具备抚养儿童的能力或缺乏抚养意愿。

像这样的"事实孤儿"，据"检察日报"称，现在可确认的在全国至少有 61 万人。而不包含在统计中的事实孤儿大量存在的可能性非常高[32]。满足法律规定的条件的"政府公认"的孤儿有 50 万人，这和"事实孤儿"的 61 万人相比，有 11 万人的差距。此外，有人指出，即使被法律承认为孤儿，也存在由于"地方政府的不作为及监管机构的缺欠"导致的没能成为支援对

---

[29] 根据 2017 年进行的采访

[30] 联 合 国 儿 童 基 金 会 官 方 网 站 （https://www.unicef.org/zh/media/%E5%AD%A4%E5%84%BF%E9%97%AE%E9%A2%98）

[31] "全国现有事实孤儿至少 61 万人救助困局亟待破解" 《检察日报》，2017 年 11 月 22 日

[32] 同上

象的孩子[33]。作为这种情况的典型，熊丙奇（2013）列举了因贫困 导致地方政府没有设立儿童福利院的河南省的事例[34]。

上述这种"事实孤儿"，虽然是现实上的"孤儿"，但是却被排除在官方支持对象之外。换言之，他们是由于儿童福利制度的不完善而从安全网中遗漏的儿童，也显示了中国的儿童福利制度中的"灰色空间"。

（3）与日本的比较

日本在上世纪中叶，以 1945 年战败而激增的战争孤儿为契机，1947 年制定了儿童福祉法，在早期就建立起了包含战争孤儿在内的儿童保育体制。现在在日本，需要抚养的未满 18 岁的儿童全部为儿童保育制度的对象，接受保护，支持以及经济上的保障。其中，除父母双亡或父母生死不明的弃婴之外，父母未死亡但是由于疾病或服役等理由无法抚养儿童或没有抚养意愿的儿童，受父母虐待的儿童也包含在内。判断儿童是否成为儿童保育的对象，是由地方政府的负责部门"儿童咨询处"对每个儿童进行调查，来确定保护的方法。和中国政府的这种由孤儿提供"弃婴证明"或"父母死亡证明"的制度相比，可以看出日本的制度更具有包容性。这种包容性是由该制度设立 70 年来积累下的经验而产生的，但和西方国家相比，投入到儿童福利政策的财政支出还很少。

日本的儿童福利院大多是地方政府批准的民间团体"社会福利法人"来经营的。地方政府仅限于经营接管重度残障儿童的福利机构，或接管违背道德及使用暴力的案例中的儿童的福利机构。政府对于民间的社会福利法人，全额援助其人员开支和儿童的养育费用。民间的法人则接受政府对其运营状况的监督。

关于宗教团体，主内宗教或佛教的团体在历史上作为社会福利法人多被认可。是否有宗教背景不会影响对这些团体批准

---

[33] 张惠，2014. 当前我国孤儿救助体系的现状与问题，《中南林业科技大学学报》，2014 年 2 期
[34] 熊丙奇，2013. "非法收养"和"黑幼儿园"，《商周刊》2013 年 02 期

的过程。在日本，传统的主内宗教和佛教团体有着自战前开始经营慈善团体的历史，因此现在，他们有稳定的资金，更容易被政府批准为社会福利法人。

2. 由家庭教会信徒组织的民间机构

笔者通过进行持续性的田野调查，考察了主内基督教信徒从事残障儿童的看护和教育工作的事例。该事例是位于中国北部大都市 A 近郊的民间儿童福利机构 B[35]。至今为止的调查结果显示，基督徒经营的福利机构的特色有两个。第一，这些机构中已 形成了基于福音信仰的独立自主的教育、保育方针；第二，这些机构与多家地方政府有着复杂的政教关系。

（1）位于大城市郊区，抚养重度残障儿童

在中国的大都市 A 市，解放前从 19 世纪开始，就有多个基督教教会在此建立教会，欧美差会通过教会学校和儿童福利院来支持当地的儿童福利和教育工作。从社会主义革命到文化大革命，信徒数虽有暂时性的减少，但进入 1980 年代后，和中国其他地方一样基督教会的活动重新兴起了。特别是进入 1990 年代后，A 市随着快速的城市化进程，不属于那些政府公认的"三自系统"的"新兴城市家庭教会"陆续的建立起来了。

新兴城市家庭教会中，白领，学生，知识分子等集中到一起，这些信徒，对于社会贡献和志愿者活动的热情很高。福利机构 B 就是由这样的新兴城市家庭教会的信徒设立的草根型NPO。

在中国国内，弃婴中残障儿童的比例很高，这是中国政府也认识到的严重的社会问题之一[36]。残障儿童的养育需要很高的医疗和护理技术，教育方面也需要特殊性的支持。而且对于包含残障儿童在内的弃婴，要让他们有健全的人格，有赖于

---

[35]为保护协助调查人员及儿童的隐私，人名地名均为化名。

[36]民政部等、民发〔2013〕83 号

培养他们与福利院职工之间一对一的、具有信任感的人际关系的形成。但是到现在为止，国内的儿童福利院中，照顾残障儿童的经济上和人员上的资源匮乏，重视一对一的人际关系的照顾更是不可能的。残障儿童中很多人是脑瘫等疾病的患儿，这类疾病需要定期接受医疗诊断，但是因为上述的理由，他们并不能接受到必要的诊断，甚至有时会危及生命。

针对这种情况，在 1990 年代，将儿童福利院中的残障儿童接出来，让他们在一般家庭中生活一段时间的家庭寄宿，以及让他们接受医疗机构的会诊的救助活动在中国民间推广开了。B 机构的创始人张女士就是从外地的福利院接收了一名全身麻痹的男孩儿来自己家里家庭寄宿。后来张女士发现，本来面无表情的男孩儿，因为自己一直在身边陪伴，男孩儿在很短的时间里有了明显的喜怒哀乐的表达。对于这段经历，张女士幽默的开玩笑说："那是我的初恋。"同时她感到，在照料残障儿童的同时，重视与他们的一对一的人际关系的建立是非常重要的。于是她联系了同属家庭教会的朋友们，一起设立了残障儿童保育为主的 B 机构。

在 B 机构，生活着 20 位未满 20 岁的残障儿童。他们都是因为看护困难，经各地的福利院同意而接收的孩子。他们全部都是脑瘫或癫痫，或者唐氏综合症等身体或精神障碍的患儿，需要 24 小时的看护。在工作的分工上，同为机构创始人的张女士的朋友孙女士，负责机构的经营方针，以及筹集资金。机构雇佣的 15 名职工，负责昼夜交替的照顾孩子们的饮食和大小便等生活上的照料。另外，A 市的基督教信徒以及他们的朋友们，主要作为志愿者，在周末参与照看孩子们的工作。B 机构的活动，靠着国内外的捐赠资金和物资来维持。超过一半的捐赠者是基督徒，在中国国内，来自非基督徒的社会人士的捐赠的资金和物资也很多。

包含张女士在内，机构职工的工资水平是"和 A 市从事相同工作的人相比要低一些。"B 机构不属于某家特定的基督教会，但它的创始人和职工全部是基督徒。

（2）以信仰为基础的"模拟家庭"

B 机构最大的特点就是，儿童和职工保持着"长期性的关系"的家庭式的养育模式。如在第一节论述过的，张女士意识到"大规模的儿童福利院中孩子太多，孩子们得不到必要的关心"的问题才设立了 B 机构，所以 B 机构的人际关系是偏向于"模拟家庭"的关系的。张女士被孩子们以及职工称为"妈妈"，她担任的是母亲的角色；父亲的角色则由性格像男性的孙女士来担任，入园儿童则全部是妈妈的"孩子们"。当然，一个母亲与 20 个孩子每个人都保持着紧密的关系是不可能的，所以承担孩子们成长的重任的是被称为"阿姨"、"叔叔"的职工们。

在 B 机构中，孩子们以年龄性别以及残障程度划分成 3～5 人/一间房间来生活。每个房间有固定的负责职工，这些职工与孩子们保持着长期且稳定的关系。很多孩子不能说话，但职工们通过孩子的细微的表情或声音的变化，就能读取孩子们想表达的意思，比如"抱我"、"想吃东西"、"想听音乐"。职工们对于从婴儿期就开始照料的孩子们有强烈的感情，每个人都有各自的"喜欢的"孩子。同样，每个孩子都有他们喜欢的职工。这样一对一的感情关系的建立，对孩子们的精神上的发育有促进作用。

在卧床不起的脑瘫患儿的房间里看到的细节，打动了笔者。在帮忙给孩子换尿布时，笔者无意识的看了一下天花板，发现白色的天花板上贴满了长颈鹿、狮子、大猩猩等孩子们喜欢的动物的画。我们"健康人"平时日常生活中不会一直盯着天花板看，但卧床不起的孩子几乎整天，或者说一生都要看着天花板。这个动物装饰的天花板动物园，可以看出这里的职工们对孩子们的无微不至的照料。

弃婴孤儿得不到充分的学校教育的机会，是一个全国性的问题，这个问题在 B 机构也存在。B 机构位于郊区，而向残障儿童提供特殊教育的学校并不在他们可以上下学的区域范围内。而且 B 机构的大多数孩子的户籍，还留在送出他们的儿童福利院的集体户口里，并不在 A 市，所以在 A 市的学校入学就很困难。因此，B 机构将有身体残障的儿童，送去基督徒建立的特殊学校上学。这所特殊学校，是针对有身体残障的儿童，进行职业教育的学校。

而对于那些有身体残障和智力残障的复合型残障的上学困

难的儿童，由 B 机构的职工和志愿者们对他们进行初级教育。比如绘画，身为职业画家的志愿者每周一次教孩子们绘画。因为有残疾，连保持固定的姿势都困难，但职工将孩子的身体固定在自制的椅子上，有的孩子要把画笔固定在自己的额头上，有的要让他的弯曲变形的手指握紧画笔，每次 3 小时，来完成一幅油画。

张女士很希望中度残障的儿童可以通过在职业训练学校的学习，将来可以独立生活。中度残障人士虽然需要在饮食，大小便和洗澡等日常生活上的照料，但是他们可以完成服务业或制造业当中担任较简单的劳动。但张女士找不到面向中度残障人士的合适的学校，所以只能不断摸索对残障儿童进行职业训练。

B 机构是通过主内网络筹得机构运营的主要资源的，包括运营资金物资，教师和医生的志愿者等。运营资金不仅来自国内的基督徒，还有来自朋友介绍以及通过网络得知 B 机构活动的国外基督徒的援助。残障儿童日常需要的治疗，由在中国医疗水平首屈一指的某家私立医院作为慈善事业来提供的。还有不在主内的，由主内朋友的介绍来当志愿者或捐赠物资的人也有。

事实上，给 B 机构介绍入园的弃婴残障儿童的，也是通过主内信徒的网络。各地的儿童福利院从事志愿者活动的信徒们，特别是在公立的福利院中，遇到福利院职工"残障程度严重，我们自己没办法照顾"的情况，就会介绍给 B 机构。福利院和当地地方政府同意后，残障儿童就会被转移到 B 机构。

B 机构是不属于特定的教会，但全体职工都是基督徒，在机构内也会定期自主开展祷告会，房间内经常播放着赞美诗。职员和儿童一起唱赞美诗、一起跳舞已经成为他们日常生活的一部分。

笔者也作为志愿者体验了照顾残障儿童，可以说，同样是残障儿童，每一个人的残障程度状态都不同，表达喜怒哀乐的方式也不同。只是照顾他们吃一次饭，笔者就累到没力气说话的程度。职工们能坚持着像这样的重体力劳动，一年 365 天，一天 24 小时，是靠着主内的信仰。在 B 机构的祷告会中，他们反复宣唱的，第一是"同一价值"，第二是"互动"。

有一天在祷告会上张女士祷告，"主啊，我们看到这些孩子们；孩子们跟我们一样，有灵，神圣，一同在地上"。祷告里面她说，她们职工和有残障的儿童是"一样"，就是在神的面前平等。张女士继续祷告，"这里的每一个人，无论是健康的照顾者还是被照顾者，我们都需要神的照顾，都需要神的保护，保护我们的心，保护我们的身体。"主内的"神前平等"这个教义，使他们以照顾残障儿童的自己的立场，强调了残障儿童和"健康人"，都是神的被造物，在神的面前不论谁的生命都有同一的价值这一理念。这个"同一价值"的理念，在 B 机构中形成了共识，对于有残障的孩子，B 机构中常被称为"宝贵价值的生命"残障儿童和健康人有"同一价值"，因此两者的关系也不是单方面的健康人照顾残障儿童的关系，而是被理解为"互动"的关系。"互动"不仅仅是一个口号，而是从职工们与残障儿童度过的每一天的体验中得来的。比如共同创始人孙女士在笔者采访时说"因为孩子们，我才了解了爱和信仰"。孙女士由于天生的性格和出于教师的职业需要，"经常抑制自己不要感性，所以自己一直是人生的旁观者"。后来，通过参与 B 机构的工作，她说，"因为孤残的孩子们，我才能够投入到人际关系中"。孙女士至今，也经常会彻夜不眠的照顾孩子。

（3）关系网的扩大和政教关系的恶化

B 机构位于 A 市郊外，是由基督教家庭教会的信徒设立的残障儿童专门的儿童福利机构。支撑他们的，是跨越了主内外，体制内和体制外，以及中国国内和国外境界的基督教信徒的巨大关系网。B 机构的人员、资金、教育、医疗等资源，都很缺乏。正因为缺乏这些资源，为了弥补这些不足，从国内外来了各种各样的人，出于各自的想法来支持他们的活动。因此，B 机构就成为了把集中到他们那里的人们联结在一起的关系网上的一个结点。由 B 机构联结成的关系网，与主权国家政府的金字塔的性质不同。他们虽然平缓，却是超越地区和国境，全球化的巨大关系网。这也可以说是包含华人华侨在内，信徒遍布全球的基督教会的特色。

出于"作为被造物，神前皆平等"这一信仰的理念，也是将各种各样的人吸引到 B 机构的原因。对于有重度残障，沟通困难的儿童，B 机构站在"被神祝福的宝贵生命"这一信仰的视角上，提出了不为义务或利益，而是为了"喜悦"而投入和孩子们的关系中这一概念。

但是，我们把目光投向 B 机构处在的中国社会中的状况，就会看到，围绕 B 机构的政教关系现在正日趋严格。

B 机构在长达 20 年中，收容了儿童福利院不能照顾的重度残障儿童，给与他们尽可能的教育机会，补充了公立儿童福利院的职能。相反，B 机构将照顾和教育残障儿童视为神给与自己的使命，是不能放弃的义务。因此，将残障儿童移交给 B 机构的公立福利院和 B 机构是相互依赖的关系。作为福利院的母体，地方政府也默许了这种互相依存关系。

从法律的角度来看，B 机构作为福利团体不具有任何法律上的地位。可以经营儿童福利机构的宗教团体，根据民政部和国家宗教事务局的规定，只承认"依法登记的宗教团体、宗教活动场所和经认定备案的宗教教职人员"组织的"宗教界举办的机构"[37]。而体制外"家庭教会"的信徒设立的 B 机构，无法成为宗教界举办的机构。宗教以外，如果有县级政府的批准，民间团体也可以作为"社会福利机构"来经营儿童福利机构[38]。但是 要经过县级政府的批准，其批准条件非常复杂，审批过程也 是"黑箱操作"。B 机构过去曾多次申请批准为福利机构，县级政府都没有接受他们的申请。设立人为家庭教会的信徒这一点，影响政府判断的可能性非常高。

另外，2013 年 1 月，在河南省兰考县发生了由民间个人运营的孤儿院发生火灾导致 7 名儿童死亡的惨痛事件，这个事件的发生吸引来自全国的关心。由此兰考事件为契机，中国政府对各地方政府下达了命令，要求地方政府强化对民间团体收养弃婴和孤儿的机构的监管。B 机构所在的 A 市也不是例外。B 机构收养的儿童中，一部分被送出的福利院接回，B 机

---

[37] 民政部等、民发〔2013〕83 号

[38] 社会福利机构管理暂行办法（民政部 1999 年 12 月 30 日中华人民共和国民政部令第 19 号发布　自发布之日起施行）

构的儿童数也有所减少。

B 机构过去一直与各地公营儿童福利院是互相依存的关系，而与 A 市地方政府比较疏远。2013 年兰考事件，以及习近平政权缩紧了宗教政策之后，B 机构与地方儿童福利院的关系淡化，被当地 A 市的基层政府敌视，政教关系开始变得严峻起来。

3.天主教体制外教会的儿童福利机构

（1）由"地下"教会神父在农村中设立

下面是有天主教背景的民间团体的事例，笔者考察了中国北部的 C 县的非公认教会 D（即所谓的"地下教会"）经营的民间儿童福利机构的事例。D 教会的福利机构和机构 B 一样是以主内信仰的价值观为基础，专门从事重度身心障碍的孤残儿童的保育工作的机构。在政教关系上，由于是地下教会直接运营的福利机构，基层政府和教会之间的关系，和机构 B 相比情况更为紧张。

与河北省或福建省一样，C 县是自 17 世纪开始就有天主教宣教活动的地区[39]。在位于农村地区的 C 县，世世代代信教的农民信徒 是天主教会的中心。主教或神父，以及修女们也都是从这样的信徒家庭出来的，天主教会已经融入了农村社会之中。现在在 C 县，估计有人口的 10%为天主教信徒。

D 教会是 1949 年"解放"以前就开始在这里进行教会活动的。1949 年新中国建立后，在共产党政权的指导下，中国国内一部分的天主教团体开始自己任命国内主教。这就是所谓"自选自圣"主教。但是 D 教会的神父和修女认为这种政策是"对教宗的亵渎行为"，所以一直没有遵从，也没有承认过自选自圣的主教。文化大革命时期，所有宗教活动都被弹压，发生了 D 教会的神父死于狱中的事件。1980 年代后，改革开放使宗教活动得以进行，但 D 教会的神父和修女，依然只遵从于

[39]Daniel H. Bays（2012）"*A New History of Christianity in China*"、25-28 页

罗马教皇任命的主教，拒绝了中国政府任命的主教以及参加体制内天主教会的活动。因此，D 教会作为"地下教会"，受到了县政府各种形式的迫害。C 县公安局 24 小时监视 D 教会，而教会的神父现在还被软禁。全国人民代表大会，G20 等大型政治外交活动期间，以及中国政府和梵蒂冈进行外交交涉前后，当地政府都会逮捕关押神父。中国政府所畏惧的是，作为"敏感人物"的神父，向海外政治人物或宗教相关人士以及西方媒体告发中国政府人权侵害以及宗教活动的状况。

D 教会开设儿童福利院，是由于 1980 年代发生有人将耳目有残疾的婴儿遗弃在教会门口的事件。教会在院子里修建了一座简单的房子，在此开始照顾被遗弃在教会的婴儿。"本地教会收养残疾弃婴"的传闻很快在 C 县传开，后来不断有人将婴儿遗弃在 D 教会中。在第 2 章例举的机构 B 里的重度残障儿童是来自从全国各地的福利院，而在 D 教会生活的残障儿童全部是直接被遗弃在 D 教会的儿童。人数最多时，有超过 100 人的脑瘫、癫痫、畸形等残障儿童在 D 教会生活。现在通过信徒家庭收养以及儿童的死亡，人数减少到 50 人左右。

儿童福利机构的运营以及照看孩子们的工作，是由 D 教会的修女约 30 个人承担。重度残障儿童的 24 小时看护虽是重体力劳动，但修女们住在教会宿舍中，除了生活费以外拿不到额外的报酬，休息日也照样需要工作。福利机构的运营费用，来自教会信徒的奉献，国内外天主教会的经济援助，以及天主教之外的中国民间人士的捐赠。

（1）调查结果

D 教会的福利机构活动，是以天主教信仰的"依靠祷告的力量去行动"作为行动准则，与天主教会的宗教活动并为一体。弃婴的名字也是用"方济各"等天主教圣人的名字来命名。修女和神父每天通过弥撒来确认他们的信仰。能够使用轮椅代步的孩子，每周日必须要参加弥撒，从神父那里接受神的祝福。对于修女们来说，将自己的人生全部奉献给残障儿童，是她们信仰耶稣的表现。

再来看一下福利机构的环境。和第 2 章的机构 B 相比，D

教会的福利机构在人员和资金方面都更缺乏。D 教会的福利机构挨着教堂。笔者几年前第一次访问该机构的时候，刚一进去，就能闻到唾液和粪便混合在一起的刺鼻味道，昏暗的房间里苍蝇乱飞，在这样的环境中修女们正在给一个光着下半身的小男孩儿喂饭。可以看出，这是因为做卫生的人手不足才导致这样的状况的。

在教育方面，D 教会的机构的儿童要接受学校教育是非常困难的。由于多为脑瘫等重度的身体残障儿童，上下学很困难，而且在农村地区的 C 县也没有针对残障儿童的特殊学校。对于智力障碍程度较轻的儿童，由修女们在机构内进行教育。但是，D 教会不像 B 机构那样，可以利用基督教信徒的关系网来给入园儿童提供教育机会，在 D 教会的机构能够得到的教育机会少之又少。

D 教会的困境，究其原因，还是由于 D 教会作为天主教地下教会，没有宗教团体法律上的地位而导致。C 县基层政府，让公安局职员住进 D 教会，监视外部人员进出以及资金的动向。另外，C 县政府以地下教会违法为理由，将他们的福利机构也视为违法，以"D 教会在没有批准的情况下抚养的儿童不是孤儿，而是违反计划生育政策而出生的孩子，所以 D 教会是长期妨碍计划生育政策的"为依据，十年前开始每年都对 D 教会发出停业封锁的命令。同时，C 县公安部门没有给 D 教会机构的儿童进行户口登记，使这些儿童处于"黑户"的状态。因此，这些残障儿童没有户口，很难接受医疗救治，更无法正常接受学校教育。

但是，就是在这样资金和人员极度缺乏的 D 教会，在短时间的访问中，看到她们给孤残儿童喂饭的场景，笔者的心被深深的打动了。D 教会的机构中，孩子们由性别和残障程度被分在不同的房间。当时笔者在一个女孩子的房间里，看到修女把煮的软烂的面条弄短，一点一点用勺子喂给女孩儿吃。当时，有一个女孩，很努力的把自己的面条喂给一个比自己更小的孤残女孩。那个女孩自身因为脑瘫，手有麻痹，自己吃饭已经很困难了。但是她学着修女的样子，照顾着周围比自己更小的孩子们。这些有着身心残障的孩子们，通过和修女的相处，学会了"爱"、"对他人的关怀"这些感情和行动，并付诸于行动。

(2) 天主教传统与政教关系的恶化

D 教会的儿童福利机构，是继承了在 19 世纪开始在中国各地进行儿童慈善事业（儿童福祉活动）的天主教传统。天主教这种通过社会事业来体现信仰的传统，不仅仅在中国，还遍布于世界各地。D 教会也是通过各种途径得到了国外天主教团体的奉献，同时，也接受了来自中国国内包括佛教徒的持续性援助。由此，D 教会及其儿童福利机构的关系网正在不断扩大，并超越了地区、国境以及宗教境界。

但是，D 教会关系网经常因受到基层政府的迫害而被阻断。另外，在中央政府层面，习近平政权对天主教地下教会实施高压政策，D 教会及其儿童福利机构也处在紧张的政教关系当中。与和个别地方政府建立起互相依存关系的机构 B 相比，能够援助 D 教会的政府部门则完全不存在。基层政府甚至希望地下教会 D 及其儿童福利机构能够彻底消失，像这样的政教关系只会越来越紧张。

4.总结：政教关系的紧张与"非法多米诺骨牌"

中国政府针对儿童福利和教育的预算一直有限，针对社会最弱势群体，残障弃婴的福利和教育，一直是依靠民间团体的补充来进行。而在法律上没有地位，处于灰色空间的民间团体又有很多。但是民间团体与政府部门不同，由于受到的制约较少，所以能够从中国国内外的各种团体和基金会来筹集人才及资源。

特别是主内民间团体，拥有全球化的信徒关系网络，并且在中国国内有着超过百年的救助弃婴的传统。因此，到 2000 年代，在孤儿的福利教育方面，一直有着默认的职能分配，就是"公立机构接收比较容易照顾的孤儿弃婴，在看护上难度很高的重度残障儿童（孤残）则由民间机构，特别是主内机构接收"。主内团体利用丰富的地上、地下关系网，筹集了经济资源和医疗资源等，用于重度残障儿童的看护和教育，他们有时还要从国外来调集这些资源。

围绕从事儿童福利的主内团体的政教关系，反映了中国多样的地区情况，一直以来都是多元化的。儿童福利教育的预算不足的部分地方政府，把接收重度残障儿童的主内团体当做"福祉的安全阀"来利用。这些地方政府，几乎完全没有考虑过这些团体是否受到政府部门批准。

中国政府对于未登记的宗教民间团体来运营的福利机构的态度，是摇摆于管理和默认两极之中。中央政府放缓宗教政策，在一定范围内允许未登记宗教团体的活动时，一些地方政府就会利用宗教背景福利机构来补充福利教育政策。特别是主内的未登记宗教团体和信徒，身处于"没有法律上的地位，但政府默许他们的活动"这样的灰色空间中，并发挥着这种优势。

但是，2013 年在民间儿童福利机构发生了"兰考事件"，受其影响，再加上习近平政权加强了宗教政策的紧缩，加紧了对民间儿童福利机构的强化管理和规范化管理的步伐。

2013 年以后，中央政府强化了对未登记宗教团体的取缔。兰考事件以后，受到"不能重蹈这样悲惨事件的覆辙"的舆论批判，民政部公布了新的针对民间儿童福利机构的"规范化管理"以及"清理"方针。民政部对于宗教团体和信徒运营的"宗教团体"，明确规定了只有在政府登记的宗教团体才能运营儿童福利机构。然后，对于没有在政府登记的宗教团体运营的儿童福利机构，基层政府做出了将这些儿童带走，转移到公立儿童福利院的措施。现在，未登记的宗教团体和信徒所运营的福利机构，都面临着要登记还是要关闭的决断。

与宗教毫无关系的一般民间团体的登记，也需要县以上政府部门的批准。但是批准的标准不明确，家庭教会和地下教会这样的体制外宗教相关的团体能够得到批准的可能性几乎没有。

因为这些儿童福利机构作为福利团体是不被法律承认的，这导致生活在这些儿童福利机构中的儿童的基本人权问题层出不穷。主内团体和个人运营的儿童福利机构，作为其母体的教会如果没有在政府部门登记，首先这个教会在中国的法律上就是"违法"的。在这种情况下，这些儿童福利机构，不论是作为

"民间宗教机构"还是作为一般的民间"社会福利机构"，都不具备法律上的地位。因此，基层的公安部门就不会批准在这些福利机构中生活的儿童的户口登记。因此，这些儿童处于"黑户"状态，没有去医院看病和去学校上学的权利，也不受法律的保护，更没有人权的保障。这就是中国共产党的宗教管理政策中，政府公认的"爱国宗教团体"以外的宗教活动在法律制度上不被承认的具体结果。换言之，由于中国的宗教政策限制信教自由，所以社会最弱势群体的残障遗孤儿童的基本人权得不到保障，这就是"非法多米诺骨牌效应"。这与宣称"贯彻落实以人为本的执政理念和儿童优先的原则，促进弃婴健康成长[40]"的中国政府的理念明显矛盾。

5. 主内民间儿童福利机构的意义及可能性

现在的中国，随着经济发展和社会多元化进程，有更多的体制外宗教参与教育福利事业。同时，援助这些事业的关系网也在中国国内外扩展开。本文中例举的这些体制外教会的信徒从事孤残儿童为主的儿童福利教育事业，正是这样的典型。

主内宗教团体开展这些社会事业，在全体社会中起到了什么样的作用，又有什么样的可能性呢？

以效率和实际利益优先的主流社会理论，是无法说明这样细心周到的照料别人的孩子的理由的，而且这些孩子能否对社会做出贡献还是未知的。特别是需要 24 小时看护的孤残儿童，在效率优先的社会中，常常会成为率先被抛弃的对象。但是，圣经和神学的价值体系中却是完全相反的。弱者与强者是对等的，甚至有时是比强者更重要的存在。将社会的弱者视为神圣而珍贵存在的基督教信仰，例如从新约圣经，马太福音第25 章"这些事你们既作在我这弟兄中最小的身上，就是作在我身上了"里可以看出。

基督徒们为何能够和残障儿童一起生活呢？这不是出于义务或者为了受到报答。接受调查的信徒表示，是出于对"所有

---

[40]民政部等、民发〔2013〕83 号

的生命都是有同等价值，都是受神的祝福的存在"。拥有这样的"生命的价值"，"神的祝福"的信仰，才能和孤残儿童一起生活度过一生。照顾孩子们的大人，并不是单方面的照顾"孩子们"，她们也受到了孩子们的祝福。信徒们通过和孩子们一起生活，自己的精神也发生了变化，自己的内心中发生的这些变化，又自觉的通过祷告或弥撒来转化成语言。

主内信仰改变了残障儿童的照料和教育的质量，另一方面对残障儿童的照料和教育的经验，又使得信仰更具有生命力。主内团体的残障儿童福利教育事业，是通过信仰和行动的互动，创造并实践出新的价值。这些团体通过对孤残儿童的照料和教育，向主流社会展示了弱者与"健康人"之间相互支撑的意义，并且承担了这些责任。

本文中例举的两个儿童福利机构，他们重视看护人和残障儿童之间的人际关系，照顾到儿童的个性，这样的照料和教育方式，可以成为中国国内其他儿童福利机构的范例。现在，已经有地方政府来 B 机构进行非正式考察了。

另外，主内信徒的关系网也使这些机构能够筹集教育、医疗、人才等各种资源。和公营的福利院不同，民间儿童福利机构常常缺乏资金和人才。但是正是因为这些不足，才让更多人和更多的资源超越了宗教和国界，来填补这些不足。这其中，显示了与国家中央集权的官僚组织不同的各界人士紧密联系的范例。

主要参考文献

1. 民政部、国家发展和改革委员会、公安部、司法部、财政部、国家卫生和计划生育委员会、国家宗教事务局,关于进一步做好弃婴相关工作的通知,民发（2013）83 号

2. 冯华, 朱峻仪. 让大龄孤儿更好融入社会（观点），《人民日报》（2017 年 06 月 09 日 17 版）

3. 联合国儿童基金会（UNICEF）.孤儿问题，https://www.unicef.org/zh/media/%E5%AD%A4%E5%84%BF%E9%97%AE%E9%A2%98

4. 全国现有事实孤儿至少 61 万人 救助困局亟待破解,

2017 年 11 月 22 日《检察日报》

5. 张惠, 2014. 当前我国孤儿救助体系的现状与问题,《中南林业科技大学学报》，2014 年 2 期

6. 熊丙奇, 2013. "非法收养"和"黑幼儿园",《商周刊》2013 年 02 期

7. 民政部，社会福利机构管理暂行办法, 中华人民共和国民政部令第 19 号发布，1999 年 12 月 30 日

8. Daniel H. Bays, 2012. A New History of Christianity in China, Wiley-Blackwell

中国在校儿童的宗教自由岌岌可危

凯瑟琳·凯普斯
2018 年五月

作者按：本文的目的是披露中国对儿童的人权和宗教教育权的侵犯。自今年出台了新规定以来，侵权的案例不断增加，本文只是不断涌现的相关研究的一部分而已。文中的披露也许能够令人们更加关注应该如何保障儿童接受宗教教育的权利，也帮助国际社会认清中国政府对国民施加的限制，以及这种限制对下一代的影响。

一、背景介绍

在过去的几十年来，中国的国民一直活在宗教规定和条例的桎梏里，而目前当权的习近平政府更是大大强化了这种桎梏。自 2018 年 2 月以来，对地下教会和官方认可的教会以及教会领袖的打压一直有增无减。出台的新条例甚至波及到儿童，进一步收紧了儿童在家里和家以外的地方参加"宗教"活动的自由。

出台的新规定也延伸到了儿童教育领域。任何形式的"宗教教育"都受到猛烈的攻击。新规定禁止学生在课堂和宗教场所诵读经文，要求所有学生和教师一起强化政治教育和宣传。新规定还禁止学生在寒暑假期间参加任何宗教活动。

毋庸置疑的是，教育是一切人类社会最重要的基石。换句话说，一个社会如何养育下一代是在它的教育制度里得到最先和最重要的体现。

二、世界各国对"儿童"的定义

追根溯源，"儿童"这个词出自拉丁语的"infans",意为"不会说话的人"。在罗马帝国时期，儿童是指 0 到 7 岁的人。这个概念随着时代不断演化，产生的一个负面效果是：虽然全世界都认可"儿童"这个概念，但不同文化对儿童到成人的年龄分界却有不同看法。目前，"儿童"被普遍定义为年龄在 18 岁以下的人。[41]

三、 涉及儿童权利、宗教自由和教育的国际法规

对宗教教育的保障虽然已有好几个世纪的历史，国际法对儿童权利的保障却是在第一次世界大战之后才正式出台，以 1924 年通过的"日内瓦宣言"作为标记。1959 年通过的"儿童权利宣言"进一步扩大了国际影响，这种关注和认可也随着时代不断扩大和加深。[42]

1.联合国 1948 年通过的《世界人权宣言》

联合国大会通过的《世界人权宣言》是第二次世界大战的一个产物，它史无前例地列出在全世界范围都应当受到保护的基本人权。《宣言》第十八条指出："人人有思想、良心和宗教自由的权利；此项权利包括改变他的宗教或信仰的自由，以及单独或集体、公开或秘密地以教义、实践、礼拜和戒律表示他的宗教或信仰的自由。"[43]《宣言》始终激励人们在矛盾冲突中、在压迫权利和自由的社会中对公义的缺席做出反抗，追求普世人权的落实。

2.《取缔教育歧视公约》（1960 年）

公约的第一条、第二条和第五条指出，出于宗教原因设立和维持分开的教育机构如果提供的是一种与学生的父母或法定监护人的愿望相符的教育，并且达到了主管当局设立的教育标

---

[41] 儿童的权利，Humanium, https://www.humanium.org/en/declaration-rights-child-2/.

[42] 儿童的权利，Humanium, https://www.humanium.org/en/declaration-rights-child-2/.

[43]《世界人权宣言》，联合国，http://www.un.org/en/universal-declaration-human-rights/.

准，就不构成歧视。这些教育机构必须致力于充分发展人的个性并加强对人权和基本自由的尊重。[44]

3. 联合国《消除基于宗教或信仰的不容忍和歧视宣言》（1981 年）

这份宣言强调了宗教自由的概念，在联合国大会通过。宣言第五条针对儿童做出下列规定：

父母或法定监护人有权根据他们的宗教或信仰，并考虑到他们认为子女所应接受的道德教育来安排家庭生活。

所有儿童均应享有按照其父母或法定监护人意愿接受有关宗教或信仰方面的教育的权利；不得强迫他们接受违反其父母或法定监护人意愿之宗教或信仰的教育，关于这方面的指导原则应以最能符合儿童的利益为准。

所有儿童都应受到保护，使其不受任何形式的基于宗教或信仰原因的歧视。儿童所受的教育应贯彻谅解、容忍、各国人民友好、和平、博爱和尊重他人的宗教或信仰自由等精神，并使他们充分意识到应奉献自由的精力和才能为其同胞服务。[45]

宣言第八条进一步提出"本宣言任何规定均不得解释为对《世界人权宣言》和《国际人权公约》所规定的任何权利有所限制或克减"。[46]教育制度中的宗教自由出自这样一个理念，即在儿童的教育问题上，父母才是决策者。

4.《儿童权利公约》（1989 年）

---

[44]《宗教自由与国际社会》，基督复临安息日会：公共事务与宗教自由，http://www.adventistliberty.org/current-issues.

[45]联合国的《反对宗教不容忍宣言》，宗教容忍（2006 年 9 月 7 日），http://www.religioustolerance.org/un_dec.htm.

[46]联合国《关于消除一切基于宗教或信仰的不容忍和歧视宣言》，"联合国人权"，http://www.ohchr.org/EN/ProfessionalInterest/Pages/ReligionOrBelief.aspx.

这份公约再度声明儿童是有权利和尊严的人。正是出于这个考量，很多份国际公约都提出了对儿童的保护。公约第十四条提出儿童享有宗教自由和信仰自由，并且提出要以符合儿童"不同阶段"接受能力的方式指导儿童行使其权利。[47]这是第一份全面承认儿童基本权利的国际公约。

综上所述，国际社会协商通过了若干份有关儿童受教育过程中拥有宗教自由的宣言和共识。虽然在原则设立上已颇有成效，但这些原则在实际操作中却是千姿百态。

四、这一话题和它与中国的关联

在中国共产党的统治下中国常年对宗教进行管控，其背后的理念是马克思主义的反宗教立场，社会组织和管控的历史模式，以及对宗教可能破坏民族稳定和领土完整的忧虑和担心。[48]中国的领导人认为普世人权会威胁到他们的统治，所以将之宣传为外来的入侵，并且惩罚那些推动普世人权的人。

在中国共产党的统治下中国常年对宗教进行管控，其背后的理念是马克思主义的反宗教立场，社会组织和管控的历史模式，以及对宗教可能破坏民族稳定和领土完整的忧虑和担心。[8]中国的领导人认为普世人权会威胁到他们的统治，所以将之宣传为外来的入侵，并且惩罚那些推动普世人权的人。

有人提出宗教认同在一个人降生伊始就已经注定，然后通过教育得到不断的发展，因为教育影响个人做选择的方式。中国有关宗教教育之选择的政府规定也决定了家长们在塑造儿童宗教认同的教育上没有发言权。

根据今年出台的新《宗教事务管理条例》，有八条规定是所有为儿童提供教育的宗教学校都必须遵守的，其中第十一条，第十二条和第十八条提出：

---

[47] 《宗教自由与国际社会》，基督复临安息日会：公共事务与宗教自由，http://www.adventistliberty.org/current-issues.

[48] "中华人民共和国：法律与宗教框架总览"，Religlaw (2017)，https://www.religlaw.org/common/document.view.php?docId=7279.

宗教院校由全国性宗教团体或者省、自治区、直辖市宗教团体设立。其他任何组织或者个人不得设立宗教院校。

设立宗教院校，应当由全国性宗教团体向国务院宗教事务部门提出申请，或者由省、自治区、直辖市宗教团体向拟设立的宗教院校所在地的省、自治区、直辖市人民政府宗教事务部门提出申请。省、自治区、直辖市人民政府宗教事务部门应当自收到申请之日起 30 日内提出意见，报国务院宗教事务部门审批。

宗教团体和寺院、道观、清真寺、教堂（以下称寺观教堂）开展培养宗教教职人员、学习时间在 3 个月以上的宗教教育培训，应当报设区的市级以上地方人民政府宗教事务部门审批。[49]

我们要问：这些侵权的条例最终会怎样影响儿童的宗教教育权？中国政府怎样用行动表达对儿童宗教教育权的认可？如果中国政府拒绝遵守国际公约，国际社会又该怎样回应？

这些复杂的问题需要我们认真回应：

1. 这些侵权的条例最终会怎样影响儿童的宗教教育权？

这些侵权的条例夺走了塑造美德、道德和建造良好社会根基的最积极正面的力量。儿童必须拥有学习宗教原则的自由；为了中国文化自身的益处，这项自由必须不受限制，被大力推动。如果这些侵权的条例被执行下去，势必导致新一代的中国公民在价值伦理观念上的缺失。

2. 中国政府怎样用行动表达对儿童宗教教育权的认可？

理想的情况是，中国政府遵守《联合国人权宣言》、《取缔教育歧视公约》、《联合国消除基于宗教或信仰的不容忍和歧视宣言》和《儿童权利公约》。

---

[49] 网站声明：本网站上的一切翻译内容均非官方翻译，仅作参考之用。《宗教事物管理条例》，中国法律文件翻译，2017 年 9 月 9 日

3. 如果中国政府拒绝遵守国际公约，国际社会又该怎样回应？

中国既然于 2016 年再次当选联合国人权理事会理事，就当积极推动各国联手保障和推动人权，而不是意图分裂、击破和压制反对的声音。[50]出于公平，理事会应当回击中国对联合国人权论坛的挑战，并且处理中国国内外出现的践踏人权事件。如果中国拒绝守约，其他成员国应当采取制裁措施，中国也不应该继续保有联合国人权理事会的席位。

五、结论

综上所述，中国目前宗教政策的通过往往是为了实现国家的经济和社会目标，而非提升宗教自由。中国政府要求所有宗教在法律规定的范围内活动，去适应政府定义的社会和文化发展目标。这一观点对中国教育中的宗教自由有着负面的影响。

人们常常发现自己生活在一个荒唐的"政治正确"的世界里，这个世界教导儿童敌视宗教，并且不准儿童学习和实践宗教。回望历史，你会发现，成百上千年来，宗教教育对文明的发展一直很重要。根据《塔木德》的记载，公元前 100 年就出现了第一间为儿童设立的学校。公元前 600 年，经济状况普普通通的家庭的孩子就已经在学习读书写字，特别是要认真学习托拉（摩西的律法）。 男孩从四岁开始，也就是刚刚能够口语表达的时候，就接受宗教训练。女孩的宗教生活也是很早就开始了。再大一点儿，儿童就要参加安息日和逾越节的活动，男孩子则要固定去会堂和上学。[51]

---

[50] "联合国权利机构需要挑战强大却滥权的中国"，人权观察，2018 年 3 月 14 日https://www.hrw.org/news/2018/03/14/un-rights-body-needs-challenge-powerful-and-abusive-china.
[51] 《儿童：国际标准圣经百科全书》，BibleHub (2017), http://biblehub.com/topical/c/child.htm.

自 1949 年中华人民共和国成立和政府强制推行共产党的无神论教育以来，中国的基督徒就一直受到压迫。然而中国有很多基督徒和其他信仰的人从信仰中获得正面和强大的力量。"但主耶和华必帮助我，所以我必不羞愧，因此我板着脸好象坚硬的燧石，我也知道我必不会蒙羞。"[52] 生活中各个领域的真自由，包括宗教自由，都来自信靠那位掌管我们命运的主，全能的上帝。

---

[52] 以赛亚书 50：7（圣经英文标准版）

八福公学事件原始材料

八福公学

1. 2018/03/15 警情通报

北京昌平北七家王府农场燕园 2 号
2018 年 3 月 15 日下午 17:00 左右

车号为 EM8780 的带有保安标志的车带 8-9 名身份不明人员，自称为北七家镇政府所派，但拒绝出示任何凭据，闯入王府农场小区在燕园 2 号聚集，野蛮对准正在回家的孩子拍照。

家长随即报警 110，警号为 055857 的自称姚姓民警赶往现场，该民警通了一个电话以后认为保安是北七家镇政府派的，并说不方便讲为什么他认定是镇政府所派。

民警现场讲所来保安姓名身份证号逐个登记后，口头令保安删除所拍照片，并称警方已经保留所有记录，如果有对该保安行为的诉讼，可以向人民法院起诉。后并未有人监督保安是否删除照片，保安后驱车离开现场。

2. 2018/03/21 情况通报

我们于 2016 年 7 月份与《燕园 2 号》房东签署了租房协议，协议中约定租期为十年。租用后，我们投入大量资金进行了内部装修，并与房东保持着良好、融洽的关系。但房东在 2018 年 2 月份因不明原因突然提出中止租房协议，我们理解房东似乎有难处，为了顾全大局和本社区的安宁，也愿意协商解决。但房东仍然于 2018 年 3 月 1 日向昌平区人民法院提起诉讼（法院已经立案），目前正在民事诉讼程序中。

然而，房东竟然无视争议已经进入司法程序的现实，在我们仍拥有房子合法使用权的情况下，知法犯法，挑起争端（如此急迫，原因让我们费解），在 2018 年 3 月 12 日上午用车辆堵住房子大门，禁止我们进出。虽然我们已经于 3 月 12 日报警（警方已对双方做了笔录），但房东仍然不将车辆撤离，此举必将激化矛盾，破坏我们对房东处境的理解和尊重，不利于争议的解决，也不利于社区的和谐稳定。

请社区邻居和居民理解并共同维护社区和谐环境，并支持协商解决和司法公正。我们也再次声明，我们始终愿意与房东友好协商，并已尽量克制，因此强烈要求房东尽快将车辆撤离，否则由此造成的车辆或人员伤害，房东必须承担所有法律责任和舆论谴责！

燕园 2 号承租人

2018 年 3 月 21 日

曾经融洽，相煎何急？
如此急迫，究竟为何？
知法犯法，后果自负！

3. 紧急代祷

教养孩童，使他走当行的道，就是到老他也不偏离。(箴言 22:6 和合本)

孩子是神所赐的产业，按着圣经教导孩子是每个神儿女的心愿，请大家同心合意为八福共学现在所面临的逼迫祷告，一起为信仰持守从今年 1 月 3 号开始，八福面临各方压力，牧者、老师、家长共同祷告共同站立，并诚恳与相关部门沟通，但他们无视家长和孩子的困难，1 月 30 日，在租期未满的情况下，小学的孩子被迫离开了 5 年的家园；目前幼儿园的租约仍未到期，房东却强行让老师和孩子搬离，而且似乎有某些方面指使，在拒赔违约金的同时调动 40 名保安强行入园，把课桌、书本等园内物品搬到社区路边。该极端行为严重破坏了社会治安和国家有关民事刑事法律规定！请众弟兄姊妹为八福代祷。

八福共学全体家长

2018 年 3 月 30 日

4. 承租人声明

我们于 2016 年 7 月份与燕园 2 号房东签署租房协议，协议中双方约定租期为十年，按照合同约定，目前该房屋仍在租赁有效期，我们仍然拥有承租人的合法权益。

租赁合同签订后，我们和房东保持良好、融洽的关系，在合同中达成一致意见后，我们投入大量资金进行装修。2018 年 1 月，房东在没有理由、未提前告知的情况下，提出终止合同的要求，经查明，得知房东因为突然遭受不便说明的压力、不得已提出终止租赁关系，我们向房东了解到，其极端行为是出于某些方面的指使。对此，为了顾全大局和本社区的安宁，我们作为承租人，在受到干扰且产生巨大损失的情况下，仍对房东表示理解，并同意按照《民法通则》及《合同法》中关于违约金责任的一般原则配合解决。

根据《合同法》规定，租赁合同中一方当事人不履行合同义务或者履行合同义务不符合约定的情形，应当向守约方支付违约金，约定的违约金若低于违约方造成的损失的情形，当事人可以请求人民法院或者仲裁机构予以增加或减少。

但目前房东拒绝赔偿，并且于 2018 年 2 月非自愿向昌平区人民法院提起诉讼，在我们作为无辜遭受损失的守约方期待法院作出公正判决的同时，却在 2018 年 3 月 12 日上午用车辆堵住该房屋大门，影响承租人进出。对此我们于当天报警（警方已对双方做了笔录），房东仍未撤离其拦截车辆，此举或许将激化矛盾，破坏社区的和谐环境，同时这种不合理不合法解决问题的态度给房东及其背后支持者带来极其恶劣的负面影响，甚至失去了人与人之间的理解和尊重，更不利于争议的解决。

在房东没有诚意谈判的情况下，3 月 23 日继续采用入室抢劫等极端行为故意损坏财物，在 3 月 28 日房东指使 40 名保安强行进入燕园 2 号不准承租人进入，致使家长和孩子受到惊吓，不能正常进行亲子教育活动。三次恶劣事件，承租人均报警。对此，我们会积极地为捍卫司法公正请求有关部门、专家、学者的帮助和支持。

我们再次声明，我们始终愿意积极与房东友好协商解决问题，请房东和相关部门能够尊重法律，理解群众关系和社区和谐环境的重要性，不用非法行为挑起事端，否则由此造成的财产或人员伤害，房东必须承担社会道义的谴责和相应的法律责任。恳请邻居、物业管理及社区群众给予公平、公开、公正的监督，我们仍然相信正义犹存，相信良知犹存！

燕园 2 号承租人

2018 年 3 月 30 日

编者注：原始材料中八福共学实为八福公学，为因应逼迫，学校主办方临时改称为八福共学。

患难的日子
若胆怯，你的力量就微小

厦门市思明区教育局对"麦种学堂"告知书

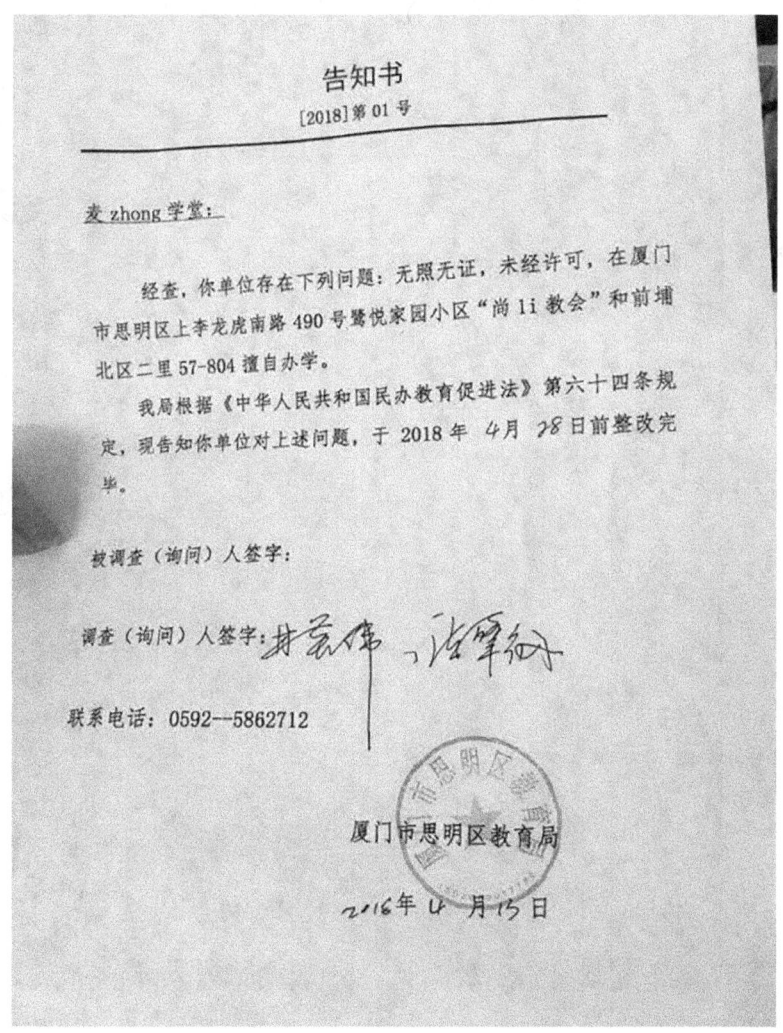

告知书

[2018] 第 01 号

麦 zhong 学堂：

　　经查，你单位存在下列问题：无照无证，未经许可，在厦门市思明区上李龙虎南路 490 号鹭悦家园小区"尚 1i 教会"和前埔北区二里 57-804 擅自办学。

　　我局根据《中华人民共和国民办教育促进法》第六十四条规定，现告知你单位对上述问题，于 2018 年 4 月 28 日前整改完毕。

被调查（询问）人签字：

调查（询问）人签字：

联系电话：0592--5862712

厦门市思明区教育局

2016 年 4 月 15 日

河南省天主教爱国会，河南省天主教教务委员会通知

通　　　　知

根据 4 月 3 日省宗教局关于"坚持宗教与教育相分离原则"、和落实《宗教事务条例》"宗教活动场所不得举行各种形式的培训班向未成年传播宗教教育"的要求，请各地市两会依照执行，现通知如下：

一、全省宗教活动场所内不得举办未成年人宗教教育培训、或其它如冬令营、夏令营等形式的学习班。

二、劝戒去教堂做礼拜望弥撒的教友把孩子交给别人托管，不要带进教堂。

三、针对以上这些问题，过去是以宣传教育为主，现在却是红线高压线，不要不当回事。

四、如果不听要求，会对场所负责人追究责任、取消教职人员备案资格、关闭活动场所。

五、请各地市两会及时传达到教堂各场所。

河南省天主教爱国会
河南省天主教教务委员会
2018 年 4 月 8 日

维吾尔族学生、父母在斋月期间被迫放弃禁食

2018 年 5 月 21 日

中国西北部新疆维吾尔自治区当局迫使维吾尔族学生及其父母签署承诺书，在伊斯兰斋月期间不要禁食，进一步破坏了穆斯林族群的宗教传统。

在斋月期间，官方通常强迫餐馆保持开放并限制人们进入清真寺。去年消息来源告诉自由亚洲（RFA）维吾尔部，为了对社区中的其他维吾尔人树立榜样，维吾尔族共产党干部、公务员和政府退休人员签署了文件，他们被要求在斋月期间既不禁食也不祈祷。

但是喀什（Kashgar）地区伽师县（Peyziwat）县的一名学生最近告诉自由亚洲（RFA），学校官员让他和他的同学与他们的父母签署了在斋月（5 月 16 日至 6 月 14 日）期间不要禁食的协议 。这是我们第一次了解到当局为学龄儿童实施这样的措施。

该报道表明，当局正在对维吾尔人的个人生活进行前所未有的骚扰，以在该地区消除当局称之为的宗教"极端主义"表现。

"因为我们是学生，所以我们不会斋戒，"这位不愿透露姓名的学生对自由亚洲（RFA）说，"我们已经与学校签署了一份协议，并且还写了一封承诺书。"

当被问到他的父母在斋月期间是否禁食时，该学生说他们不会，因为"他们不允许在自己的孩子面前做这样的事情"，"作为榜样，他们当然不会斋戒，"他补充说。

来自伽师县（Peyziwat）的一位女干部说，在斋月之前，"所有干部和党员都被召集到县办公室召开会议，我们被告知要'更加警惕'，并且要'特别关注'任何抱怨政府宗教极端主义政策的人。"

"这些干部正在努力......教育[居民]禁食是错误的，"她补充道。

当被问及禁食是否被认为是"非法的宗教活动"时，该女干部承认不是，但说，"人们在这样好的条件下生活，不应有抱怨。"

她还确认了本月早些时候纽约人权观察（Human Rights Watch）（HRW）的一份报告，当局正在对穆斯林维吾尔族干部家庭定期进行"家庭住宿"，记录他们的生活和政治观点，并对他们进行政治灌输，这是该地区日益深入开展"严打"活动的一部分。

她谈到了"家庭住宿"政策，说政府的该政策让被住宿家庭有机会接受有关技术技能的培训，"他们正在帮助农民摆脱贫困，"教中文普通话，并帮助居民找到更好的工作。

其它消息来源，包括阿克苏（Akesu）地区警察局的一名警官表示，在斋月期间，该地区加强了安保措施。"我们加强了巡逻以保持稳定，目前没有不稳定问题，"该警官在挂断电话前说。

现行措施

围绕斋月新的限制做法符合新疆近年来针对宗教"极端主义"的现行措施。

自 4 月以来，新疆各地数千名维吾尔人因被指控"极端主义"和"政治上不正确"的观点，而被关押在政治再教育营和监狱中，维吾尔人抱怨在中国统治下普遍存在歧视，宗教压迫和文化压制。

自从去年 8 月份，陈全国被任命为中国共产党新疆党委书记以来，新疆当局出台了一系列严厉的政策侵犯维吾尔人的合法权利和自由，包括按照去年年初发布的"75 种宗教极端主义表现"清单，关押维吾尔人。清单上极端主义的表现包括：斋月期间"照常营业"和"妇女穿着宗教服饰工作"，"家庭储存或购买大量食物"和"行为异常"，以及"在清真寺外公开聚集祈祷"。另一份清单告诉官员要注意所谓的"非法宗教活动的 28 种表现"。

中共官员告诉自由亚洲（RFA），去年 4 月他们还接到了有关几个新的"极端主义表现"的指示，包括：在祷告时两腿分开站立，用指甲花染发，穿短裤，右手腕戴手表，突然戒酒等。

在今年的斋月之前，总部设在慕尼黑的世界维吾尔代表大会（WUC）流亡组织发表声明，敦促中国政府确保维吾尔人享有宗教自由权利，并允许他们在不受限制的情况下遵行斋月。

"因为限制的增加，每年斋月都会变成一种恐惧和焦虑，这对维吾尔人的日常生活造成了极大的干扰，"世界维吾尔代表大会（WUC）主席 Dolkun Isa 当时说。

中国警方定期在新疆进行"严打"活动，包括骚扰维吾尔族家庭，限制伊斯兰教做法，查禁体现维吾尔人文化和语言的视频和其它材料。

因为压制性的国内政策导致暴力事件高涨，自 2009 年以来新疆已有数百人死亡。虽然中国指责维吾尔人搞"恐怖主义"袭击活动，但中国以外的专家称，中国政府夸大了维吾尔人的威胁。

（自由亚洲(RFA)维吾尔部 Shohret Hoshur 报道；翻译：自由亚洲(RFA)维吾尔部；英文撰稿：Joshua Lipes；中文翻译：对华援助协会（CAA）孟元新）。

新疆当局监禁送儿子到未经批准的宗教学校的维吾尔族

伊玛目

2018 年 5 月 10 日

因为带儿子到未经批准的宗教学校与其他孩子在一起，中国西北部新疆维吾尔自治区和田地区一位著名的伊玛目，被中共新疆当局判处五年以上有期徒刑。

乌尔其乡党委书记告诉自由亚洲（RFA）维吾尔部，2017 年 5 月，和田地区墨玉县乌尔其乡东巴赫清真寺的伊玛目 Abduheber Ahmet 被拘留，一个月后被判处五年半监禁。

在要求匿名的情况下，该党委书记说，这位四十六岁的父亲"把他的一个儿子带到了东巴村的一所地下宗教学校"。

"据说他只带他儿子去过一次……我想是四、五年前……他带他儿子去那里，以便他儿子能和其他孩子一起玩。"

"作为伊玛目，艾哈迈德曾得到国家认可，并获得'五星'评级，在一次认罪会议上他供述了自己的罪行，"该党委书记说，并且因为认罪而得到了"宽大处理"。

"因为政府和党是公平的，所以他被判处五年半的徒刑，否则他将被判七年徒刑。"该党委书记补充说。

据该党委书记介绍，"大约 11 个月前"，艾哈迈德被送到了监狱，现正在巴音郭楞蒙古自治州库尔勒市的劳改监狱服刑。

"两面"维吾尔人

自 2017 年 4 月以来，在新疆，被认为有"极端宗教观点"和"政治上不正确"观点的维吾尔人遭到囚禁或拘留进行再教育，维吾尔人长期以来一直抱怨中国统治下普遍存在歧视、宗教压迫和文化压制。

在 2016 年 8 月任职后的几个月里，新任党委书记陈全国对维吾尔人开展了前所未有的镇压，并对所谓的"两面"维吾尔族官员（政府对不愿意遵守命令并有"不忠诚"表现的维吾尔官员使用的一个术语）实施意识形态清洗。

自由亚洲(RFA)获悉，去年 10 月，当局曾监禁墨玉县(Qaraqash）县哈拉克(Hanliq)清真寺前伊玛目库班.巴拉特(Qurban Barat)的四个孙子，库班.巴拉特曾因为将两名所谓的"分离主义分子"送交警察，而被共产党认为是"爱国宗教学者"。

巴拉特的儿子当时告诉自由亚洲(RFA)，这四名人士因为"听宗教教义"并且拥有"非法宗教材料"，被判处五年半至八年徒刑，他还说，他们县里至少有三名党员的子女或配偶因宗教违法行为被判处监禁或被安置在再教育营地。

中国警方定期在新疆进行"严打"活动，包括骚扰维吾尔族家庭，限制伊斯兰教做法，查禁体现维吾尔人文化和语言的视频和其它材料。

因为压制性的国内政策导致暴力事件高涨，自 2009 年以来新疆已有数百人死亡。虽然中国指责维吾尔人搞"恐怖主义"袭击活动，但中国以外的专家称，中国政府夸大了维吾尔人的威胁。

（自由亚洲(RFA)维吾尔部 Shohret Hoshur 报道；翻译：自由亚洲(RFA)维吾尔部；英文撰稿：Joshua Lipes；中文翻译：对华援助协会（CAA）孟元新）

新疆维吾尔自治区教委关于在学校禁止
宗教活动的规定
（新教党字 [1996] 5 号）

为了保证社会主义的办学方向，维护学校正常的教育教学秩序，依照《中华人民共和国宪法》、《中华人民共和国民族区域自治法》、《中华人民共和国教育法》、《新疆维吾尔自治区宗教事务管理条例》以及党和国家的民族、宗教、教育、政策的有关规定，结合我区学校实际，制定本规定。

社会主义的学校是用马列主义、毛泽东思想和邓小平建设用中国特色的社会主义理论教育学生，传播科学文化知识，培养社会主义"四有"新人的阵地，禁止任何形式的宗教活动，任何宗教组织和个人不得在学校内（包括校办工厂、农场、实习基地等）和学校毗邻的地方修建和设立清真寺及寺庙、道观，已经修建或成立的有限期拆除或搬迁；不得招收在校学生学习经文；不得妨碍学校进行辨证唯物主义、历史唯物主义、无神论和科学文化知识的教育；不得在学校和学生中传播宗教思想，进行宗教仪式；不得胁迫、引诱在校学生参加宗教活动。若发现上述行为，学校、教师、学生和其它社会组织、个人都应及时向当地政府和有关部门报告，由当地政府和有关部门依照法律和规定处理。

人民教师是科学文化知识的传播者，担负者教书育人的光荣职责，必须认真贯彻执行党和国家的教育方针，坚持对学生进行马克思列宁主义、毛泽东思想教育，进行科学世界观、人生观和无神论的教育，进行维护祖国统一、民族团结的教育、教师不得参加宗教活动，不得向学生传播宗教思想，不得胁迫和带领学生参加宗教活动，对违反上述规定的，学校应进行批评教育，教育不改的，要取消教师资格，情节严重的，要清除出教师队伍。学生是社会主义事业未来的建设者和接班人，必须自觉接受爱国主义、集体主义和社会主义教育树立科学的世界观和人生观、学生不得参与宗教活动，不得到经文学校、唱诗班读经颂诗，不封斋，不佩戴宗教标志、学生家长和他人不得强迫学生信教和参加宗教活动，对参与宗教活动的学生，学校应进行批评教育。教育不改者，要给予纪律处分。

教职员工和学生中的共产党员、共青团员应当是马克思主义无神论者，应当严格遵守党、团章的规定，带头宣扬马列主义、毛泽东思想，学习科学文化知识，树立辨证唯物主义和历史唯物主义世界观，而不得信仰宗教和参与任何宗教活动。党、团员组织要进行批评教育，教育不改的，应劝其退党（团）或予以除名。

各级各类学校要进一步加强思想政治教育工作，在大、中、小学校政治思想品德课中要保证一定课时的无神论教育，并把这种教育融于各科教学之中。学校党、团组织和工会、妇联、少先队等群众组织要经常组织师生学习时事政治，进行辨证唯物主义教育，开展丰富多彩的文体科技活动，把学校办成健康向上，追求真理，学习科学的园地，增强青少年抵御唯心主义和宗教思想的能力。

各级教育行政部门和学校要进一步加强管理，完善各类规章制度，把全国贯彻党的教育方针、正确执行党的宗教政策和对学生进行爱国主义教育，民族团结教育，无神论教育列入干部、教师考核考评内容与教师资格的认定、评优、晋职、晋级挂钩，同时学生操行评定要有是否正确对待宗教问题的内容。

学校、社会、家庭要紧密配合，认真贯彻执行以上规定，反对宗教对教育的渗透和干预，保护青少年学生健康成长。

本规定适用于除宗教学校以外的各级各类学校。

新疆维吾尔自治区教育委员会

1996 年 2 月 2 日

中共中央办公厅、国务院办公厅转发教育部
《关于正确处理少数民族地区宗教干扰学校教育问题的意见》

(一九八三年二月二十七日)

　　教育部《关于正确处理少数民族地区宗教干扰学校教育问题的意见》[1]，已经中央书记处和国务院批准。现转发你们，望结合实际情况，参照执行。

　　近年来，在一些少数民族地区出现宗教干预教育、冲击学校的问题，虽然是在落实党的宗教政策取得显著成绩的情况下出现的局部问题，但是仍然需要引起各级党政领导机关的重视。望各地结合贯彻中共中央关于印发关于我国社会主义时期宗教问题的基本观点和基本政策的通知，在充分地耐心细致地做好信教群众的思想工作，做好爱国宗教职业人员和宗教界上层人士工作的基础上，通过民主程序，制定必要的行政性法规和地方性法规，认真加以解决。对于极个别披着宗教外衣，借机进行煽动破坏社会主义教育事业和其它反动活动的反革命分子，则必须坚决予以揭露和打击。

　　发展民族教育事业，是少数民族地区物质文明和社会主义精神文明建设的重要组成部分，也是直接关系到增强民族团结、巩固和保卫边疆各族人民利益的大事。因此在做好少数民族地区经济建设工作的同时，必须把民族教育工作认真抓上去，争取在不长的时间内，使民族教育状况有较大改善，以逐步适应少数民族地区社会主义现代化建设的需要。

教育部关于正确处理少数民族地区 宗教干扰学校教育问题的意见

(一九八三年一月十五日)

中央书记处、国务院：

　　党的十一届三中全会以来，党的宗教政策逐步得到贯彻落实，群众的正常宗教活动得到恢复，这对改善党和政府同群众的关系，增强民族团结，促进政治上的安定团结，起了重要作用。但是，据新疆、甘肃、宁夏、青海、云南、四川等省、自治区调查反映，在信奉伊斯兰教、小乘佛教和喇嘛教一些少数民族地区，近年来出现了宗教干预教育，争夺学生，冲击学校的问题；有的地方还出现了天主教、基督教干预教育的现象。这种宗教干预教育的情况，在有的地方还比较突出。有些地区把阿訇请到学校念经做礼拜，向青少年儿童灌输宗教思想，诱使他们参加宗教活动，有的阿訇向学生宣传"不学经文，将来死了进不了天堂"。云南楚雄自治州禄丰县一大队干部是天主教徒，他竟规定：一、学生不信上帝不准读书；二、上课时要《圣经》；三、教师不信教不准教书。新疆有个别阿訇利用宗教破坏民族团结，在青少年学生中煽动说："我们要为宗教而战，让汉人死于水中"；并诬称红领巾是"把人拉到地狱的绳索"，致使一些学生把红领巾和政治课本、汉语课本都烧了。在新疆、甘肃、宁夏等一些信仰伊斯兰教的民族地区，有人擅自开办经文学校(多设在清真寺，也有的设在宗教人士家里，还有的实行寄宿制)，已有大批学龄儿童弃学念经。1981 年 3 月，甘肃临夏自治州广河县有弃学念经儿童近 6000 人，占学龄儿童总数的 38．8％。临夏全县入学儿童 12000 人，入经文学校念经儿童却达 14000 人。新疆喀什地区 1981 年 3 月以后半年多时间，弃学念经儿童就从 4000 人增加到 18000 人。云南、四川、青海、甘肃等省信奉小乘佛教和喇嘛教的傣、藏族地区，大批少年儿童退学到寺里当喇嘛、当和尚。云南西双版纳自治州勐海县近两年已有 2000 名学生退学到寺里当和尚，占全县傣族在校生人数的 30％。四川甘孜藏族地区农村，有些还俗喇嘛以"私人办学"名义，招收藏族儿童教经文，甚至提出不要国家派去的教师。1958 年宗教制度改革以后和十年内乱中，有些寺院被学校占用，近年来，信教群众借口落实宗教政策强占校舍，拆校建寺，造成学校被迫停办，学生无处上课的情况也屡有发生。

　　所以出现上述这些情况，当然绝不能归于正确地贯彻落实宗教政策，其中有宗教影响的问题，也有我们工作上的问题。从宗教本身来说，伊斯兰教、喇嘛教和小乘佛教在一些少数民族中历史很长。影响很深，群众中存在着较浓厚的宗教信仰和宗教感情，这不能不影响宗教信徒的子女，而有些宗教职业人员，则通过宗教干预教育，违反政策规定，擅自举办经文学校等方式，借机扩大宗教影响，这是一个方面；另一方面，有些干部对宗教政策缺乏全面的认识，在落实宗教政策过程中，对出现的问题不愿管，不敢管，或者认为不好管，有些放任自流。同时，有些少数民族地区对教育不够重视，因而教育长期落后，科学文化远没有普及，也是一个重要原因。特别是其中有些边远地区，学校少，条件差，教育质量低，群众对办好学校缺乏信心，送子女入学的积极性不高。在蒙、傣族地区，曾因受"左"的思想影响，长期不重视学习民族语文，甚至明令取消民族语文教学，至今尚未完全恢复。所以，有些群众为了使孩子学点民族语文，就把他们送到寺里念经，除上述原因外，极少数披着宗教外衣的反革命分子进行煽动破坏，也是不容忽视的原因之一。1981 年新疆叶城县发生的一起利用宗教煽起的反革命事件，就有许多青少年(多是经文学校学生)被诱骗参加。

　　当前的问题，基本上都是属于人民内部矛盾问题，解决的办法，主要靠党的政策，靠耐心细致的思想政治工作，同时也必须制定必要的行政法规。为了正确地、全面地贯彻党的宗教政策，处理好宗教干预教育、冲击学校的问题，特提出下列几点意见：

一、必须坚持宗教与教育分离的原则。

　　这同我国实行的宗教信仰自由政策并不矛盾。解放前，藏、傣族中的佛教寺院既是宗教机关，又是那个封建社会的文化教育机关，宗教同教育是合一的。现维吾尔、回等民族中，情况稍有不同，既有专设的宗教学校，也有普通学校。解放后，我们实行教育同宗教分离的原则，经过大量工作，大部分宗教学校逐步解散，一般学校中的宗教课也早已取消，这是改革旧教育的重要成果。今天，要不断巩固和完善我国的社会主义教育制度，对于宗教与教育分离的原则仍应继续坚持，不能有丝毫动摇。

二、必须坚持宗教不得干预教育的原则。

这一条已正式写进党的十一届六中全会一致通过的《关于建国以来党的若干历史问题的决议》，《中华人民共和国宪法》中也作了明确规定，**任何人不得利用宗教进行妨碍国家教育制度的活动。**这个原则，得到广大信教群众和爱国宗教职业人员的拥护。为了避免和制止宗教干预教育、妨碍国家教育制度的情况继续发生，我们认为，除按《中共中央关于印发(关于我国社会主义时期宗教问题的基本观点和基本政策)的通知》(中发[1982]19 号文件，以下简称《基本政策》)中有关政策规定举办的宗教学校外，在普通学校应当明确规定：

(1)不得在学校向学生宣传宗教，灌输宗教思想；(2)学校不得停课集体进行宗教活动；(3)不得强迫学生信仰宗教，不得强迫他们当和尚、喇嘛或满拉等；(4)不得以任何形式在学校开设或讲授宗教课；(5)不得利用保教干扰或破坏学校的正常教学秩序；(6)不得以任何形式干扰或阻挠学校向学生进行马列主义、毛泽东思想教育和科学文化教育。

三、要正确处理各地擅自开办的经文学校或经文班。

现在摆在全国各族人民面前的根本任务，是把我国建设成为现代化的高度文明、高度民主的社会主义国家。全国各地，包括少数民族地区在内，要进一步发展科学文化教育事业，逐步普及小学教育，培养造就各类人才，不断提高人民的科学文化水平。上述大量开办经文学校，使大批学龄儿童弃学念经的情况，同社会主义现代化建设。的艰巨任务，同建设"两个文明"的要求，是背道而驰的。这样做对下一代的健康成长，对民族教育事业的发展，对提高少数民族的科学文化水平，十分有害。对此，绝不能放任不管。对未经政府批准擅自开办的经文学校，要有关部门协同配合，积极做好疏导工作，逐步予以解决。

四、对某些信奉伊斯兰教地区的民族中、小学要求开设阿拉伯文课的问题，不能予以同意。

因为从历史上看，阿文从没有成为我国任何一个少数民族的通用文字，只是作为宗教经典文字曾在少数人中使用过。1953 年 9 月《中共中央转发中央民族事务委员会党组关于中国伊斯兰教协会成立会议的报告》中指出：**"阿文不是回民的民族通用文字**，而是伊斯兰教的经典文字，因此在宗教方面学习或使用阿文是可以的。**但把阿文当作回族全民族的文字，而企图推广使用的作法，则是非常错误的。这种作法对回族人民政治、经济、文化的发展十分不利。"**因此，在学校开设阿文课是不必要的，更不能借学习阿文之名，恢复宗教课。

五、关于学校占用寺产的遗留问题，应根据有关政策规定，分别不同情况，经当地政府同有关方面充分协商，妥善加以解决。

今后，任何人不得强占学校，强拆校舍，毁坏设备，任何人都不得以任何理由强迫学校停课、停办。

六、党的十二大指出："普及教育是建设物质文明和精神文明的重要前提"。

我们一定要按照十二大的精神，切实加强少数民族地区的中、小学教育，采取各种有力措施，吸收更多的学龄儿童入学读书。从长远来说，这是解决宗教干扰学校教育问题的一个关键。**首先要加强学校的思想政治教育，应对学生进行爱国主义、民族团结的教育，还应进行生动的普及科学文化的教育。**为此，要改革政治课教材，力求内容生动活泼。要努力改善办学条件，改进教学，提高教育质量，积极开展文娱、体育和各种有益的课外活动。在有民族文字的少数民族中小学中，应尽快恢复民族语文教学，使学生首先学好本民族语文，并根据需要同时学好汉语文，要积极培训民族师资，加强民族文字教材建设。

七、处理好宗教冲击、干扰学校教育的问题，关键在于领导。

各级党委和政府应当通盘考虑，动员各有关部门密切配合，共同做好这项工作。为此，首先要认真学习和坚决贯彻执行《基本政策》这一重要文件，统一认识，统一政策，名有关部门应切实负起责任，敢于做干部、群众及宗教职业人员的工作，讲明政策，讲清道理，对广大信教群众和爱国的宗教职业人员进行爱国守法教育，使他们自觉维护学校教育，遵守宗教不得干预教育的原则。《基本政策》指出："使全体信教和不信教的群众联合起来，把他们的意志和力量集中到建设现代化的社会主义强国这个共同目标上来，这是我们贯彻执行宗教信仰自由政策，处理一切宗教问题的根本出发点和落脚点。任何背离这个基点的言论和行动，都是错误的，都应当受到党和人民的坚决抵制和反对。"我们在处理宗教干预学校教育问题的时候，也必须切实贯彻这一基本原则。

以上意见如无不当，请批转各地参照执行。
注释，此件略有删节。

来源：中国共产党新闻网

http://cpc.people.com.cn/GB/64184/64186/66704/4495671.html.

学校里基于宗教或信仰的歧视

编辑：凯瑟琳·凯普斯

本文节选了"全球基督教团结阵线"所做的研究。有关这项研究和一些重点国家的全面深入报导，可参考： *"Discrimination on the Basis of Religion or Belief in Education – Faith and a Future", http:// faithandafuture.com/wp-content/ uploads/2018/02/Faith_and_a_Future_HR.pdf.*

简介

《世界人权宣言》第 18 条、《公民权利和政治权利公约》和《联合国儿童权利公约》第 14 条都提出要保障儿童的宗教信仰自由权，除美国以外的其他联合国成员国也都签署了《联合国儿童权利公约》。然而在全世界范围内，儿童和青少年仍然因着宗教信仰的原因受到歧视，并且这种歧视也发生在他们受教育的场所。

教育既能塑造一种具有包容性的文化，也能助长刻板印象、敌对情绪和极端主义。它既能加速社会的流动性，也能加深强势和弱势群体之间的鸿沟。

对儿童宗教信仰自由权的侵犯有以下表现形式：

1. 偏见

带有偏见的教育，包括教师的不宽容和课本里传达的歧视，能够制造出一种有害的氛围，使持非主流宗教信仰的学生感到孤立和无所适从。在那些因着课本里的偏见和刻板印象已经形成了宗教偏执的国家，当务之急是改革教学内容和提供培训，帮助教师了解和尊重主流以外的宗教信仰和传统。

2. 歧视

"全球基督教团结阵线"发现，基于宗教或信仰的歧视和不宽容是损害受教育权的一个重要因素，例如缅甸若开邦的罗兴亚族儿童就得不到基于本民族特色和宗教的教育。在那些因着儿童或父母的宗教信仰强迫儿童辍学的国家和族群中，必须采取有效的措施保护儿童的权利。

3. 虐待

千万不要低估在学校遭受虐待会对儿童产生的心理影响。"全球基督教团结阵线"的许多受访者讲述了在学校遭受歧视和不宽容给他们造成的"心理折磨"。被同龄人和师长拒绝所带来的折磨将对一个人的一生产生深远的影响。

政府必须处理和终止对儿童权利的践踏，并且追究肇事者的责任。为了那些在学校遭受宗教歧视的孩子，国际社会必须立刻采取行动制止宗教歧视，并且投入资源进一步推动宗教信仰自由权和受教育权这两者之间的互动。

受教育权的重要性早已得到各国法律和国际法的认可，并且很多国家在普及基础教育和提升中高等教育方面已经取得巨大的进步。然而，虽然国际社会充分强调了受教育权的重要性，成百上千万的儿童仍然没能充分享受到这项权利。2016年联合国秘书长在有关"可持续性发展目标"的报告中强调，"现有的最新数据，即 2013 年的数据表明，5900 万小学学龄儿童没有在学校上学。根据预测，其中五分之一的儿童是辍学儿童，最近的趋势显示，五分之二的未在校儿童永远不会踏足校园。"还有更多的孩子被剥夺了优质教育以及通过教育获得更多机会的权利。"

国际法框架：受教育权和宗教信仰自由权

人权公约和监督机构以及联合国各部门的工作都对儿童的受教育权给予了极大的关注，2015 年通过的"可持续发展目标"对这一权利的重点强调就是明证。相比之下，儿童的宗教信仰自由权只得到很少的关注，而联合国人权理事会的特别程序任务负责人也注意到了这一点，所以继任的宗教信仰自由权特别报告员都越来越关注儿童的权利，也对宗教信仰自由权和包括受教育权在内的其他权利之间的交集提出了关键性的指导。

除此以外，侵犯宗教信仰自由权和侵犯受教育权这两者之间的交叉在国际人权制度中尚未得到足够的关注。学校对宗教信仰自由权的侵犯、基于宗教或信仰的歧视和由于儿童/家长/法定监护人的宗教身份对儿童的受教育权实施的侵犯都会对儿童的成长产生有害的影响。这种侵犯的短期影响是一目了然的，对儿童成长过程中的长期影响却是不可估量的。因此，必须充分认识到这种对儿童发展的限制，并在国际、地区、国家和地方等各个制度层面进行有效的干预。

联合国教科文组织的《取缔教育歧视公约》

联合国教科文组织在 1960 年的联合国大会上通过了《取缔教育歧视公约》。这份 1962 年开始生效的公约提出了无歧视和受教育权的原则。公约的第一条将"歧视"定义为基于一系列受保护的特征，例如宗教，所采取的"区别、排斥、限制或特惠"，其目的或效果为取消或损害教育上的待遇平等"，包括禁止任何人或任何一群人接受教育、限制任何人或任何一群人只能接受低标准的教育、或者维持分开的教育制度。

在三种具体的情况下，公约允许设立分开的教育制度：对男女学生设立或维持分开的学校；为宗教或语言上的理由设立或维持分开的教育制度；设立或维持私立学校。为男女分设的学校必须为男女提供同等质量的教育；为宗教或语言理由分设的学校必须提供一种与学生的父母或法定监护人的愿望相符的教育；而私立学校的目的不在于"排除任何一群人，而在于在公共当局所提供的教育设施之外另再提供其他教育设施。"

公约第三条要求各缔约国承担起消除和防止歧视的责任，确保立法、行政惯例、学校和公共当局都不得在教育上歧视或限制任何一群人。更进一步的是，公约第九条提出缔约国对本公约不得作任何保留。也许正是这个原因，接受和签署这个公约的国家要少于签署其他类似国际公约的国家， 如《公民及政治权利国际公约》和《经济、社会和文化权利国际公约》。

学校教育的重要性

伸张受教育权的国际人权惯例采纳的是一种非此即彼的立场，即某个儿童要么能够得到初级、中等或高等教育，要么无法得到。评估和认定对宗教信仰自由权的侵犯通常要求我们进一步深入分析涉案事实，而对侵犯受教育权的评估只要基于初步证明就可以认定了。

在学校教育中，联合国上一任特别报告员比勒费尔特专门强调要区分"宗教教导"和"宗教信息"：

"宗教教导的目的是让学生了解自己的宗教传统，包括神学教义和规范，而有关宗教的信息却是为了拓宽学生对各种宗教和信仰的了解，特别是那些他们会在社会生活中接触到的宗教和信仰。"

强迫儿童接受与自身信仰不符的宗教教导违背了宪法第十八条的规定，该条宣称"拥有或接受"某个信仰的自由是人内在的权利，在包括公共突发事件在内的任何情况下都不应该被剥夺。国际人权法规定，用强制性手段、法律或政策对"拥有或接受"某一宗教或信仰的权利施加的任何限制都是无效的。实际上，根据第十八条第二款，"不得用任何胁迫手段损害一个人拥有或接受他自愿选择的宗教或信仰的自由。"

下列国家的学校教育中存在基于宗教信仰的歧视

缅甸

宪法的承诺：虽然第三十四条貌似保障所有人的宗教信仰自由，却额外附加了条件，即宗教自由只有在不损害"公共秩序"、"道德"、"健康"或"其他宪法条款"的前提下才能得到法律的保护。第三十六条声称："联邦认可佛教作为绝大多数公民的信仰的特殊地位。"把佛教的特殊地位写入宪法为那些以保护佛教之名歧视非主流宗教的政策提供了合法性，势必导致定义含糊的"公共福祉"凌驾于宗教信仰自由之上。

摧毁学校：信教的民族主义分子以集体施暴的方式摧毁穆

斯林学校，有时甚至得到政府的支持，而政府尚未重建被摧毁的学校。

伊朗

宪法的承诺：第十三条指出："信仰拜火教、犹太教和基督教的伊朗人，作为受到认可的宗教少数派，在法律许可的范围内，可以自由执行他们的宗教仪式，并且按照他们的宗教正典的教导处理私人事务和实施宗教教育。"第十四条则指出非穆斯林人士必须受到尊重，只要他们不从事反对伊斯兰教或者伊朗的活动。虐待：有些信仰巴哈伊教的儿童在学校被殴打，还有一些和父母一起因信仰的缘故被收押。

墨西哥

宪法的承诺：针对教育和宗教信仰之间的关系，宪法第三条第一款指出："宪法第二十四条保障宗教信仰自由，其指导教育的准则必须与一切宗教教义完全分离；基于科学的发展和进步，指导教育的准则必须尽力反对无知、奴役、宗教狂热和偏见。"强迫参与：儿童有时候被强迫参加打着"文化教育"旗号的宗教性活动。在有些地方，宗教少数派人士常常遭受来自地方政府的压力，强迫他们皈依主流宗教或者出钱赞助甚至亲自参与与主流宗教相关的节日庆典。如果他们拒绝，地方政府往往会剥夺他们本应享受的服务，包括不准他们的孩子上学。

纳米比亚

宪法的承诺：第三十八条第二节指出："在任何学校受教育的任何人都不应当被要求接受与他本人或其家长或监护人所持宗教不同的任何其他宗教教导，或被迫参加任何其他宗教仪式。"强制皈依：信仰基督教的女童的教育常常被绑架、强制皈依和未经父母同意的童婚打断。

编者按：如文中所示，虽然国际法保障儿童的宗教自由权，许多国家仍在践踏这项普世人权。

本文也通过曝光上述国家指出，中国目前也在推行类似的做法，剥夺在校儿童的宗教自由。虽然中国是联合国人权理事会的理事国，却在自己的国家里侵犯最基本的人权。

宗教或信仰自由及学校教育

——宗教或信仰自由问题 2010 年 12 月份报告（节录）

海纳·比勒费尔特

三. 宗教或信仰自由及学校教育

A. 介绍性发言

20. 迄今为止，学校是最重要的落实受教育权的正式机构，若干国际人权文件均规定了受教育权，例如《世界人权宣言》(第二十六条)，《经济、社会和文化权利国际公约》(第十三条)，《儿童权利公约》(第 28 条)及《残疾人权利公约》(第二十四条)。区域性人权保护体系的基本文件中也规定了受教育权。受教育权对有效享有人权具有战略意义，这似乎是世界范围内的共识。不仅是由于这个原因，《儿童权利公约》第 28 条要求实现全面的免费义务小学教育，并使所有儿童均能享有和接受中学教育。

21. 学校教育不仅可以为学生提供不同科目的必要知识和信息，还能促进来自不同种族、经济、社会、文化和宗教背景的学生间的日常交流。学生之间进行定期的面对面互动的可能性与发展智力技能同样重要，因为这样的定期互动能够养成一种共同感，这种共同感与对多样性的珍视——包括对宗教或信仰多样性的珍视——是齐头并进的。体验相结合的共同性与多样性也是宗教间和文化间对话项目的主要目标。因此，学校提供了独特的机会，令年青人能够在其发展成长阶段、在基层每日都进行这样的对话。

22. 《德班宣言和行动纲领》(2001 年)旨在促进实现"包容性社会"，从而使种族或社会背景各异的人在平等的基础上参与社会。从另一角度看，《残疾人权利公约》最近也着眼于这一目标，在《公约》中，包容性原则成为一个关键性概念，与其他原则紧密相关，例如尊重个人自主性及理解多样生活状况等原则。

《残疾人权利公约》正是基于这样一个复杂的认识而规定了包容性教育这一权利。尽管这一权利只明确涉及残疾学生，是否应将以及如何将包容性教育的原则适用于其他情况，包括学校生活中宗教或信仰的多样性，这至少是值得讨论的。就宗教多样性问题而言，包容性教育将使学校成为宗教或非宗教倾向各异的学生以自然的方式来互相认识的地方。

23. 然而，应该小心处理宗教或信仰自由及学校教育的问题。这主要是因为，学校不仅提供了学习和社会发展的场所，同时也是行使权威的地方。正是在学校教育期间，年青人获得或未能获得至关重要的文凭，而他们未来的生活和工作机会很大程度上取决于此。此外，特别是对于年幼的儿童来说，教师可能是具有巨大影响力的权威，接近于——有时甚至超越了——家长和其他成年家庭成员的权威。因此，学校生活能够使人处于单方面依赖或特别脆弱的境况之中。学生们可能感受到来自同学、教师或学校管理人员的压力。家长可能担心学校使其子女脱离家庭传统。无论如何，与其他社会机构相比，学校更能触发一系列矛盾的情绪：从希望和高度的期许到怀疑和各种恐惧心理。

24. 对少数群体成员——包括宗教或信仰少数群体——而言，这种矛盾的感觉往往更为明显。一方面，他们可能希望学校教育能够有助于消除其所遭受的负面成见和偏见。另一方面，宗教少数群体的成员——学生和家长——可能担心在学校里遭到歧视、滋扰或压力，甚至是要促使他们放弃其信仰以融入主流社会。必须认真对待这种担心，无论其合理与否。

25. 根据《公民权利和政治权利国际公约》第十八条第4款，各国"承担，尊重父母和(如适用时)法定监护人保证他们的孩子能按照他们自己的信仰接受宗教和道德教育的自由"。《消除基于宗教或信仰愿意的一切形式的不容忍和歧视宣言》第五条第 1 款重申了这一规定："父母或法定监护人有权根据他们的宗教或信仰，并考虑到他们认为子女所应接受的道德教育来安排家庭生活。"《儿童权利公约》将尊重家长的权利与尊重儿童不同阶段接受能力的原则联系在一起。

《公约》第 14 条第 2 款规定各国应"尊重父母并于适用时尊重法定监护人以下的权利和义务：以符合儿童不同时期接受能力的方式指导儿童行使其权利"。

26. 鉴于这一法律背景，需要以高度的敏感性来处理与宗教或信仰相关的学校教育的基本问题，包括对教育原则的定义、汇编学校课程专题、基本的制度和组织安排等等。只要有可能，都应与所有相关方——包括宗教或信仰群体的成员——充分协商以作出有关这些问题的决定，同时注意尊重各项国际人权标准。在这种情况下，特别报告员想要提及其前任指导下进行的一项研究，其中指出：

"同样地，人权仍是主要焦点，相关问题是以公平客观的方式，提供关于宗教趋势、传统、运动和信念的教育，刺激受众的好奇心，鼓励他们质疑自己关于文化、宗教以及异于其自身认同的观念的偏见和成见。成功地描述他人，从而使他们能够认识自身，这不仅提供了有启发性的宝贵教育体验，还有助于在不同的群体或世界观持有者间建立理解和相互尊重。"

B. 消除成见和偏见

27. 依照国际人权法，各国不仅有义务尊重宗教或信仰自由，还应保护这一自由不受第三方横加干涉。此外，各国应促进形成容忍和理解宗教多样性的氛围。儿童"所受的教育应贯彻谅解、容忍、各国人民友好、和平、博爱和尊重他人的宗教或信仰自由等精神，并使他们充分意识到应奉献自己的精力和才能为其同胞服务。"此外，《儿童权利公约》第 29 条第 1(d)款规定，缔约国一致认为教育儿童的目的应是"培养儿童本着各国人民、族裔、民族和宗教群体以及原为土著居民的人之间谅解、和平、宽容、男女平等和友好的精神，在自由社会里过有责任感的生活"。

28. 鉴于学校教育的巨大意义和潜力，这种努力不可避免地涉及到学校课程、社会和组织等所有方面。在这种情况下，特别报告员推荐对学校教育与宗教或信仰自由、宽容和不歧视的关系问题国际咨询会议所通过的最终文件的研究。此次咨询会议于 2001 年 11 月 23 至 25 日在马德里举行。这一会议是由宗教或信仰自由问题的第二位任务负责人奥马尔先生与其他人一起发起的。2002 年，奥马尔先生在向人权事务委员会提交的报告(E/CN.4/2002/73,附件，附录)中纳入了马德里最后文件的全文，并提出了重要的发现。2007 年，第三位任务负责人贾汉吉尔女士在制定《关于公立学校讲授宗教和信仰的托莱多指导原则》的过程中提出了意见。以下意见和建议应结合马德里最后文件及《托莱多指导原则》一并解读，且需要进行回顾及进一步落实。

29. 学校教育能够且应该有助于消除负面成见，这些成见常常影响不同群体间的关系，对少数群体特别有害。对于不同倾向——有神论、非神论或无神论——的宗教或信仰群体来说亦是如此。事实上，在许多国家，宗教或信仰少数群体成员所遭到的公众反感甚至仇恨达到了令人震惊的程度，这种仇视往往滋生于既恐惧又蔑视的矛盾情绪。有时甚至一些小团体也被描绘成"危险"的，因为据称他们具有某种神秘的"传染性"效应，会破坏国家的社会凝聚力。这种指控可以升级成由竞争团体、媒体甚至国家当局编造的完整的阴谋论。与此同时，由于谣传宗教或信仰少数群体成员缺乏任何道德观念等原因，他们常常遭到公众的鄙视。正是由于这种妖魔化的阴谋论推断与公众的鄙视相结合，常常触发针对少数群体成员或发生在不同社群之间的暴力行为。因此，消除构成恐惧、不满和仇恨之根本原因的成见和偏见，就是对防止暴力行为及随之而来的侵犯人权的行为的最重要的贡献。

30. 学校教育在这一努力中发挥着复杂的作用。一方面，学校教育应提供关于不同宗教和信仰的公正信息。另一方面，学校提供了独特的机会，令不同社群的成员得以面对面地交流。要争取克服偏见，这两种途径都同样重要，应尽一切可能同时利用。

31. 必须从概念上将学校教育中提供的关于宗教和信仰的信息与基于某特定信仰而提供的宗教教育加以区分(见下文第47 至 56 段)。宗教教育旨在使学生熟知其宗教传统，即神学教义及其特定信仰的规范，与其相反的是，宗教信息是为了丰富学生关于宗教和信仰的一般知识，特别是那些他们将在社会中接触到的宗教和信仰。从这个意义上讲，提供有关宗教的信息并非神学教育的一部分，而是更贴近于其他学科，例如历史或社会科学。

32. 然而，如果想令有关宗教和信仰的信息对消除成见和偏见产生积极的影响，就必须用公正中立的方式来教授这些信息。此外，在公立学校里，如果故意将教授此类关于宗教的信息作为有关宗教或信仰的国家宣传，或实际上造成这种影响，那么就可能侵犯了家长和法定监护人"保证他们的孩子能按照他们自己的信仰接受宗教和道德教育"的权利。然而，根据从各种渠道获得的信息，在许多国家，学校里使用的提供宗教信息的课本实际上远未能达到中立的要求，有些时候甚至强化了针对少数群体的现有成见。各国有责任采取适当措施，纠正这一不幸的局面。

33. 以中立的方式来介绍关于宗教和信仰的信息并非易事。甚至可以这么认为，严格来说，没有人能持有完全"中立"的立场，超越于相互竞争的宗教或信仰体系所提供的不同意义之上。但是，如果没有克服偏见这一起码的愿望——并在这个意义上实现中立——关于宗教的信息就无法对学生的思想产生积极的影响。克服现有偏见的一种方式是与各社群成员进行协商，积极地将他们对其传统和做法的理解纳入学校教育之中。这种协商在编写课本和其他教学资料的过程中尤为有用。它们也可成为教师和其他目标团体培训的一部分，使其在学校教育中提供关于宗教和信仰的公正准确的信息。

34. 关于宗教和信仰的信息应总是包括一个关键的观点，即宗教——作为一种社会现实——并非铁板一块；这也同样适用于非宗教的信仰体系。这一观点非常重要，因为其有助于解构现有的关于集体心理的观念，人们总刻板或消极地认为所有宗教或信仰的信徒都具有这种心理。在极端的个案中，这种关于集体心理的观念甚至可能造成对人产生"去个人化"的看法，随之产生破坏性的"去人性化"的影响。特定宗教或信仰的信徒得不到尊重，没有被当作不可替代的个人，没有个人面貌，也没有个人的性格，见解和生活计划等等，他们被简单地刻画成"面目不明的群体"，其成员似乎或多或少都是可替换的。无需多言，如果持这一观点，任何严肃的沟通互动从一开始就注定会失败。

35. 宗教或信仰——在社会现实中——从来都不是铁板一块的，从这一关键的观点来看，它们亦可能随着时间而改变。对基本教义的诠释能够且实际上确实适应了不同的社会环境。此外，信徒们能够且确实一次又一次地挑战传统做法。例如，当一些做法有可能对妇女或女童的境况产生负面影响时，一些妇女曾呼吁进行改革，提倡并追求对相应信息来源、教义和规范的创新性解读。

36. 尽管公立学校在介绍关于宗教和信仰的信息时，并无权决定争议性的神学问题，但重要的是，教科书和其他资料应充分介绍各种宗教或信仰及其内部多元化的复杂情况。此外，应该总是给予宗教传统内现有的替代性意见——包括妇女的意见——适当且公平的关注。总的来说，尊重差异不应只局限于不同宗教间的差异，还应认识到各种宗教或信仰群体内部存在的差异。我们只有摒弃了这种以铁板一块看问题的方法，才能认识到人与人——在人权方面有权利的人——之间真正的多样性。

37. 与传播公正准确的宗教信息同样重要的，是宗教或信仰背景各异的学生之间的日常互动。这是消除负面成见和偏见的第二种途径。教师和学校行政机构负有特殊的责任，以确保学生们本着豁达、尊重和公正的精神来进行互动。通过自愿的会议和校际交流，教师和学生有机会在国内外与有不同宗教或信仰的同行和同龄人会面。这样做的目的是推广一种行为方式，表明认识到在现代多元化的社会里，差异——包括在宗教或信仰方面的差异——是"正常"的。

38. 学校应本着尊重和公正的精神来处理宗教和信仰多样性的问题。针对一类典型的误解，特别报告员还想强调，尊重他人的态度并不是要回避敏感的问题——例如妇女的状况——或甚至将此类问题作为禁忌。只要是本着公平的精神，坦诚地讨论敏感的宗教或信仰问题、提出问题、开展辩论并且可能求同存异，这都可能是更尊重对方的。在这方面，尊重和公正这两个概念是紧密相连的。

39. 针对学校处理宗教或信仰多样性的问题，值得重申的是，从宗教或信仰自由的角度来看，必须始终以人类的自我理解作为出发点，人类是人权领域唯一的权利人。此外，宗教或信仰自由既有其"正面"，也有其"反面"，正反两面都源自对人类尊严的尊重，都作为不言自明的原则被载于所有基本人权文件之中。宗教或信仰自由的正面是积极表达和表现个人宗教或信仰的自由，而其另一面(反面)则是不受任何压力——尤其是来自国家或国家机构的压力——而违背自身意愿来进行宗教或信仰活动的自由。学校既是交流和社会交往的场所，又是可能产生弱势境况的地方，鉴于这种矛盾性，宗教或信仰自由中的正面和反面这两个元素应永远结合在一起考虑。忽略这两个相互关联的元素中的任何一个，都将最终从整体上损害宗教或信仰自由这一人权。

40. 因此，从人权角度来看，应该主要由学生(或他们的家长或监护人)以他们认为合适的方式，在学校内表达其宗教或非宗教的信念，只要这不与其他人的权利相冲突。教师们既不应淡化目前的宗教多样性，也不应过分强调宗教差异。忽视在学校教育中可能出现的宗教差异是错误的，同样，在预先指定的团体间，主要以宗教交流的神圣名义组织学生交流，这也是有问题的。相反，基于宗教或信仰自由而尊重差异，这要求有这样一种态度：让学生(或他们的家长或监护人)有机会自行决定是否、以何种程度及在何种情况下愿意表现、或不表现他们的宗教或信仰。这样一种轻松开放的气氛能营造一种有利环境，养成这样一种意识，即多样性是现代多元化社会的正常现象。国家有义务提供有助于实现此目标的适当框架，永远铭记儿童的最大利益这一《儿童权利公约》第 3 条第 1 款所规定的总体原则。

C. 校园范围内的宗教标志

41. 在一些国家，宗教标志一直以来并将继续是一个争议性的问题，包括在学校内穿着宗教服饰以及在教室内展示宗教标志。在一些国家，遵循宗教着装规定的——包括伊斯兰头巾和锡克教头巾——学生和教师被学校开除、被剥夺接受高等教育的机会或被停职。此外，当局在接受政府监督的特定场所——特别是在教室内——强制展示例如十字架之类的宗教标志的行为，已在国家和区域一级引发了无数法庭判决。此外，执行宗教着装规定的个案也令人关注。

42. 要正确处理这一错综复杂的问题，就必须记住一些重要的区别。例如，鉴于教师特有的作用和地位，宗教标志是由教师还是学生佩戴的，这就有明显的差别，也许应该在相应的立法或法庭裁决中反映这一差别。考虑到学生的年龄，也许可在小学和高等教育机构内实施不同的规定。同样地，当局毫无例外地规定在公立学校的教室内放置特定宗教标志，或国家本身被认为是要表达一种宗教信仰，这两种情况也是不同的。此外，在社会上或特定学校内，多数派和少数派宗教团体的动态也是一个需要考虑的重要因素。因此，不同的情况需要不同的解决方案，必须在个案基础上进行准确的评估。

43. 然而，在不影响具体情况的前提下，有理由进行一项一般推定，即学生有权在学校内佩戴宗教标志。根据《公民权利和政治权利国际公约》第十八条第 1 款，思想、良心和宗教自由权包括以礼拜、戒律、实践和教义来表明其宗教或信仰的自由。毫无疑问，遵循和实践个人的宗教或信仰也包括依照其信仰穿着特别的服饰或头饰。此外，人们行使宗教或信仰自由时，既可以单独一人，也可以与社群其他人一道，既可以在公共场所，也可以私下进行。因此，在公共场所——包括学校内——佩戴宗教标志的可能性似乎是表现个人宗教或信仰的自由的自然结果。此外，学校内的宗教标志也可以反映社会中存在的宗教多样性。

44. 另一方面，表现个人宗教或信仰的自由并不是毫无限制的。根据《公民权利和政治权利国际公约》第十八条第 3 款中设定的标准，此限制只受"法律所规定以及为保障公共安全、秩序、卫生或道德、或他人的基本权利和自由所必需"。无论如何，在使用这些标准对表现个人宗教或信仰的自由加以可能的限制时，需要勤勉、准确、并小心谨慎。鉴于学校状况的矛盾性，学生——特别是少数群体学生——可能会不时处于个人或结构性的弱势状态中，因此关于可以佩戴宗教标志的一般推定必须与一些注意事项相联系。例如，在某些情况下，对佩戴宗教标志这一表现宗教或信仰的自由加以限制可能是有道理的，这是为了保护少数群体学生免遭同学或其社群的压力。

此外，教师在课堂上佩戴宗教标志可能对学生产生不当的影响，这取决于教师的一般行为、学生的年龄以及其他因素。此外，一方面强制要求在所有教室放置宗教标志，另一方面，国家有义务在公立教育中保持信仰中立，以在平等和不歧视的基础上纳入不同宗教或信仰的学生，然而，这两个方面可能是难以调和的。

45. 为有关学校内宗教标志的冲突寻求适当的解决方式显然并非易事，也不存在适用于所有情况的一般性解决办法。与此同时，我们的目标很显然应始终是要平等地保护宗教或信仰自由的正反两方面，即表现个人信仰的积极自由，例如穿着宗教服饰的自由，以及免遭任何进行宗教活动的压力——特别是来自国家或国家机构的压力——的自由。此外，在这种情况下认为有必要的对遵循宗教着装规则之自由的限制都必须是以无歧视的方式制定的。例如，如果这些限制措施中存在例外条款，只倾向于有关国家的主要宗教，那么这些限制就是不合法的。

46. 在这方面，特别报告员希望提请大家注意其前任务负责人在向人权事务委员会提交的最后一份报告中提出的意(E/CN.4/2006/5，第 51 至 60 段)。在该报告中，贾汉吉尔女士为评估关于宗教标志的冲突——特别是学校内发生的此类冲突——制定了一系列一般性标准。她对以下两类规定做出了区分；一种是以中立的方式适用于所有宗教标志的规定；一种是在法律或事实上倾向于某些宗教标志，而不顾其他宗教或信仰的规定，这种做法可能违反了不歧视的原则。她还表示，在某些情况下，根据所涉人群的弱势状况而顺应不同的情势，这被认为是合理的，例如是为了保护未成年的学生，以及其父母保证他们的孩子能按照他们自己的信仰接受宗教和道德教育的自由。此外，还应适当考虑妇女权利。

D. 学校的宗教教育

47. 如上所述(见第 27 至 40 段)，从概念上区分有关宗教或信仰的信息和宗教教育是至关重要的。而在实践中，这两方面却有一些重叠，因而在实际进行区分时造成了一些问题。此外，不同的教学方式也可能增加细微差别，例如某种教学方法鼓励学生"了解宗教"或是"从宗教中学习"。无论如何，在规范层面，概念清晰对采取人权方式仍然具有战略意义，同样地，其对正确处理学校的矛盾性——既是学习、社会发展和沟通互动的场所，又是可能产生特别弱势状况的地方——也仍然具有战略意义。

48. 宗教教育，即基于特定宗教或信仰之信条的教育，可在不同的情况下进行。以下各段将主要集中于公立学校体系，即国家提供的公立教育体系内的宗教教育。尽管特别报告员也会提及私立学校，包括教会学校，但他在本章中将不涉及由宗教机构——例如教堂、清真寺、佛塔、犹太教堂或寺庙——组织的、校外学 生参与的宗教教育。

49. 在许多国家，上文所定义的宗教教育构成了公立学校教育不可分割的一部分，甚至可能是学校的必修课程。这种做法可能反映了大部分人口的利益和要求。许多家长可能希望他们的孩子能够了解他们自己宗教或信仰的基本教义和规则，而学校在这一工作中发挥着积极作用。在许多家长看来，如果学校教育不包含对宗教的认识及对自己宗教或信仰的了解，那么他们的孩子的知识和社会技能的发展将是不完整的。因此，在公立学校体系内提供宗教教育，这可能是基于该国大部分人民明示或暗示的意愿。

50. 然而，鉴于学校情况的矛盾性——可能出现某些个人或团体特别弱势的情况——公立学校体系内的宗教教育必须始终伴随着针对宗教或信仰少数群体成员的专门保障措施。人权事务委员会还强调，宗教方面的教学应"尊重不信奉任何宗教的父母和监护人的信念"。一个最起码的要求是，少数群体成员能够'选择退出"违背其自身信仰的宗教教程。这种免修措施应该也适用于所教授的宗教本身的信徒，只要他们感到其个人信仰——包括可能持有的异见——没有受到尊重。此外，选择退出这一可能性不应被繁琐的官僚程序所累，也不能招致任何法律或事实上的处罚。最后，只要有可能，因其不同的信仰而不参与宗教教育的学生应该能够上学校提供的替代课程。

51. 必须由学生或其家长或监护人——在这方面的决定性权利人——作出是否选择退出宗教教育的决定。关于《公民权利和政治权利国际公约》第十八条第 4 款的规定，人权事务委员会指出"包括特定宗教或信仰在内的公共教育，除非规定了能够符合父母和法定监护人愿望的不歧视例外办法或备选办法，否则即不符合 第十八条第四款的规定"。此外，必须关注家长和法定监护人(适用时)的权利和义务：以符合儿童不同时期接受能力的方式指导其行使思想、良心和宗教自由权。"不同时期接受能力"的概念是至关重要的，因为它承认儿童在某时"达到了法定年龄"，因而应该能够作出宗教或信仰上的个人选择。应该根据儿 童的年龄及其成熟程度对其意见给予应有的重视，这需要依照个案的具体情况加以评估。

52. 然而不幸的是，来自不同国家的报告显示，上述各项原则——构成了宗教或信仰自由不可分割的一部分——并未始终得到尊重。在一些国家，据称少数群体学生遭到正式或非正式的压力，以使他们参加完全基于该国主流宗教传统的宗教教育。对作为学校教育基础的主流宗教持替代性诠释或异见的信徒也遭受到这样 的压力。更糟的是，据报道，在某些学校，少数群体或持异见的学生不得不批判他们自己的信仰，以作为参加学校考试的前提条件。信奉其他宗教或信仰(并非学校所教授的)的学生要获得免修(如果确实有的话)，有时需经受繁琐的申请程序或侮辱性的做法，结果使得学生和家长往往不要求免修。

53. 在这方面，值得强调的是，违反学生意愿，强迫其接受宗教教育的做法违反了《公民权利和政治权利国际公约》第十八条第 2 款的规定，即"任何人不得遭受足以损害他维持或改变他的宗教或信仰自由的强迫"。宗教或信仰自由中的内心悔悟元素得到国际人权法的特别保护，因为《公约》第十八条的规定不得受到任何减损，哪怕是在威胁国家命运的公共紧急状态时期。此外，强制性做法可能还侵犯了家长"保证他们的孩子能按照他们自己的信仰接受宗教和道德教育"(《公约》第十八条第 4 款)的权利。

54. 私立学校的宗教教育状况则需要不同的评估。原因是基于其特定的理由和课程安排，私立学校可能会顺应家长和孩子更为具体的教育利益和需求，包括宗教或信仰方面的利益和需求。事实上，许多私立学校都属于某特定教派，故而对该教派的信徒特别有吸引力，但常常也接纳具有其他宗教或信仰倾向的家长和儿童。从这个意义上讲，私立学校是构成现代多元社会中机构多样性的一部分。根据国际人权法，国家并无义务为建立在宗教基础上的学校提供资助，然而，如果一国决定向宗教学校提供公共资金，那么就应该以无歧视的方式进行资助。

55. 此外，私立教会学校的存在——或建立这类学校的可能性——并不能成为一个国家不充分关注公立学校教育中宗教和信仰多样性的理由。尽管私立教会学校可能是家长保证他们的孩子能按照他们自己的信仰接受宗教和道德教育的一种途径，公立学校体系也必须尊重宗教和信仰的多样性。在这种情况下，2008 年 12 月举行的少数群体问题论坛首届会议建议"在基于语言、宗教或文化的原因而为少数群体设立单独的教育机构的情况下，不得设置任何障碍，防止少数群体成员在一般的教育机构学习，只要他们或其家庭愿意这样做"。

56. 另一个需要注意的事实是，在特定的地区或区域，私立教会学校具有事实上的垄断地位，使得学生和家长没有选择的余地，只能接受以异于他们自己的宗教或信仰的教派为基础的学校教育。在这种情况下，国家作为人权的保障者，有义务确保宗教或信仰自由得到有效地尊重，包括学生不被迫接受宗教教育的权利，以及家长保证他们的孩子能按照他们自己的信仰接受宗教和道德教育的权利。

四. 结论和建议

57. 宗教或信仰自由和学校教育是一个多方面的问题，既带来重大的机遇，也蕴含深远的挑战。学校是实现受教育权的最重要的正式机构。它提供了学习、社会发展和社会交往的场所。与此同时，学校也是实施权威的场所，因此一些人——包括宗教或信仰少数群体的成员——可能处于弱势境地。鉴于学校这一矛盾性，实行保障措施，保护个人的宗教或信仰自由权是有必要的。必须特别关注宗教或信仰自由中的内心悔悟元素，这一元素受到国际人权法的绝对保障。至于表现个人宗教或信仰的自由，必须平等地确保该自由的正反两方面，即表达个人信念的自由和不受任何压力——特别是来自国家当局或国家机构内的压力——而被迫进行宗教或信仰活动的自由。

58. 学校可提供独特的机会，在整个社会内部进行建设性的对话，特别是人权教育能够有助于消除负面成见，这种成见常常影响宗教少数群体的成员。然而，在许多社会里，宗教或信仰自由和学校教育的问题也引发了争议，尤其是关于学校内的宗教标志和宗教教育等有争议的问题(见上文 20 至 56 段)。

59. 关于宗教标志——特别是公立学校内的宗教标志——的问题，特别报告员希望重申，要根据每个个案的具体情况作出决定。如果认为对佩戴宗教标志的限制是有必要的，那么就不可用歧视性的方式来实施这些限制，而且必须与实施这些限制的具体需要直接相关且相称。与此同时，例如，为保护儿童、其父母或法定监护人的权利，可能有必要限制教师们通过佩戴宗教标志以表现其宗教或信仰的自由。针对所有涉及孩子的行动，孩子的"最大利益"应该是首要考量因素。至于由国家规定在教室内摆放宗教标志的问题，各国应在公立教育中持信仰中立的态度，以在平等和不歧视的基础上纳入信奉其他宗教或信仰的学生。

60. 一般来说，教育政策应着眼于加强对人权的保护和促进，消除与宗教或信仰自由相抵触的偏见和观念，确保尊重并接受宗教或信仰领域的多元化和多样性，确保个人有不接受不符合其信仰的宗教教育的权利。应努力在不同层面建立咨询机构，采取包容性的方式，使不同的利益攸关者都参与到制定和实施有关宗教或信仰问题的学校课程及教师的培训中来。

61. 特别报告员要提到他的前任们关于这些问题的报告，以及他们为制定学校教育与宗教或信仰自由、宽容和不歧视的关系问题国际咨询会议最后文件和《关于公立学校讲授宗教和信仰的托莱多指导原则》所做的工作。在这方面，特别报告员重申，各国应在适当的政府一级，根据其教育体系，积极考虑：

(a) 为教师和学生提供自愿机会，与宗教或信仰不同的同行和同龄人进行会面和交流；

(b) 鼓励教师和学生的交流活动，推动出国留学；

(c) 强化教育中的不歧视观念，并在各适当层面强化有关宗教或信仰自由的知识；

(d) 确保男女在教育领域的平等权利以及宗教或信仰自由，特别是要加强对女童受教育权利的保护，尤其是那些来自弱势群体的女童；

(e) 采取适当措施，打击所有形式的基于宗教或信仰的不容忍和歧视行为，它们常常表现在学校课程、教材和教学方式中；

(f) 评估公立学校内目前所使用的涉及宗教和信仰教学的课程设置，以确定其是否促进了对宗教或信仰自由的尊重，是否是公正、平衡、包容、适合学生的年龄、无偏见且符合专业标准的；

(g) 评估制定宗教和信仰教育课程的过程，以确定这一过程顾及了各种宗教和信仰群体的需求，且所有利益相关者均有机会发表意见；

(h) 审查现有的教师培训机构能在何种程度上为教师提供教授宗教和信仰知识的必要专业培训，从而促进对人权——特别是宗教或信仰自由——的尊重；

(i) 确定教师培训机构能在何种程度上提供：关于人权问题的充足知识；对社会上宗教和非宗教观念之多样性的认识；对各种教学方法(特别关注以跨文化方法为基础建立的教学方法)的牢固掌握；以及对如何以尊重、公正和专业的方式教授宗教和信仰的知识的真知灼见。

62. 最后，特别报告员重申，家长、家人和法定监护人对儿童在宗教或信仰领域所接受的教育发挥着重要的作用。因此，应给予特别关注，鼓励积极态度，并着眼于儿童的最大利益，支持家长行使其权利，充分发挥他们在容忍和不歧视教育领域的作用，同时考虑到《世界人权宣言》、《公民权利和政治权利国际公约》、《经济、社会和文化权利国际公约》、《消除基于宗教或信仰原因的一切形式的不容忍和歧视宣言》和《儿童权利公约》中的相关规定。

(节选自联合国宗教或信仰自由问题特别报告员海纳·比勒费尔特"宗教或信仰自由问题 2010 年 12 月份报告",不含注释)

《中国法律与宗教观察》内含中国颁布、发行的涉及法律、政治、政府的政策文件、学术作品及其完整的英文译本。

欢迎访问：

对华援助协会中文网站：http://www.chinaaid.net

中国观察网：http://www.monitorchina.org

——完——